D1564541

Unless Recalled Earlier

THE TRAGEDY OF LIN BIAO

林彪的文革悲劇

孫萬國
泰偉斯 合著

FREDERICK C. TEIWES
WARREN SUN

The Tragedy of
Lin Biao

Riding the Tiger during the
Cultural Revolution
1966–1971

UNIVERSITY OF HAWAII PRESS
HONOLULU

© Frederick C. Teiwes and Warren Sun, 1996

Published in North America by
University of Hawaii Press
2840 Kolowalu Street
Honolulu, Hawaii 96822

Published in the United Kingdom by
C. Hurst & Co. (Publishers) Ltd., London

Printed in Hong Kong

Library of Congress Cataloging-in-Publication Data

Teiwes, Frederick C.
    The tragedy of Lin Biao : riding the tiger during the Cultural Revolution,
    1966–1971 / Frederick C. Teiwes, Warren Sun.
      p.   cm.
    Includes bibliographical references and index.
    ISBN 0–8248–1811–3 (alk. paper)
    1. Lin. Piao, 1908–1971. 2. China—History—Cultural
Revolution,
1966–1971. 3. China—Politics and government—1949–1976. I. Sun,
Warren. II. Title.
DS778.L4725T38 1996
951.105'6—dc20   95–44130
                                             CIP

To our children
Inge and Jack Teiwes;
and Ru-shih and Ruo-fei Sun

CONTENTS

PHOTOGRAPHS

Between pages 102 and 103

Lin Biao in 1937, as a commander of the 115th Division of the Eighth Route Army.

Lin Biao in Guangzhou, c. 1960, as Vice Chairman of the Military Affairs Committee.

Lin Biao's family with Air Force Commander Wu Faxian, early Cultural Revolution period.

Lin Biao and Mao Zedong during the Cultural Revolution period.

Lin Biao with Mao and Zhou Enlai at Eleventh Plenum, August 1966.

Lin Biao reading a speech to a mass reception of Red Guards, Tiananmen, 31 August 1966.

Mao, Zhou Enlai and Lin Biao during a Red Guard reception, 1966.

Mao and Lin Biao on rostrum at Ninth Party Congress, April 1969.

Lin Biao with the 'four generals', Lushan, September 1970.

Mao receiving Edgar Snow, with Lin Biao and others.

On the rostrum of Tiananmen during May Day celebrations, 1971, when the Mao-Lin relationship was under strain.

Lin Biao's last public appearance, at a reception for Ceauşescu.

A note taken as evidence of Lin Biao's alleged order to assassinate Mao.

Wreck of Lin Biao's *Trident* after it crashed in Mongolia, 13 September 1971.

PREFACE AND ACKNOWLEDGEMENTS

In China today it is possible to purchase a new series of postage stamps bearing the likenesses of the *ten* marshals of the People's Republic – that is, of the great military heroes of the Chinese revolution *including* Lin Biao. How can this be? How can a man who allegedly planned to assassinate Chairman Mao Zedong and died fleeing the country to the hated Soviet Union be treated with such official respect? The aim of this book is to use the varied sources which have become available in recent years to re-examine this still obscure instance of Chinese Communist leadership conflict in hopes of explaining this paradox and uncovering the long suppressed truth of the case. In this endeavour we have provided a new assessment of Lin Biao during the Cultural Revolution both as Mao's designated successor and then as his purported mortal enemy. The result is an analysis contrasting sharply with existing Western scholarship which, we believe, to be profoundly mistaken on a wide variety of specific events and in general characterization. Our study is important in two senses, first as a revisionist interpretation of one of the crucial developments in post-1949 Chinese political history. But perhaps even more important, through this historical study we have been able to make a critical evaluation of the assumptions which have dominated scholarship concerning leadership conflict during the Maoist era. Given that these assumptions retain their influence notwithstanding the accumulation of significant amounts of recent Communist Party materials pointing in different directions, such an evaluation is crucial in advancing the larger debate in the nature of Chinese élite politics.

The Lin Biao affair is one of the most elusive leadership conflicts of the post-1949 period, clearly of enormous significance given the tumultuous context of the Cultural Revolution, certainly the most explosive in that without warning or preparation the Chinese public was required to accept that Lin, hitherto the Chairman's 'best student', was in fact the most heinous of

ix

counterrevolutionaries, but nevertheless a case underexamined in the West. The events of 1966–71 analysed in this study must be seen against the larger sweep of Lin Biao's career. One of the great commanders of the revolution, the greatest in the opinion of many Chinese scholars, Lin was undoubtedly a man in poor health by the time victory was achieved, and spent much of the 1950s in positions of high honour but little operational significance. This changed in 1959 with the disgrace of Minister of Defence Peng Dehuai at the first Lushan plenum, and Lin's assumption of Peng's duties at Mao's behest. As Minister of Defence Lin remained in poor health and reclusive in personal style, but he was clearly the ultimate authority within the military (under Mao) although delegating substantial operating responsibilities. In this period leading up to the Cultural Revolution, the army under Lin's leadership became a standard-bearer (at least in propaganda) of political work above all else and a vigorous promoter of the cult of Mao Zedong, and by 1964 it was being held up as a model for all official organizations. When the Cultural Revolution unfolded in 1966 and Mao's designated heir of the previous two decades, Liu Shaoqi, came under attack, Lin Biao was named the new successor. Moreover, with chaotic conditions threatening the country in 1967, the army emerged as the only organization retaining an effective nation-wide command structure and the institution holding China together. During 1966–8 Lin made repeated public appearances singing the praises of Mao and the Cultural Revolution, but at the second Lushan plenum in summer 1970 the Chairman rebuked Lin and set in train a series of events which ultimately led to the successor perishing in a plane crash while fleeing the country in September 1971.

Understandably, in view of these events and the persistent official presentation of Lin Biao as a Cultural Revolution proponent, virtually all contemporary observers regarded Lin as nothing other than a firm supporter of the Cultural Revolution and Mao. Arguably less defensible, Western scholars also followed, albeit with scepticism concerning important details and different glosses on the main actors and general process, official *ex post facto* explanations of Lin's demise – explanations emphasising a bitter Mao-Lin power struggle, various alleged policy differences, and a fundamental institutional conflict between Lin's alleged desire to establish military rule and Mao's effort to restore civilian Party control. In all of these aspects Western interpretations not only drew on official claims, but perhaps even more significantly linked those claims to Western assumptions about Communist power struggles, policy contention and the significance of institutions. Our investigations demonstrate that these (and other) assumptions and conclusions are misplaced for the 1966–71 period, and by implication must be reassessed for the entire Maoist period – particularly the Chairman's last two decades. In the matter at hand, we conclude that Lin not only did not engage in a power struggle with Mao but in fact had little interest in politics in general and in being Mao's successor in particular. His basic political posture was passive, his few active interventions sought to limit the disruption caused by the Cultural Revolution, and the inevitable tension between military men and civilians did not translate into a Bonapartist challenge since army leaders to a man accepted Mao's authority. Instead, an extreme form of one-man rule existed which both stimulated court intrigue and stifled normal policy and institutional conflict.

After the initial attempts to explain the Lin Biao affair in the years immediately following 1971, little scholarly attention was given to the matter. Even with the appearance by the late 1980s of new material with quite different implications from the official version, there was little revived interest in Lin Biao apart from overviews in *The Cambridge History of China*, parts of larger narratives concerning court intrigues under Mao, and a few studies in the '20 years after' mode. While these writings incorporate recent information, they largely adhere to orthodox interpretations. Moreover, even educated Chinese hostile to the regime and Mao ironically still accepted the Party's view of an ambitious Lin Biao brutally clashing with the Chairman, as in the case of the reform intellectual now in exile, Yan Jiaqi, and the late personal physician to Mao, Li Zhisui. All of these assessments, foreign and Chinese, have missed the true story which can be gleaned from the variety of new Chinese sources now available.

These sources can be grouped in three broad categories. The first is works by Party historians which have been constrained in what they can say given the continuing official verdict on Lin's 'crimes' but which, through a careful examination of specific events and, in a few cases, finely judged general comments, provide important raw material for a strikingly different interpretation. Secondly, a variety of unofficial studies such as memoirs of secretaries and bodyguards serving Lin Biao and his wife, Ye Qun, and books by investigative writers who have interviewed many of the concerned individuals, while not explicitly challenging the orthodox view, nevertheless paint a picture of a man far different from what has been asserted. And finally, interviews with Party and military historians, and with individuals connected to important actors in the story, enable these people to say openly in private what they cannot express in public, as well as to answer many concrete questions. The results of these interviews point in the same direction as the written sources. While endless questions concerning specific events remain, a clear picture of a Lin Biao who was nothing like what has been generally accepted emerges from all these sources.

Despite some rumours of an imminent 'reversal of the verdict' on Lin Biao's case, we do not believe this to be likely in the short run. Although it is true that elements associated with Lin's Fourth Field Army have been sympathetic to their former leader and perhaps are seeking a re-examination of the case, it is most unlikely that the present leadership under Deng Xiaoping or any likely successor group would address the issue since it would involve a devastating blow to both Mao's reputation and the Party's legitimacy. Yet the very fact that scholars have been able to drop pointed hints in their work, and that former secretaries have been able to publish relatively benign accounts of their boss – not to mention Lin's resurrection on the nation's stamps – suggest a recognition of the weakness of the official conclusion. Similarly, the fact that key Party historians privately query that conclusion with their peers and foreigners also indicates that this weakness is understood by those with the greatest professional interest in the truth of the matter and the greatest capacity to analyse objectively. What is involved is more than a mechanical 'truth from facts' approach which distinguishes the good general of revolutionary days from the 'wicked careerist' of the Cultural Revolution, but seemingly a tacit acknowledgement that the Party's historical judgment on Lin is open to eventual reconsideration.

We have appended to our study a critical *nianpu*, a chronology or chronicle of Lin Biao's activities and related events from the founding of the People's Republic through 1965, virtually the eve of the Cultural Revolution, along with a brief summary of his pre-1949 career. This modified version of the traditional Chinese chronicle of a notable's life is very different from the form the Communist Party has adopted for various of the 'good' leaders in our story such as Mao himself, Zhou Enlai, and Lin's alleged victim, He Long, but has not extended to 'evil' figures in the Party's history. Such official *nianpu* are largely compilations of factual data about events, but compilations restricted by taboos which steer clear of any questionable activities or politically embarrassing situations involving the leader concerned. In contrast, our chronology, which draws on the various sources consulted in the preparation of the body of the study as well as additional works, explores complex and contentious issues, and comments on the likely motives of Lin and other actors. It serves as a companion to the study itself, allowing the reader to observe the traits so characteristic of Lin during the complex and confusing events of 1966–71 in less stressful periods, while providing background information to the various developments of our story. In addition, the summary of these events, similar to our analysis of 1966–71, demonstrates how misguided much of the conventional wisdom concerning Lin Biao, the politics of the army, and élite politics generally has been for the earlier period.

In addition, our select bibliography directs the reader to sources used or otherwise encountered in our research. It first of all lists all those items cited in the notes, except that in selecting articles from Chinese journals we have excluded a few items that are tangential to our story. To this core list we have added sources consulted in the research but not cited in the notes, including a number of major documentary collections and chronologies that will be of use to anyone wishing to pursue the period further. Finally, we have added a small number of additional studies which have come into our possession after the completion of the manuscript. The information and findings of these studies have not been incorporated into our analysis, but in broad terms, while not adopting our interpretation they provide additional piecemeal evidence in its support, even though in a few cases they suggest that we have only exposed the tip of the iceberg. Indeed, these studies and further interviews with people directly concerned reinforce our feeling throughout the original research that there is still a long way to go before the full Lin Biao story can be told, and when told this story will reveal even more extreme erratic behaviour on Mao's part, and personal power almost beyond imagination.

Various people have contributed to this study, none more so than the oral sources noted above. While those with personal connections to major actors on several sides of the drama (both 'good' and 'bad' according to present orthodoxy) of course had particular interests to advance, careful questioning produced both invaluable detail and a sense, in nearly all cases, that the respondents were telling the truth – at least as they saw it. Of particular significance are the important insights and detailed information obtained from discussions with roughly two dozen Party historians from civilian and military institutions. These people varied considerably in their views from those basically accepting the official version of an ambitious Lin Biao to a minority rejecting the orthodox story as a gross distortion of the truth. Yet as in previous research we were struck by the intellectual seriousness and empirical orientation of these researchers regardless of their overall conclusions, and even those inclined to support the official verdict presented evidence in a balanced fashion – evidence, we believe, that ultimately supports our revisionist interpretation. As for those questioning the orthodox view, we were especially moved not only by their passion for the truth, but by expressions of self-reproach for having been taken in by official misrepresentations at earlier stages of their own work on Lin Biao. These people (as with all oral sources) must remain nameless, but they have our special admiration.

In addition to our unnamed Chinese colleagues and contacts, thanks are due to Tim Cheek, Dai Qing, Keith Forster, David Goodman, Nancy Hearst, Jia Qingguo, Lin Yousu, David Shambaugh, Shum Kui-Kwong, Sun Shen-shu and Wang Qiming for their helpful comments on an earlier version of this study and/or the generous provision of research materials. Kathy Dempsey of the University of Sydney's Department of Government meticulously and cheerfully proof read the text and prepared the index. Robert Ash of the School of Oriental and African Studies gave repeated support at an earlier stage when the study was earmarked as a monograph in the Contemporary China Institute's Research Notes and Studies series, and Martin Daly of SOAS provided editorial assistance. We are particularly grateful to Christopher Hurst who had the wit to see a book in an expanded manuscript, the result of which has materialized in these pages. Research funding was generously given by the University of Sydney's Research Grants Scheme, the University's Research Institute for Asia and the Pacific, the Ian Potter Foundation, the Pacific Cultural Foundation, and especially the Australian Research Council. Without this financial support the project could not have been undertaken or executed in anything like the form in which it now appears.

Finally, no acknowledgment of the support which has sustained this project would be complete without mention of the love of our families, Kath and Jack in Sydney, Inge in Oregon, and Julie, Ru-shih and Ruo-fei in Canberra.

Sydney and Canberra
November 1995

ABBREVIATIONS

Organizations and policies

CCP	Chinese Communist Party
CRG	Cultural Revolution Group
GPD	General Political Department
MAC	Military Affairs Committee
NPC	National People's Congress
PLA	People's Liberation Army
PLACRG	PLA's Cultural Revolution Group
PRC	People's Republic of China
SPC	State Planning Commission

Publications and publishing agencies

AJCA	*Australian Journal of Chinese Affairs*
CHOC	*The Cambridge History of China*
CQ	*China Quarterly*
FBIS	*Foreign Broadcast Information Service*
RMRB	*Renmin ribao* (People's Daily)
XHRB	*Xinhua ribao* (New China Daily)
ZGDSJXCKZL	*Zhonggong dangshi jiaoxue cankao ziliao* (CCP History Teaching Reference Materials)
ZGDSRWZ	*Zhonggong dangshi renwu zhuan* (Biographies of Personalities in CCP History)
ZGDSYJ	*Zhonggong dangshi yanjiu* (Research on CCP History)

1

INTRODUCTION

'Do not lightly ride [the tiger of political power].' Lin Biao's reading notes, sometime before the Cultural Revolution[1]

'Be passive, passive and again passive.' Lin Biao's advice to his friend Tao Zhu shortly before the latter's fall, December 1966 and January 1967[2]

'At any given time, in all important questions, Chairman Mao always charts the course. In our work, we do no more than follow in his wake, and that's it.' Lin Biao at the Ninth Party Congress, April 1969[3]

More than two decades after his demise, the case of Lin Biao, who became Mao Zedong's personally anointed successor in 1966 but was denounced as an unprincipled conspirator following his death five years later, remains the most obscure and controversial case of top-level élite conflict in the history of the Chinese Communist Party (CCP). While the official version of Lin's death in September 1971 as the result of a plane crash while fleeing to the Soviet Union is widely disbelieved both in and outside China, this appears the least problematic aspect of the Party's account of Lin Biao during the Cultural Revolution.[4] More

---

[1] Guan Weixun, *Wo suo zhidaode Ye Qun* (The Ye Qun I Knew) (Beijing: Zhongguo wenxue chubanshe, 1993), p. 202. Guan, a secretary to Lin's wife (see below, n. 11), found this notation in Lin's hand as a marginal comment concerning Cao Cao's observation upon becoming Prime Minister during the Han dynasty that 'when riding the tiger it is difficult to get off.

[2] Quan Yanchi, *Tao Zhu zai 'Wenhua dageming' zhong* (Tao Zhu during the 'Cultural Revolution') (n.p.: Zhonggong zhongyang dangxiao chubanshe, 1991), pp. 196, 215.

[3] 'Impromptu remarks by Lin Biao at plenary session of the Ninth National Congress of the CCP on 14 April 1969', as trans. by Michael Schoenhals in *The Stockholm Journal of East Asian Studies*, vol. 2 (1990), p. 102.

[4] Intellectuals and urban residents in China generally have little confidence in the CCP's account while the 'inside story' published in the West, Yao Ming-le, *The Conspiracy and Death of Lin Biao* (New York: Alfred A. Knopf, 1983), which claims that Mao arranged for Lin's assassination, has considerable acceptance. Party historians, however, including those deeply sceptical of many aspects of the official verdict on Lin Biao, accept the story of the fatal flight after careful analysis of the available data. For a refutation of Yao Ming-le's book, see *Dang de wenxian* (The Party's Documents),

problematic is the story of military coup plans and an assassination plot directed against Mao by Lin in the last desperate period of his political decline – apart from the question of whether such plans actually existed, there is much to suggest that to the extent that they did, it was Lin's son, Lin Liguo, who organised these projects without his father being aware.[5] Yet it is concerning more fundamental political questions that not only the official account but also the basic thrust of Western analysis are most in need of re-examination. How did Lin Biao ascend to the position of successor to Mao? Why did he fall so precipitously in 1970–1? What were Lin's objectives, methods and role over the entire 1966–71 period? What does the case of Lin Biao tell us about the nature of Chinese politics in the Cultural Revolution period?

Any effort to reconstruct the politics of the Lin Biao case faces enormous methodological problems. Most obviously, the great political sensitivity of the affair has resulted in a distorted official account. The awkwardness of explaining how Chairman Mao's 'best student' could turn into an assassin produced confused and conflicting claims, a tendency to paint Lin as unremittingly evil,[6] and efforts to protect the reputations of both Mao and

---

no. 4 (1989), pp. 81–4. Moreover, recent investigative reporting by Peter Hannam, 'Solved: the mystery of Lin Biao's death', *Asiaweek*, 2 February 1994, pp. 32–3, provides near conclusive proof of Lin's presence on the plane in the form of interviews with the KGB experts who examined the remains of the crash victims as well as photographs of those remains which were taken to Moscow.

[5] A range of Party historians interviewed, including those relatively accepting of the official characterization of Lin, acknowledge the possibility or likelihood that this was the case. For a published comment, see Wang Nianyi, *1949–1989 nian de Zhongguo: Dadongluan de niandai* (China 1949–1989: The Years of Great Turmoil) (Henan: Henan renmin chubanshe, 1988), pp. 388–9, 421, who states there is no evidence of Lin's awareness.

[6] In the 1980s the emphasis on greater historical objectivity has led to acknowledgement of Lin's positive contributions during the revolution, but there is little sign of any official re-evaluation of his actions in the post-revolutionary period, especially during the Cultural Revolution. However, the fact that the authorities, probably reacting to pressure from veterans of Lin's Fourth Field Army, have allowed the publication of books casting major if discreet doubt on the Party's verdict concerning Lin suggests a tacit recognition that the official story is, at the very least, overstated. The key works in this respect are the scholarly study, Wang Nianyi, *Dadongluan*; and the reminiscences of two secretaries in Lin's household, Zhang Yunsheng and Guan Weixun (see below, n. 11).

Zhou Enlai. A further consequence of such sensitivity has been both severe limitations on access to materials concerning Lin for Party historians seeking a more objective evaluation and limits on what they can say in print, with the result that even the most serious scholars give contradictory accounts of the inherently confusing events of the Cultural Revolution period. The importance of these limitations for scholarship within China cannot be overstated; even the seminal work of the military Party historian Wang Nianyi, for all its excellence, has been hobbled by archival restrictions, and in the resulting analysis some of his most important points must be made indirectly. Beyond general bias, conflicting detail and restrictions on sources, a major problem concerns the reliability of key materials on the case; some were clearly fabricated by the authorities[7] while others – especially the important evidence of leading figures at the trial in 1980–1 of the 'Lin Biao and Jiang Qing cliques'[8] – are of questionable validity. In particular, General Wu Faxian who provided some of the most significant evidence concerning Lin Biao's activities is – according to a well-informed Party historian – deeply remorseful over his testimony, parts of which he claims to have invented to please his inter-

---

[7] While not created out of whole cloth, Lin's alleged '571 military coup plan' is an example. According to a Party historian in the military, the document issued in 1972 as the 'Outline of "project 571"' (see the translation in Michael Y.M. Kau (ed.), *The Lin Piao Affair: Power Politics and Military Coup* (White Plains: International Arts and Sciences Press, 1975), pp. 81–90) was constructed on the basis of confessions by collaborators of Lin Liguo. The notion of a '571 project' comes from an isolated scrap of paper bearing the circled number 571 found in the effects of one of Lin Liguo's accomplices.

[8] Although one historian denounced the trial as a kangaroo court where testimony was rehearsed, this seems overstated. According to a participant in the process, the principle of 'truth from facts' and the right to speak freely were emphasized to the defendants, and, in fact, some charges were dropped on the basis of the evidence. Nevertheless, as the following case of Wu Faxian suggests, the incentives for giving the prosecutors what they were looking for were substantial. Compilations of evidence from the trial are: *A Great Trial in Chinese History: The Trial of the Lin Biao and Jiang Qing Counter-Revolutionary Cliques, Nov, 1980-Jan. 1981* (Oxford: Pergamon Press, 1981); the more extensive *Lishi de shenpan* (The Historic Trial) (Beijing: Qunzhong chubanshe, 1981); and the more recent Xiao Sike, *Caoji shenpan: shenli Lin Biao fangeming jituan qinliji* (The Super Trial: A Participant's Account of the Trial of the Case of the Lin Biao Counterrevolutionary Clique) (2 vols, Jinan: Jinan chubanshe, 1992).

rogators.[9] Moreover, unofficial interpretive works[10] and first-hand accounts are subject to bias and limitation, even when they run counter to the official picture as in the memoirs of Lin's secretary, Zhang Yunsheng.[11]

Another methodological problem is that the public record of Lin Biao's statements, so often used by Western analysts to determine his political position,[12] have no necessary relationship to his private views. Apart from the well-known case of Lin's political report to the Ninth Party Congress in 1969, on other

---

[9] Oral source. Cf. below, p. 24, n. 38; and Barbara Barnouin and Yu Changgen, *Ten Years of Turbulence: The Chinese Cultural Revolution* (London: Kegan Paul International, 1993), pp. 216, 325.

[10] A case in point is the influential book by the reform intellectual Yan Jiaqi and his wife, Gao Gao and Yan Jiaqi, '*Wenhua dageming, shinianshi 1966–1976* (History of the 'Cultural Revolution' Decade 1966–1976) (Tianjin: Tianjin renmin chubanshe, 1986). Ironically, while frowned upon by the authorities for its relentless account of evil-doings during the Cultural Revolution, the book perpetuates many official myths as well as being sloppy on matters of detail. In the following discussion we often use this book as representative of the official view although technically this is not the case. For a critique emphasising the book's various inaccuracies by the leading historian of the period, Wang Nianyi, see *Dangshi tongxun* (Party History Bulletin), no. 4 (1987), pp. 18–29.

[11] Zhang Yunsheng, *Maojiawan jishi: Lin Biao mishu huiyilu* (True Account of Maojiawan: Reminiscences of Lin Biao's Secretary) (Beijing: Chunqiu chubanshe, 1988). A translation of roughly one-sixth of this book, together with a perceptive if brief introduction by Lawrence R. Sullivan, can be found in *Chinese Law and Government*, no. 2 (1993). In addition, Wen Feng, *Shentanxia de Lin Biao* (Lin Biao Down to Earth) (Beijing: Zhongguo huaqiao chubanshe, 1993), mirrors Zhang's book and is apparently based on a journalist's interviews with him and other of Lin's secretaries; it is useful primarily for identifying some people not identified in *Maojiawan*. While there are varying assessments of Zhang's account among Chinese scholars and it contains some significant factual errors, it can be considered broadly reliable and revealing despite the author's restrained sympathy for his former boss and his limited access to Lin while working for him in the crucial period from summer 1966 to late 1970. Another major recent book, Guan Weixun, *Ye Qun*, provides further credible information from a vantage point inside Lin's residence. The author, who had been a deputy director of the army's cultural bureau, was hired to read classical texts to Lin's wife, Ye Qun, from 1968 to 1971, and subsequently in the 1980s conducted interviews with Lin's daughter, Lin Liheng (Lin Doudou), and other members of his circle.

[12] See especially the work of Lin's contemporary biographers, Martin Ebon, *Lin Piao: The Life and Writings of China's New Ruler* (New York: Stein and Day, 1970); and Thomas W. Robinson, 'Lin Piao as an élite type', in Robert A. Scalapino (ed.), *Elites in the People's Republic of China* (Seattle: University of Washington Press, 1972).

occasions he read speeches or put his name to articles prepared
by others – even by those allegedly in opposing political camps
as in the case of 'his' celebrated 1965 treatise 'Long live the victory of people's war'.[13] This, of course, is related to the gap
between the private beliefs and public actions of politicians
everywhere, but, as this study demonstrates, this gap was often
extraordinarily wide in Chinese politics, and especially so during
the Cultural Revolution. Finally, the very nature of Lin's reclusive persona and the questions at issue – political motives, possible conspiracies and clashes of personalities over trivial matters –
contributes greatly to the difficulty of analysis. Thus we share
the assessment of the most careful chronicler of the Cultural
Revolution period, Wang Nianyi, that key materials on Lin Biao
are lacking, that research is necessarily very incomplete, and that
only individual opinions can be offered.[14] Yet the documentary
evidence which does exist, together with interviews of Party
historians, some of whom are altering their own interpretations
as new evidence becomes available and passionately seek a just
verdict on a case where 'there has never been such disregard [of
the principle of "seeking] truth from facts"',[15] does provide the
basis for analysis. At the very least such an analysis can cast doubt
on official claims as well as conventional wisdoms in Western
scholarship, and it is also possible to present an alternative interpretation, however tentative on specific issues.

As in other respects concerning Chinese élite politics,[16]
Western analyses of Lin Biao, both those appearing in the period

[13] See below, pp. 26–7, 106–8.

[14] Wang Nianyi, *Dadongluan*, pp. 368–9.

[15] The sentiment, originally articulated by General Huang Yongsheng of the 'Lin
Biao clique' (see Xiao Sike, *Caoji shenpan*, vol. 1, p. 303), was cited approvingly by
an oral source specializing in the case. On the value of interviews, see Frederick C.
Teiwes, 'Interviews on Party history', *CCP Research Newsletter*, nos. 10 & 11 (1992).

[16] See the discussion of Western adaptations of the official 'two line struggle' model
of the pre-1966 period in Frederick C. Teiwes, *Leadership, Legitimacy, and Conflict in
China: From a Charismatic Mao to the Politics of Succession* (Armonk, NY: M.E.
Sharpe, 1984), p. 5.

following his death[17] and the few recent works dealing with the case,[18] have been heavily influenced by Chinese interpretations. While there are some significant differences among Western interpretations, and of course between Chinese accounts and Western scholarly views which have demonstrated a healthy scepticism concerning aspects of the official line,[19] there has nevertheless been a substantial degree of agreement on political issues that have strong echoes in official Chinese sources. The following points, at some risk of oversimplification, fairly characterize the dominant interpretation:

1. Lin Biao was an ambitious politician who did what was necessary in terms of political manoeuvring and factional combat first to consolidate his control of the People's Liberation Army (PLA), and then to attain and retain the position of successor to Mao including an ill-fated effort to become People's Republic of China (PRC) state chairman in 1970.

---

[17] Significant studies from the immediate post-Lin period include: Jürgen Domes, *China after the Cultural Revolution: Politics between Two Party Congresses* (London: C. Hurst, 1976), parts I–II; Jaap van Ginneken, *The Rise and Fall of Lin Piao* (New York: Penguin Books, 1976); Philip Bridgham, 'The fall of Lin Piao', *China Quarterly (CQ)*, no. 55 (1973); Ellis Joffe, 'The Chinese army after the Cultural Revolution: the effects of intervention', *CQ*, no. 55 (1973); and Harry Harding, 'Political trends in China since the Cultural Revolution', *The Annals*, July 1972. In an earlier work one of the present authors, Teiwes, *Leadership*, pp. 105–13, was similarly misled into some of the same errors as these works, albeit in the context of a correctly Mao-centred interpretation; a first step in correcting said errors was idem, 'Mao and his lieutenants', *Australian journal of Chinese Affairs (AJCA)*, no. 19–20 (1988), pp. 63–7.
[18] In particular, the state of the art essays by Harry Harding, Roderick MacFarquhar, Thomas Robinson and Jonathan D. Pollack in *The Cambridge History of China (CHOC)*, vol. 15 (Cambridge University Press, 1991). The book by Barnouin and Yu which came to hand after the present analysis was drafted, *Ten Years of Turbulence*, especially ch. 6, is easily the best Western study to date. It is particularly notable for its clear understanding that 'Mao was too formidable an emperor' (p. 201) for 'Lin Biao [to] be considered a threat' (p. 208), but in our view it errs on various specific developments and most fundamentally in its characterisation of Lin as 'highly ambitious and unscrupulous in [his] attempts to strengthen [his] own position' (p. 211), and in claiming he engaged in 'acute' struggle with Mao after the 1970 Lushan plenum (p. 200).
[19] E.g., see Domes, *China after the Cultural Revolution*, pp. 130–2; van Ginneken, *Rise and Fall*, pp. 270–4; and Barnouin and Yu, *Ten Years of Turbulence*, pp. 216–17.

2. During the active phase of the Cultural Revolution from 1966 to 1968, Lin was a forceful proponent of the movement, even to the extent of advocating or at least sanctioning measures which disrupted the economy and the army, although perhaps with some restraint where his military 'power base' was concerned.

3. While initially allied with Mao, around the time of the Ninth Party Congress in April 1969 as the Cultural Revolution entered its 'construction' stage, the Chairman and his increasingly insecure successor began to fall out with an unrelenting power struggle developing by the time of the summer of 1970 Lushan plenum, if not earlier.

4. Apart from Mao himself, Lin's chief antagonist was Zhou Enlai who organized an anti-Lin coalition, while the 'Cultural Revolution left' represented possible if untrustworthy allies.[20]

5. The core of the post-Ninth Congress struggle was Lin's effort to perpetuate military preponderance over the polity while Mao and Zhou sought to restore civilian control.

6. In attempting to secure his power Lin Biao developed a programme of defence preparedness, a hard-line foreign policy, and Great Leap-style economic policies designed to appeal to China's military-industrial complex, but this programme lost out to a coalition of civilian administrators and regional military leaders who favoured more moderate policies.

Our review of the evidence suggests that all of the above points are seriously flawed. In contrast, we offer the following summary evaluation of the Lin Biao case:

1. Far from being excessively ambitious, Lin was content with an inactive albeit honoured position and was thrust into a leading role by Mao and subsequently cast aside for reasons that had little to do with any wishes he may have had for greater power.

---

[20] This view was strongly expressed in the immediate post-Lin period. Under the influence of post-Mao Chinese accounts of the struggle of the 'Lin Biao and Jiang Qing cliques', more recent Western analyses have given greater attention to conflict between these two groups.

2. While Lin publicly assumed a proponent's role during the Cultural Revolution as befitted his new status as the successor, and also seemingly took advantage of the situation to settle some personal grievances, to the extent that a personal political orientation can be deduced from his actions and private statements, it was in favour of economic moderation and limiting chaos, particularly in the army.

3. Lin never opposed Mao politically but instead operated by the prime political rule of strictly following the Chairman's wishes to the extent that they could be determined. Even in the desperate post-Lushan period his posture was passive and he most likely (although not certainly) had no knowledge of any military coup or assassination plots.

4. There was no fundamental conflict between Lin and Zhou Enlai as Zhou accepted Lin's superior status and Lin did not interfere in Zhou's activities. The conflict which did exist was between Lin and his supporters and Jiang Qing's 'group' which fundamentally developed from competition for Mao's blessing and was concerned more with trivial matters and perceptions of relative power than with policy issues.

5. Although the relationship of civilian and military authority caused considerable friction within the Party, there is little to suggest that Lin or his top associates in the PLA command were pushing for a Bonapartist outcome.

6. While Lin did have an interest in the institutional well-being of the military and the PLA as an organisation played a key role in supervising the economy, there is no evidence of his shaping a coherent programme to appeal to a military-industrial complex, or indeed of any developed policy positions throughout the entire 1966–71 period.

This interpretation suggests that Lin Biao was a tragic figure, but it is important to be clear in what sense he can be regarded as tragic. It definitely does not imply a favourable moral judgment on Lin. Instead it concerns a man who was at best an acute observer but became a reluctant player in the most turbulent years of CCP politics. As for personal morality, ironically the

most adequate summary judgment of Lin may have come in the
form of an obscure historical reference by Mao at the critical
August-September 1970 Lushan plenum – one which saw Lin's
wife, Ye Qun, seeking scholarly advice as to possible implications. According to Mao's allusion, 'King Zhou [Lin Biao?] is
no good, but he's not as bad as people think.'[21] Rather than
any virtue, what makes Lin tragic is that essentially he had little
interest in politics and did not wish to be in his exalted position.
He was the victim of his circumstances, trapped above all by the
designs and whims of Mao but also by the shifting currents of
an unpredictable political situation and the manipulation of his
own family. The following analysis elaborates on Lin's plight,
and the nature of élite politics in this period, first by examining
Lin and his context in broad terms, then by reviewing his role
during key conflicts in the active phase of the Cultural Revolution in 1966–8, and finally through the lens of major developments from the Ninth Congress to the period of Lin's decline
in 1970–1.

[21] Zhang Yunsheng, *Maojiawan*, p. 396.

2

LIN BIAO: THE MAN AND HIS CONTEXT

Lin Biao emerges from the reminiscences of Zhang Yunsheng, who served him as a secretary from August 1966 to late 1970, not only as a man of little ambition but as a detached, introverted figure[1] who usually showed little interest in national or world affairs and seldom played an active role in policy-making. Clearly poor health was a major factor, with Lin rarely attending important meetings, only able to work for one or two thirty-minute periods per day when he was briefed by his secretaries, and requiring injections before public appearances.[2] Lin's low level of interest in public affairs was graphically indicated by his falling asleep during a briefing on the Cambodian crisis in May 1970 and his nonchalant attitude toward China's first successful hydrogen bomb test in 1967, while his general detachment was illustrated by his unawareness of the construction of a swimming pool in Maojiawan, his Beijing residence.[3]

---

[1] Although someone who rarely 'knocked on other people's doors', for Lin there were several exceptions within the leadership whose company he enjoyed – Tao Zhu who had served under Lin in the Fourth Field Army and in the Central-South region immediately after 1949, and Su Yu whose military accomplishments Lin greatly admired. See Guan Weixun, *Ye Qun*, pp. 65, 208.

[2] Zhang Yunsheng, *Maojiawan*, pp. 13, 333. There have been reports that a major aspect of Lin's health problem was drug addiction: see Harrison E. Salisbury, *The New Emperors: China in the Era of Mao and Deng* (Boston: Little, Brown, 1992), pp. 285ff, 511; Xiao Sike, *Caoji shenpan*, vol. 1, p. 84; and Gao Gao and Yan Jiaqi, '*Wenhua dageming*', pp. 252–3. Possible drug abuse aside, it is clear that Lin's health problems were genuine. Apparently the result of a wound inflicted during the Anti-Japanese War, he suffered from low tolerance of light, wind and water, and he perspired heavily whenever his condition deteriorated. In addition, sleep was a constant problem which resulted in a dependence on sleeping pills and frequent late-night drives around Beijing. Some medical personnel reportedly even believed he had a mental disorder. See Guan Weixun, *Ye Qun*, pp. 171, 203, 205; and Zhang Yunsheng, *Maojiawan*, pp. 12, 165, 236.

[3] Zhang Yunsheng, *Maojiawan*, pp. 297–300, 331–2; and Guan Weixun, *Ye Qun*, p. 219. It is also of interest that the movie *Zhou Enlai*, which was filmed in the late 1980s with the assistance of the Central Documents Research Office, depicts a passive, distant Lin in contrast to the actively evil activities of his wife and son.

Zhang's picture has been confirmed in important respects by interviews with a range of Party historians. While some scholars hold to the view that Lin was ambitious, none have been able to find instances of his adopting significant positions on policy issues apart from those forced on him as the new number-two in the hierarchy by the fast-moving developments of the Cultural Revolution, nor do they have evidence that lie was involved in daily administrative affairs apart from military matters. On matters of basic domestic or foreign policy, these historians know of no input by Lin Biao. The situation was put graphically by a scholar specializing in the study of Zhou Enlai's role during the Cultural Revolution, who has seen much of the document flow among the top leaders. While there was an active exchange of ideas and suggestions between Mao and Zhou, despite the fact that all documents with rare exceptions went to Lin, the scholar in question never saw a concrete proposal from Lin who only circled his name to indicate receipt or wrote 'Completely agree', 'Act according to the Chairman's instructions' or 'Submit to the Chairman for decision' on these documents. While this clearly overstates the case in that, as the subsequent analysis shows, Lin did make a few specific suggestions concerning the events of the Cultural Revolution, it does point to a deliberate *modus operandi* on his part. Indeed, in laying down a personal political guideline of 'three dos and three don'ts', he included the injunction 'Do not make constructive proposals'.[4]

As for ambition, Lin's previous history points to contentment with a position on the sidelines since he held few active posts in the 1950s despite high status as a Politburo member, as Vice Premier and, from 1958, as Party Vice Chairman. His re-emergence in an operational role as Minister of Defence in 1959 came about not as a result of any lobbying on his part but in consequence of the sudden and unanticipated dismissal of Peng Dehuai at the first Lushan plenum. While Lin did play a significant role in support

---

[4] Guan Weixun, *Ye Qun*, p. 210. The remaining don'ts were 'Do not be critical' and 'Do not report bad news', while 'No constructive proposals' was linked to 'Not interfering with other people's responsibilities'. The three dos were 'Be ready to respond, to praise and to report good news.'

of Mao on that occasion, it was – as in subsequent years – in response to the initiative of Mao, who summoned him to the meeting after the crisis emerged. As we shall see, his public posture apparently did not reflect his private assessment of the situation.[5] From 1959 to the Cultural Revolution, Lin repeatedly praised the Chairman – something which did not distinguish him greatly from various other top Party leaders during and after the Great Leap Forward;[6] however, his actual role, according to a leading Party historian in the military, was confined to the army.

While Lin's personality and physical condition made him dependent on secretaries who selected the documents on which he was briefed, the situation was further complicated by the dominant position of his wife who served as head of his personal office and in the General Office of the Military Affairs Committee (MAC) since 1960, apparently with Mao's blessing.[7] Ye Qun, who saw her role as 'guarding the pass' (*ba guan*), controlled access to Lin Biao and was easily able to manipulate him, a fact which often makes it almost impossible to know when actions reflected Lin's will or when they were the product of Ye's initiative. In specific cases, however, Ye simply kept information from Lin – whether on personal matters such as their daughter's two attempts at suicide, or on important political questions as in approving a mid-1967 document on 'dragging out a handful in the military' in his name rather than bothering Lin with such a 'trivial' matter. In another revealing incident Ye went further and had a secretary forge in his writing extraordinarily favourable remarks concerning Jiang Qing whom she often

---

[5] On Lin's role at Lushan in 1959, see Li Rui, *Lushan huiyi shilu* (True Record of the Lushan Conference) (Beijing: Chunqiu chubanshe, 1989), pp. 223, 242, 246, 248–52, 257, 259. On his private view of that occasion, see below, p. 18.

[6] See Frederick C. Teiwes, *Politics and Purges in China: Rectification and the Decline of Party Norms, 1950–1965* (2nd edn, Armonk: M.E. Sharpe, 1993), pp. xxvii–xxviii, xxxix–xl.

[7] While Mao claimed he had 'never approved of one's wife heading the . . . office of one's own work unit' during his southern tour of 1971 when he alerted local leaders to his discontent with Lin Biao (see Kau, *Lin Piao*, p. 66), he had earlier encouraged Ye to play a more active role in view of Lin's poor health. See Guan Weixun, *Ye Qun*, p. 218.

sought to flatter, apparently feeling than Lin's antipathy towards Jiang would prevent him from being a party to such a manoeuvre.[8]

On other occasions Ye Qun deliberately disregarded Lin's instructions. For example, when Lin agreed to visit Nanchang to be received by the Jiangxi provincial leader Cheng Shiqing, of whose influence on him she disapproved, Ye simply ordered their plane to go directly to the next destination and vaguely said that they had already passed Nanchang some time previously when Lin enquired what was going on.[9] But perhaps the most spectacular instance of Ye ignoring Lin's expressed wishes, a case demonstrating that her interests were not identical to his, concerned the election of the new Politburo following the Ninth Congress. Before the Congress Mao had commented that Jiang Qing should not be a Politburo member – a situation which, if it had come to pass, would certainly have ruled Ye out and in fact led Lin to declare *his* opposition to Ye's candidacy. As matters unfolded, the three-man group consisting of Zhou Enlai, Kang Sheng and Huang Yongsheng which had been appointed by Mao to draw up the Politburo list, apparently not believing Mao was serious and unwilling to deny the ambitious women, included both of them on the list. Mao was seemingly agreeable to such an outcome but dispatched Zhou and Huang to visit Lin and solicit his views. Ye, fearful of what might transpire at such a meeting, invented the story that Lin was ill and could not receive them but that he agreed to the names on the list.[10] Such events and many others led his secretaries to conclude that it was so easy for Ye Qun to fool and cheat Lin.[11]

[8] Zhang Yunsheng, *Maojiawan*, pp. 55, 158, 172–4, 178, 233, 270–3; and Wen Feng, *Shentanxia*, p. 153. Such behaviour undoubtedly contributed to Marshal Nie Rongzhen's somewhat overstated observation in 1980 that 'Ye Qun was the real master of his affairs'; see Barnouin and Yu, *Ten Years of Turbulence*, p. 208. See also Huang Yongsheng's assessment of Ye's influence; Xiao Sike, *Caoji shenpan*, vol. 1, p. 85.

[9] Wen Feng, *Shentanxia*, p. 229.

[10] Lin did soon approve the list, however. See Zhang Yunsheng, *Maojiawan*, pp. 247–55; and a slightly different account in Guan Weixun, *Ye Qun*, pp. 220–1. The speculation concerning the thinking of the three-man group is ours rather than that of Zhang who prefers to believe Zhou was outvoted 2–1.

[11] See Guan Weixun, *Ye Qun*, p. 168.

Lin Biao's role on the national stage was thus critically influenced by the politics of the Lin family. For all his personal dependence, which even took the form of asking his wife whether he
should swallow or spit out phlegm in his throat, Lin's authority
within the family was unquestioned as both father and Vice
Chairman. Ye Qun and Lin Liguo understood that their own
positions were totally dependent on the leader (*shouzhang*), as
they referred to Lin, and this contributed to doing things behind
his back because they would not dare to confront him. Notwithstanding various tensions between Lin Biao and Ye Qun and
between Ye and their children, together with Lin and Ye's
daughter Lin Doudou, the family unit was unusually close by
CCP standards. Its four members frequently travelled together,
and Lin would request his children to prepare speeches and
articles for him.[12] Politically, the family was also unusual. Notwithstanding the case of Mao's own wife Jiang Qing, whom Ye
regarded as something of a model,[13] Ye Qun's prominence and
clout were remarkable for a Party wife, while the position of
their son Lin Liguo as deputy head of the combat department
of the air force, with the alleged (but not real) authority to decide
all air force matters from October 1969, was certainly unheard-of
for a twenty-four-year old.[14] And while, according to Zhang
Yunsheng's observations, there was little physical intimacy between Ye and Lin Biao, the larger relationship was passionate and

---

[12] Zhang Yunsheng, *Maojiawan*, pp. 196, 310; Wen Feng, *Shentanxia*, pp. 184, 224,
240; Guan Weixun, *Ye Qun*, p. 214; and Wang Nianyi, *Dadongluan*, pp. 375–8.
[13] Wang Nianyi, *Dadongluan*, p. 383.
[14] Even here the story is complex. While official histories claim Lin Biao put Wu
Faxian up to Lin Liguo's promotion, Zhang Yunsheng, *Maojiawan*, p. 328, reports
that Ye Qun instructed that Lin Biao should not be told, thus implying he might
have had a different opinion. Also, according to a report of an interview with Lin
Doudou in the Hong Kong journal *Jingbao yuekan* (The Mirror Monthly), June 1988,
p. 23, Lin not only had no knowledge of Liguo's promotion, he was also unaware
that the position existed, while Guan Weixun, *Ye Qun*, p. 172, claims that Lin dressed
down Ye Qun after becoming aware of the matter. As for Lin Liguo's reported
authority over all air force matters, this was highly exaggerated; see Wang Nianyi,
Dadongluan, p. 378. Even Lin himself required Mao's approval before units of company
size or larger could be deployed; see below, n. 31. See also Barnouin and Yu, *Ten
Years of Turbulence*, p. 216.

stormy. Despite the extent of his dependence, Lin often disapproved of Ye's actions and refused to see her for days at a time or had her ejected from his car – behaviour which led her to appeal to an amused Mao for support; but on the other hand he wrote love poems to Ye declaring that 'Although the colour of our hair is not the same our hearts share the same temperature, [and] while we were not born on the same day we are prepared to die together.'[15] Most important, Ye's personal grievances sometimes aroused in Lin a passion which influenced his political involvements. Perhaps the most remarkable example occurred during the crucial May 1966 enlarged Politburo meeting that sealed the downfall of, among others, Lu Dingyi. Lin circulated a letter affirming that Ye was a virgin at the time of their marriage. In this he was refuting charges raised anonymously years earlier by Lu Dingyi's wife, and at the meeting the normally cool man of few words launched into a particularly heated attack on Lu, declaring 'I'd love to shoot you.' While undoubtedly the key political consideration leading Lin to attack Lu was Mao's prior condemnation of Lu's reign as CCP propaganda chief, the atypical degree to which he threw himself into the task was surely linked to Ye Qun's honour.[16]

While Lin Biao was certainly manipulated by his family and most likely unaware of much of their political activity, he was inextricably linked to them and their deeds by the logic of Chinese political culture which made families a single responsible unit. Moreover, in a strictly factual perspective, as already suggested, there is no way of knowing precisely what he was aware of or responsible for. While Lin's secretaries felt sorry for him since he was repeatedly kept in the dark, they also could not completely absolve him. Perhaps the most judicious overall judgment is that offered by Zhang Yunsheng: 'Ye Qun did many things behind Lin Biao's back while holding high his banner. However, it's unfair to say that all her actions were done without his

[15] See Guan Weixun, *Ye Qun*, pp. 140, 222. Lin attached to his poem a note that it was composed for his beloved wife and that he wished their ashes to be placed together when they died.

[16] Wang Nianyi, *Dadongluan*, pp. 18–19.

knowledge. . . . [Lin] was so willing to be manipulated by Ye Qun.'[17] For better or worse, and with an uncertain degree of his own direct responsibility, Lin Biao's role in the Cultural Revolution and his subsequent fate could not be separated from the actions of his family.

If the Lin Biao seen from inside his residence at Maojiawan was somewhat pathetic, from the outside he was a figure of considerable substance. Despite evidence of reservations concerning his elevation to the position of successor, he seems on the whole to have been accepted because he was seen as having Mao's trust and as being relatively free of mistakes, and because of his enormous status and prestige as one of the great military heroes of the revolution. His high position in the Party even during the time of his inactivity in the 1950s was regarded, according to the reports of oral sources,[18] as quite proper in view of his past achievements. Moreover, even someone like Deng Liqun, who as a former secretary to Liu Shaoqi would be presumed hostile to Lin's replacement of Liu as the successor, considered the change reasonable at the time in view of Lin's perceived deeper ideological commitment and greater loyalty to Mao, as well as his better understanding of military matters.[19] And notwithstanding official attempts to picture Lin as a relentless foe of the other marshals, relations with these marshals excepting He Long and Zhu De were apparently good and marked by great respect toward Lin. In contrast to the peer group attitude toward Ye Jianying, who – according to an army Party historian – was looked down upon as someone selected as a marshal just to round off the numbers, Lin's military achievements were universally admired. Thus even in the hostile reminiscences of Marshal Nie Rongzhen, Nie acknowledged that he and his colleagues accepted

[17] Zhang Yunsheng, *Maojiawan*, pp. 428–9, 430.

[18] With regard to Lin's promotion to Vice Chairman in 1958 there are varying interpretations including Mao seeking additional support for the Great Leap Forward and an effort to redress a sense of military grievance *vis-à-vis* the civilian apparatus, but the view of it as simply reflecting Lin's accepted status was strongly argued by several senior Party historians.

[19] See Deng's 1981 recollection as cited in Harry Harding, 'The Chinese state in crisis,' in *CHOC*, vol. 15, p. 207.

Lin as the successor even after differences with him emerged over the course of the Cultural Revolution.[20]

The contrast between the pathetic Lin Biao seen within the confines of Maojiawan and his elevated public and Party reputation not only distressed his secretaries, but it also underlines the jarring contradiction with the assessment of contemporary Western biographers who depicted Lin as commanding and decisive, a master of tactics with great stores of energy and drive who sought action and 'shared in all major decisions regarding ... the Cultural Revolution'.[21] Undoubtedly much of Lin's image in both China and the West is a reflection of his genuine military achievements: on the battlefiled he did undoubtedly demonstrate extraordinary decisiveness and tactical brilliance. But while his post-1949 political life did not match these achievements, the weak figure portrayed above is only part of a more complex story. First, in dealing with Mao during the initial period after liberation Lin continued in the same vein as during the revolution – that is, he expressed his views calmly and frankly in private discussions while publicly always backing the Chairman, assigning accomplishments to him, and accepting responsibility for any mistakes.[22] But with inner-Party democracy in decline by the time of the Great Leap Forward,[23] a shrewd and increasingly cynical Lin began to tailor his advocacy to the prevailing wind. Significantly, he reflected on the Great Leap period with the observation that 'whoever did not speak

---

[20] *Xinhua ribao (XHRB)* (New China Daily, Nanjing), 18 October 1984, in *Foreign Broadcast Information Service (FBIS)*, 5 November 1984, pp. K17–18. *XHRB* serialised parts of Nie's recollections, *Nie Rongzhen huiyilu* (Memoirs of Nie Rongzhen) (Beijing: Jiefangjun chubanshe, 1984), in October 1984. For a high evaluation of his military accomplishments by another Lin Biao 'victim', see Huang Kecheng's post-Mao assessment in *Dangshi ziliao zhengji tongxun* (Collected Materials on Party History Bulletin), no. 4 (1985), p. 9.

[21] Ebon, *Lin Piao*, pp. 11–12, 147; and Robinson, 'Lin Piao', pp. 156–7, 167.

[22] This is the picture conveyed by Quan Yanchi, *Zouxia shengtande Zhou Enlai* (Zhou Enlai Down to Earth) (Taibei: Xinrui chubanshe, 1994), p. 364. This is the Taiwan edition of a book by a prolific PRC writer with a military background who has developed extensive interview sources and whose work can be taken as generally reliable.

[23] See Teiwes, *Politics and Purges*, pp. l–lvi.

falsely fell from power'.[24] Once he had been thrust into an increasingly significant role after the 1959 Lushan conference, Lin was inevitably involved in speaking falsely.

The views which Lin expressed openly during these years and into the Cultural Revolution itself stood in sharp contradiction to his private beliefs, which in turn contradicted the political interests often ascribed to him by foreign analysts. Thus, far from being the Great Leap enthusiast Mao presumably believed him to be when promoting him to a Party Vice Chairmanship in 1958, Lin commented to his daughter in this period that the Leap was 'pure idealism'. His true attitude toward Peng Dehuai, whom he attacked at Lushan and then replaced as Minister of Defence, was also quite different. While conceding that Peng's timing may have been bad, he felt like other leaders that Peng's letter critiquing the Great Leap was correct and was dismayed with Mao's ruthless reaction despite the effect which it had of enhancing his own power. With regard to another key leader, Liu Shaoqi, Lin's views were also very different from what is generally assumed. Lin had not only carefully read Liu's famous 'Cultivation of a Communist Party Member' and made many approving marginal comments, but during the Cultural Revolution he told Lin Doudou that Lin's level of theoretical understanding was superior to Mao's, declared that both Liu and Deng Xiaoping were good comrades, and commented that it did not make sense to get rid of Liu. As for the Cultural Revolution itself, Lin's dismissive 1967 comment that the movement had become 'a revolution without culture' (*wuhua dageming*) perhaps best summed up his attitude.[25] But with the onset of the Cultural Revolution Lin could no longer stand on the periphery as he had done in the 1950s, or even be the comparatively limited if still significant player he had been from 1959 to 1965.

[24] Guan Weixun, *Ye Qun*, p. 209.
[25] *Ibid.*, pp. 202, 209, 214–15; and Zhang Yunsheng, *Maojiawan*, p. 108. Less specifically, Zhang Yunsheng, *ibid.*, p. 225, reported that when he read Lin's diaries after September 1971 he found various critical remarks concerning Mao's policies in the 1950s and early 1960s. On other leaders' similar attitudes towards developments at Lushan, see Teiwes, *Politics and Purges*, pp. xxxiii–xxxv, liv–lv.

The Cultural Revolution Context

The Cultural Revolution placed Lin Biao in a completely new position. As the number-two figure in the leadership he now had overall responsibility for the full range of Party and state affairs, received all relevant documents, and was given an expanded secretarial staff to cope with the load. But while he was clearly involved in a wider range of affairs than merely military matters as had been the case since 1959, Lin as indicated above did not play an active operational role outside the army, and the burden of daily affairs fell squarely on the shoulders of Zhou Enlai and in some ways also on the civilian radicals of the Cultural Revolution Group (CRG).[26] More significant than administrative changes was that the very fact of being the successor thrust Lin into the spotlight and placed upon him the specific duty of promoting Mao. What is not generally understood in view of Lin's documented record of singing Mao's praises over the 1959–65 period is that the position of number-two carried with it extra responsibilities and expectations in this area. Even someone as different in so many ways as Liu Shaoqi also felt the need to follow Mao closely and promote his cult to demonstrate complete loyalty to the Chairman.[27] That Lin Biao may have been particularly sycophantic did not lessen the burdens or – as events were to demonstrate – the dangers of these expectations.

Mao Zedong, of course, stood at the centre of the Cultural Revolution drama. Mao, as we see later in greater detail, clearly thrust Lin into the successor role – for reasons that are subject to conjecture. Chinese scholars believe, as does much Western analysis, that Mao needed Lin because the army's assistance would be required in order to secure the Cultural Revolution, and there is no reason to doubt that the Chairman may have

---

[26] Zhang Yunsheng, *Maojiawan*, p. 5; and oral sources.
[27] On Liu in this respect, see Teiwes, *Politics and Purges*, pp. xxxix–xliv, liii, lviii; and Frederick C. Teiwes with the assistance of Warren Sun, *The Formation of the Maoist Leadership: From the Return of Wang Ming to the Seventh Party Congress* (London: Contemporary China Institute Research Notes and Studies, 1994), pp. 38–9.

thought in that way even if, on the basis of the full Cultural Revolution experience, it is difficult to believe that the military would not have obeyed Mao with someone else in charge. Nevertheless, Lin's great military prestige certainly made the objective of military support easier to achieve, and given Mao's disenchantment by 1965 with all other members of the Politburo Standing Committee, including Zhou Enlai, Lin was the only figure of sufficient status who would have appeared to him to be a reliable supporter of the new movement. In any case, Mao's trust in Lin, which most Party historians interviewed regard as the primary aspect of his relationship with his new successor at the start of the Cultural Revolution, was of long standing and well known within the top group. About 1960 he singled out Lin and Deng Xiaoping as possible future successors (presumably after Liu Shaoqi), and by early 1965 he had cooled towards Deng. Overall, Lin was the logical choice because of his institutional connection, his status in the CCP and his ostensible commitment to 'Politics in command' (*zhengzhi guashuai*), and especially because of his presumed personal loyalty over decades.[28]

More important for our purposes than Mao's motives in choosing Lin was both the general atmosphere surrounding the Chairman and the methods used by Lin to deal with the situation. While the general ambience was clearly that of an imperial court,[29] it was also one where the 'emperor' was regarded by his courtiers as increasingly unpredictable and dangerous – as we have seen, this view had already been held by Lin since the Great Leap Forward. This was perhaps put most clearly by one of the

[28] Oral sources. A further claim, that in 1956 Mao voted for Lin as Party Chairman at the Eighth Congress (see Gai Jun, *Zhongguo Gongchandang bolan zhuangkuo de qishinian* (The CCP's Magnificent Seventy Years of Surging Forward) (Beijing: Zhongguo qingnian chubanshe, 1991), p. 447; and Roderick MacFarquhar, 'The succession to Mao and the end of Maoism', in *CHOC*, vol. 15, p. 306n), is more dubious. This claim is apparently based on a 1966 report by Ye Jianying after the Eleventh Plenum, i.e. *after* Lin's elevation to the status of successor, and is regarded as unreliable by a number of senior Party historians. One well-placed historian, moreover, states that an investigation revealed the vote for Mao as Party Chairman in 1956 was unanimous. For an overview of the Mao-Lin relationship, see Teiwes, 'Mao and his lieutenants', pp. 63–7.

[29] For a discussion of life at the court at an earlier, considerably more benign stage, see Frederick C. Teiwes, *Politics at Mao's Court: Gao Gang and Party Factionalism in the Early 1950s* (Armonk: M.E. Sharpe, 1990).

new additions to the inner circle during the Cultural Revolution, Ji Dengkui: '[Mao] often contradicted himself with his thinking. In his later years, almost nobody trusted him. We very seldom saw him and . . . when we [did meet] him we were very afraid of what we said for fear of committing an error.'[30] In this context where even the trappings of collective leadership no longer existed, Lin's explicit strategy was rational if extremely reactive: 'It is essential to follow Chairman Mao,' 'If the Chairman circles [a document], I circle.' This was linked not only to excessive praise but also, despite official claims to the contrary, to efforts to limit his own publicity and keep the focus on Mao. The posture Lin adopted was illustrated by his decision to replace the character *qing* 请, 'please [comment]', or *song* 送, 'deliver to', with *cheng* 呈, 'submit a memorial to one's superior', when sending documents to Mao for approval. Great lengths were also generally taken to secure Mao's consent concerning even minor matters, as when the Tianjin Garrison Command sought Lin's approval for sending a company of soldiers to the countryside to help with the harvest. Lin hesitated to act and passed the matter on to Mao – lamely responding, when asked why the Chairman had to be consulted on such a trivial matter, that during the Cultural Revolution authority should be centralized and Mao's approval was needed. And all the while Ye Qun, as the in-house specialist for dealing with 'number-one', made sure that in public Lin always had the 'little red book' of Mao Quotations at hand and was constantly reminded of such matters as making sure he never kept the Chairman waiting and always walked a few steps behind him. Such considerations, not the large affairs of state, were the issues of concern at Maojiawan.[31]

---

[30] *Liaowang* (Outlook), overseas edition, 6–13 February 1989, in *FBIS*, 14 February 1989, p. 26. This comment, which specifically refers to Mao's nephew, Mao Yuanxin, serving as liaison between the Chairman and other leaders, may more strictly apply to 1975–6, but the general atmosphere certainly applied earlier.

[31] Zhang Yunsheng, *Maojiawan*, pp. 232, 298, 300–1; Wang Nianyi, *Dadongluan*, pp. 371–2; and oral sources. On Lin's self-effacing posture toward Mao, see also Barnouin and Yu, *Ten Years of Turbulence*, p. 202. With regard to troop movements, a regulation in fact required Mao's approval of all movements at the company level and above; see *Zhuanji wenxue* (Biographical Recollections Literature), no. 6 (1994), p. 11. This regulation was proposed by the MAC (Lin Biao?) and approved by Mao.

A major feature of the Cultural Revolution was the relentless attacks on and vicious treatment of political figures who had fallen from grace, attacks often leading to 'persecution to death'. Such persecutions, which amounted to only a small part of the human toll of the movement, reportedly resulted in over 34,000 deaths reaching to the highest levels including Politburo members Liu Shaoqi, Tao Zhu, Peng Dehuai and He Long. Many cases, involving not only politically undermining victims and framing them for imaginary crimes but also direct involvement in torture and associated cruelties, have been officially laid at Lin Biao's door. Lin is thus characterised as having an 'ubiquitous murderous hand' which reached into every corner of China, but which reserved particular ferocity for such military leaders as Peng Dehuai, He Long and Luo Ruiqing who allegedly presented a threat to his control of the armed forces.[32] Given the difficulties of knowing precisely what went on behind closed doors at Maojiawan, such claims cannot be rejected out of hand, but there is much about both the general allegations and specific cases which raises doubts, at least concerning the degree of Lin's involvement and initiative.

One of the major problems is that it is often difficult to find clear traces of Lin Biao as an individual in perfidious activities, even after formal investigation as part of the 1980–1 trial process. Many charges are directed simply against 'the Lin Biao clique' or 'Lin Biao and company', and blame is frequently assigned to the 'Lin Biao *and* Jiang Qing cliques' acting together. And indeed in specific cases elements of both groups were involved, but in such cases it often appears that the 'Lin Biao clique' was playing a secondary role. In a suggestive example, in mid-1968 a 'special case group', one of the organs assigned to investigate cadres under suspicion which were frequently guilty of torture and other forms of maltreatment, submitted a report to Jiang Qing, PLA Chief of Staff Huang Yongsheng (one of the 'principal members of the Lin Biao clique'), and two other leaders for

---

[32] See especially the damning account in Gao Gao and Yan Jiaqi, '*Wenhua dageming*', pp. 209ff. See also *A Great Trial*, pp. 82–9.

comment. Huang dutifully expressed agreement on the report but when it reached Jiang Qing she reportedly flew into a rage and demanded to know what business Huang had with 'her' special case group.[33] More generally, Huang was made responsible for the 'second special case group' dealing with military figures, yet the evidence of the trial of the 'two cliques' suggests a somewhat reactive Huang who approved the reports of groups dealing with such cases as that of Peng Dehuai, or joined in attacks on various other old marshals, rather than being a primary initiator of action.[34]

The uncertainty concerning the depth of the involvement of Lin Biao, Huang Yongsheng *et al.* points to the larger problem of how much choice these individuals had. Given the atmosphere of asserted danger from revisionist, indeed counterrevolutionary opposition, Lin, Huang and others could reasonably feel that harsh action was what Mao wanted. This was unambiguously the case where Peng Dehuai was concerned,[35] and Mao's ambivalent attitude toward various other old marshals at the very least left room for believing that strong criticism was needed.[36] Indeed, it was Huang Yongsheng's defence that while he did engage in dishonest criticism of the old marshals, in his own mind he still held them in great respect.[37] In addition to such subjective factors, the case against Lin in particular is compromised by the fact that some of the most specific charges of frameups and persecutions laid against him came from the tainted

---

[33] Wang Nianyi, *Dadongluan*, p. 386; and Zhang Yunsheng, *Maojiawan*, pp. 203–4.
[34] *A Great Trial*, pp. 84–5; and Ma Qibin *et al.*, *Zhongguo Gongchandang zhizheng sishinian (1949–1989)* (The CCP's Forty Years in Power, 1949–1989) (revised edn, Beijing: Zhonggong dangshi chubanshe, 1991), p. 333. Huang's distance from the persecutions is also suggested by the fact that they had begun in 1966 but he only assumed a role in 1968.
[35] On Mao's relationship with Peng, see Frederick C. Teiwes, 'Peng Dehuai and Mao Zedong', *AJCA*, no. 16 (1986); and idem, *Politics and Purges*, pp. xxxi–xxxvi, liii–lvi, lix–lx.
[36] When Lin sought Mao's advice concerning the old marshals at the time of the October 1968 Central Committee plenum, Mao replied 'Criticize first, then protect'; Zhang Yunsheng, *Maojiawan*, p. 200.
[37] Xiao Sike, *Caoji shenpan*, vol. 1, p. 231.

testimony of Wu Faxian.[38] Moreover, there is evidence of Lin
Biao's efforts, at least initially when Mao's position was unclear,
to *protect* military leaders who had come under radical attack.
This not only included old revolutionary subordinates such as
Yang Chengwu and Xiao Hua, and local commanders such as
Xu Shiyou, but even Marshal Ye Jianying in the spring of 1967.
Indeed, according to Zhang Yunsheng, Ye Qun felt caught between 'following Mao closely and supporting the CRG firmly'
on the one hand and taking account of 'Lin Biao's affection for
the marshals' on the other.[39] All of this suggests the difficulty
of getting at the truth, but a better understanding of this important question may be possible through examining two cases
where Lin clearly was significantly involved: the cases of Luo
Ruiqing and He Long.

Luo Ruiqing, the PLA Chief of Staff, was one of the first
victims of the immediate pre-Cultural Revolution period in
late 1965. At the time, Luo was charged with both pushing
military professionalisation in opposition to Mao's and Lin's
emphasis on political work, and with seeking to wrest leadership
of the army from Lin. In addition, contemporary Western
scholars – but not Chinese sources – added another policy issue,
Luo's alleged advocacy of a united front with the Soviet Union
to resist the United States in Vietnam in opposition to the
views of Mao and Lin Biao.[40] In the post-Mao era the accusation

[38] See *A Great Trial*, pp. 84, 86; and *Jingbao yuekan*, June 1988, p. 23 (see above,
n. 14). It should be made clear that the sources indicating Wu's remorse for making
up testimony did not specify these instances, but the general picture of giving the
prosecutors what they wanted suggests that this may have been the case. Wu was
not the only source of tainted testimony but the most significant given his status and
the several hundred thousand words of written testimony he provided in 1971–81.
Wu was acknowledged by trial officials as the most cooperative and enthusiastic of
the defendants, and he surreptitiously marked some of his testimony with dots to identify fabrications. See Xiao Sike, *Caoji shenpan*, vol. 1, pp. 224, 273, 279, 280–1.
[39] See Zhang Yunsheng, *Maojiawan*, pp. 31, 65, 73, 103, 105, 218; and Guan
Weixun, *Ye Qun*, p. 212. On Xiao Hua, see below, p. 41.
[40] See, e.g., Uri Ra'anan, 'Peking's foreign policy "debate," 1965–66', in Tang Tsou
and Ping-ti Ho (eds), *China in Crisis*, vol. II (University of Chicago Press, 1968);
and the critique of this interpretation by Michael Yahuda, 'Kremlinology and the
Chinese strategic debate, 1965–6', *CQ*, No. 49 (1972). The standard account of

of seeking military power has been considered a frame-up
organised by Lin Biao, and Luo's fall has been officially interpreted as Lin's initiative which succeeded in winning Mao's
support,[41] a view still held by some serious scholars.

The Luo Ruiqing case is unusually difficult to unravel because
of, first, the secrecy surrounding the events themselves and,
secondly, contradictory evidence from credible sources, particularly concerning the key question of the degree of initiative on
Lin Biao's part. There is one basic feature of the case which may
go far to explain the difficulties of analysis and any unusual
initiative by Lin – precisely the fact that this was to a large
extent a *pre*-Cultural Revolution development. In contrast to the
mass-movement politics and extensive leaking of information
during the Cultural Revolution, the crucial events of
November–December 1965 took place behind closed doors and
were kept within very narrow circles.[42] And while the matter
was clearly linked to Mao's larger concern with revisionism
within the CCP as a whole, the immediate issues *did* relate to
military policy and thus were a genuine concern of Lin's portfolio in the normal pre-1966 sense. Thus even a scholarly account
hostile to Lin admits – in contrast to its accusations concerning
the Cultural Revolution itself – that 'on the surface' Lin's moves
against Luo in the military sphere were quite legitimate, while
the memoirs of Navy Commander Xiao Jingguang conclude

Luo's purge focusing on policy matters is Harry Harding and Melvin Gurtov, *The
Purge of Lo Jui-ch'ing: The Politics of Chinese Strategic Planning*, RAND Report
R-548-PR, February 1971, an account emphasising the professionalisation *versus*
politics issue but rejecting conflict over the united front question.
[41] For the standard view, see Gao Gao and Yan Jiaqi, *'Wenhua dageming'*,
pp. 192–202.
[42] In daughter Luo Diandian's account based on post-Mao discussions with Tan
Zhenlin, even ordinary Politburo members at the key December meeting in Shanghai
where Luo was first denounced were unaware of the very existence of a 'Luo Ruiqing
case', thus implying that the affair was dealt with secretly within the Standing Committee. See [Luo] Diandian, *Feifan de niandai* (Those Extraordinary Years) (Shanghai:
Shanghai wenyi chubanshe, 1987), pp. 199–200. This is most likely in error since other
sources indicate a wider participation, although one still restricted to very high levels.

that criticisms of Luo regarding naval matters were not improper, even though he disagreed with their content.[43]

In any case it is clear that by 1964–5 Lin had become disenchanted with Luo although they had had close ties in the revolutionary period, Lin had nominated Luo for the Chief of Staff post in 1959, and their working relations had been generally harmonious up to about 1964. Indeed, oral sources report that there was no question of Luo challenging Lin's leadership, and all important military issues were referred to Lin for decision. Yet while, in the opinion of one Party historian working on the case, it would have been impossible for Luo to raise different opinions to Lin face-to-face given the strong sense of hierarchy in the army, different policy perspectives did emerge concerning the emphasis on politics and the crudeness of the Mao cult, something Luo reportedly felt the Chairman would not agree to. These clashing policy views were arguably the main source of tension between the two PLA leaders as seen in 1964 when Luo's military training programme attracted Lin's attention. Lin sent Ye Qun to investigate and came to the critical conclusion that 'politics should figure prominently', yet Luo issued his own criticisms of 'empty politics' which seemingly resulted in the Defence Minister's frustration over his subordinate's attitude.[44] On the Vietnam question, however, there is not only no direct evidence of a Luo-Lin clash, but the chief basis

[43] See Tan Zhongji (ed.), *Shinianhou de pingshuo – 'Wenhua dageming' shilunji* (Critical Explanations after Ten Years – Collected Historical Essays on the 'Cultural Revolution') (Beijing: Zhonggong dangshi ziliao chubanshe, 1987), p. 67; and *Xiao Jingguang huiyiluxuji* (Sequel to Memoirs of Xiao Jingguang) (Beijing: Jiefangjun chubanshe, 1989), p. 250.

While the personal grievances of Jiang Qing and Ye Qun were present in this case, they appear to have been less critical than in various developments during the Cultural Revolution itself. Tensions reportedly existed between Luo and Jiang about this time as a result of Luo's ignoring of her invitation to attend a forum on literature and art and his earlier denial of her request for a military uniform; see Gao Gao and Yan Jiaqi, *'Wenhua dageming'*, p. 195. On Ye Qun's grievances, see below, p. 28.

[44] See Cong Jin, *1949–1989 nian de Zhongguo: Quzhe fazhan de suiye* (China 1949–1989: The Years of Circuitous Development) (Henan: Henan renmin chubanshe, 1989), pp. 631–3.

of the Western scholarly argument – a Pekinological comparison
of Luo's May 1965 article celebrating the defeat of Germany in
the Second World War with Lin's September piece, 'Long live
the victory of people's war' – is undercut by the fact that,
although issued in Lin's name, the latter article was primarily
written by Wu Lengxi of the 'revisionist' Central Propaganda
Department while the whole project was organised by none
other than Luo Ruiqing.[45]

Another factor apparently contributing to estrangement was
the vast array of operational powers which Luo held within the
PLA, involving no less than twelve major posts, so that – in the
words of a Party historian – 'his hands reached everywhere'.[46]
The story that Luo 'shouted' that Lin Biao, being ill, should get
out of the way and let him take over may have been the result
of a misunderstanding or a fabrication by Lin (or, more likely,
Ye Qun) as claimed by official historiography.[47] However, such
an array of powers monopolised by a capable and ambitious official, together with the fact that Luo was very close to Marshal
He Long who also had great clout as the MAC Vice Chairman
in charge of daily work since late 1962 and whose initial

---

[45] Ye Yonglie, *Zhonggong shenmi zhangquanzhe* (The CCP's Mysterious Powerholders)
(Taibei: Fengyun shidai chuban youxian gongsi, 1993), p. 198. As with Quan Yanchi
(see above, n. 22), this is the Taiwan edition of a work by a noted mainland writer
with extensive interview sources. He too can be treated as generally reliable, and,
if anything, he is more thorough in his research than Quan.

[46] Tan Zhongji, *Shinianhou*, p. 65; [Luo] Diandian, *Feifan*, p. 209; and oral source.

[47] The misinterpretation thesis is suggested by the fact that Luo had raised the question of the retirement of cadres in poor health in the context of a general discussion
of cadre policy (see *Zhonggong wenhua dageming zhongyao wenjian huibian* (Collection
of Important CCP Documents on the Cultural Revolution) (Taibei: 'Zhonggong yanjiu' zazhishe bianjibu, 1973), p. 30), and this was perhaps taken by Lin and/or Ye
Qun as applying to the Defence Minister. The more general notion of Luo pressuring
Lin to retire is largely based on the claim that before Air Force Commander Liu
Yalou's death in February 1965 Luo sent Liu to Ye with a message to that effect;
see Barnouin and Yu, *Ten Years of Turbulence*, pp. 68–9. But as Deng Xiaoping
reportedly commented (in a version that may be too kind to Deng; see below), with
Liu dead the claim rested solely on Ye's word. Jiang Bo and Li Qing (eds), *Lin Biao
1959 yihou* (Lin Biao after 1959) (Chengdu: Sichuan renmin chubanshe, 1993), p. 198;
and oral source.

political decline coincided with Luo's,[48] undoubtedly gave some cause for concern. Petty irritants also played a part. Lin reportedly told Luo that in view of his own poor health, Luo could report directly to Mao and other MAC Vice Chairmen, but when Luo actually did so, Lin was dissatisfied and felt excluded. On the other hand, when Luo did report to Lin, the Defence Minister sometimes believed that he was being troubled over small matters which did not need to be brought to an unwell man.[49] More specifically, in the summer of 1965 Lin Biao's office told Luo, in response to his request, to come and report, but when Luo hurriedly arrived Lin complained of a 'surprise attack' because he knew nothing of the meeting until Luo arrived at the gate of his residence.[50] Finally, Luo had run foul of Ye Qun on several matters where personal pride was involved. In the early 1960s Luo promoted Ye to colonel according to regulations, while she assertedly wanted the rank of senior colonel, and in 1965 Luo removed her name from an order by Lin concerning the emphasis to be placed on politics, an effrontery on her part that reportedly also angered Lin.[51] Indeed, in the view of one historian, the tension between Luo and Ye Qun was much greater than any between him and Lin Biao, while one of the secretaries at Maojiawan claimed that a big role had been played by Ye in the Luo Ruiqing affair.[52]

Thus, whatever the precise mix of factors, dissatisfaction existed within Maojiawan concerning Luo Ruiqing in late 1965,

[48] Lin Biao was reportedly angered in April 1965 by the fact that Luo and He Long briefed Mao on military work without his prior knowledge although, as the following shows, he had granted permission for such a step. In addition, He strongly promoted military training in 1964 along with Luo and Ye Jianying, and both He and Luo worked together on defence industry matters. [Luo] Diandian, *Feifan*, pp. 189–90; and *Jiefangjun jiangling zhuan* (Biographies of PLA Generals) (Beijing: Jiefangjun chubanshe, 1985), pp. 354–5. On He's decline, see below, pp. 32–6.

[49] Tan Zhongji, *Shinianhou*, p. 67.

[50] [Luo] Diandian, *Feifan*, p. 194. This incident suggests that relations between Lin and Luo may have been exacerbated by Ye Qun withholding information from her husband. For another instance where Ye clearly used underhand methods to deceive Luo when he visited Lin, see Guan Weixun, *Ye Qun*, p. 223.

[51] Gao Gao and Yan Jiaqi, '*Wenhua dageming*', pp. 197–8.

[52] Guan Weixun, *Ye Qun*, p. 223; and oral source.

but even in accounts emphasising Lin's initiative the role of Mao was crucial. Some Chinese scholars believe that Mao's warning in October 1965 about possible revisionism in the Central Committee moved Lin to act while, more narrowly, one Party historian specialising in the case believes that a visit to Lin in Suzhou in late November from 'a Party Centre comrade', who discussed the case of Yang Shangkun, the recently sacked head of the CCP General Office, convinced Lin that he could now move against Luo.[53] And by this logic Lin would have been further encouraged by the cooling in 1965 of Mao's formerly close relationship with Luo, who had always previously accompanied him on trips outside Beijing but was now excluded.[54] In the official account, but one which is also supported by some careful historians, Lin then fabricated materials and dispatched Ye Qun to Hangzhou to present the case against Luo to Mao, and the Chairman immediately accepted her account and set in motion Luo's purge.[55]

Certainly there is evidence of an initiative on Lin's part which may have been influenced by signs of the Chairman's dissatisfaction with Luo before Mao's meeting with Ye Qun in early December. In particular, Lin asked in late November for materials from the navy's political commissar, Li Zuopeng, concerning differences with Luo over ideological work in the navy, although it is likely, but not completely certain that this came after an initial complaint by Li.[56] This conflict, however, not only concerned ongoing military work that was a proper concern of the Defence Minister; it also reflected longstanding tensions, rather than being something concocted for the moment. Lin then wrote to Mao on 30 November addressing problems involving

---

[53] Ma Qibin, *Sishinian*, p. 260; and oral sources.
[54] See the 16 May 1966 CCP Centre document, 'Remarks on the report concerning Luo Ruiqing's mistakes', in *Zhonggong wenhua dageming zhongyao wenjian huibian*, p. 26.
[55] The Lin Biao initiative thesis gains credibility from the endorsement of the excellent Party historian, Cong Jin, *Quzhe fazhan*, p. 633.
[56] Three events took place on 27 November – a letter from Li Zuopeng to Lin Biao, Lin's phone call to Li requesting materials, and a visit to Lin by Luo Ruiqing. The sequence of these events, however, is not clearly stated in available sources.

Luo Ruiqing, and attached various materials exposing Luo. Lin's letter, however, oddly made no direct reference to Luo and indicated that, before the Yang Shangkun affair he saw no compelling need to inform the Chairman. Moreover, according to well-placed Party historians in the PLA, the official version distorts what actually happened. It would be naive, one commented, to believe that Mao would simply accept Ye's story. In fact, they claim, it was Mao who summoned Ye to Hangzhou and expressed *his* discontent with Luo on the political work issue, thus arguably changing the issue from an irritation over professional matters within Maojiawan to an ominous political question. Whoever took the initiative, the key development was Mao's warning on 2 December against *opportunists* 'who don't believe in giving prominence to politics'.[57]

Whether the sceptical version or the official account is closer to the truth, events then quickly unfolded with Lin seemingly active in taking advantage of the situation to rid himself of Luo, allegedly developing the bogus case, and convening a meeting of the PLA General Political Deparment (GPD) at the turn of the year to promote 'Politics in command', the principle that political considerations should guide army work. Even for this crucial period, however, there is evidence suggesting less than wholehearted action on Lin's part. A case in point was the performance of Li Zuopeng whose disputes with Luo over navy affairs had set the stage for Lin's initial action, but who remained silent at the crucial conference in Shanghai in December which first attacked Luo, and only joined in criticism at the subsequent meetings in March.[58] Moreover, if Lin participated in the escalating moves against Luo, others were not blameless. Marshal Ye Jianying was placed in charge of a group investigating the case which did not absolve Luo, and General Yang Chengwu of the General Staff Department launched one of the first major attacks on his colleague.

---

[57] Cong Jin, *Quzhe fazhan*, p. 633; Tan Zhongji, *Shinianhou*, pp. 66, 68; *Xiao Jingguang huiyiluxuji*, pp. 241, 246, 249–51; and oral sources.
[58] Xiao Sike, *Caoji shenpan*, vol. 1, p. 250.

Liu Shaoqi, Zhou Enlai and Deng Xiaoping as well as various marshals[59] attended the December and subsequent meetings which targeted Luo, with Zhou and Deng relaying Mao's verdict on Luo to the December session, and the three went along with his purge despite their grave but largely unexpressed doubts about the evidence.[60] If Lin had more to gain personally and was indeed active in the machinations which framed Luo, the clear political logic for all concerned was to give Mao what he wanted. While there are accusations of Lin's subsequent involvement in the physical abuse of Luo as well,[61] the overall picture painted by our well-placed sources, which include one of the most meticulous students of the period, suggests that although Lin was active in the purge of Luo Ruiqing, he was fundamentally following Mao's lead. And indeed not only evidence concerning the time but also later developments suggest that Mao had built up a particular animus toward Luo by late 1965, perhaps based on the belief that he was following Liu Shaoqi's 'line'. Thus in contrast to other leaders such as Deng Xiaoping and Chen Yun, Luo was not even informed of Lin Biao's death until a year after the event and was only released from custody for medical treatment more than two years after it.[62] The remaining question is whether Lin Biao was bold enough to initiate action on the basis of Mao's ambiguous clues before he had clearly indicated the depth of his dissatisfaction with Luo,

[59] Moreover, in addition to Ye Jianying, Marshals Chen Yi, Liu Bocheng and Xu Xiangqian were promoted to be MAC Vice Chairmen in January 1966; *Zhonghuaren-mingongheguo dang zheng jun qun lingdao renminglu* (Namelists of PRC Party, Government, Military and Mass Organization Leaders) (Beijing: Zhonggong dangshi chuban-she, 1990), p. 13.

[60] See Ma Qibin, *Sishinian*, p. 262; [Luo] Diandian, *Feifan*, pp. 203–4; *Lishi de shen-pan*, p. 378; Kau, *Lin Piao*, p. 493; Harding in *CHOC*, vol. 15, p. 126; and Teiwes, 'Mao and his lieutenants', pp. 33–4n. Cf. above, n. 47.

[61] In 1968 Lin, Ye Qun and Huang Yongsheng reportedly delayed surgery that Luo urgently needed. Gao Gao and Yan Jiaqi, '*Wenhua dageming*', p. 237; and *A Great Trial*, p. 86.

[62] [Luo] Diandian, *Feifan*, pp. 246, 250. Another indication is that in contrast to his attitude toward other 'rightists', Mao showed no interest in ever seeing Luo again even after his release from confinement; *ibid.*, p. 196. On the question of whether an opposing Liu 'line' actually existed, see Teiwes, *Politics and Purges*, pp. xxxvi–xliv.

or if Lin only became involved in a major way after the Chairman made his attitude fully known.

The He Long case also raises questions about the official characterization of Lin Biao's role. In this version Lin again takes the initiative to frame a long-time associate, this time overcoming the reservations of a less receptive Mao. In August 1966 Lin allegedly began to concoct materials and spread slanders against He who, like Luo Ruiqing, was seen to have great power in the PLA which thus blocked his designs for total control, and in September convened a MAC meeting where he accused He of subversive activities. Meanwhile, the fabricated material reached Mao who expressed his continuing confidence to He in mid-September and suggested that he see Lin to sort matters out. In the ensuing meeting Lin assertedly demanded to know who He supported, and when the old marshal replied 'the Party and Chairman Mao', Lin took this as a rejection of his effort to pull He over to his side. With Lin's hostility reinforced, efforts to undermine He peaked at the end of the year, forcing him out of Beijing. Zhou Enlai's efforts to protect He proved of no avail as Mao gave increasing credence to the false accusations of Lin Biao's followers, and from mid-1967 Lin increased his control over the marshal and denied him proper medical treatment with the result that he was 'persecuted to death' in 1969.[63]

While not resolving all the uncertainties, the available evidence suggests a rather different picture. As with Luo Ruiqing there was tension between Maojiawan and He Long, although it appears much sharper and more personal, with little sign of any significant policy differences.[64] He, according to oral sources, was one of the few marshals whom Lin did not get along with, and probably a major cause of Lin's attitude and certainly the reason for

---

[63] For the standard account, see Gao Gao and Yan Jiaqi, 'Wenhua dageming', pp. 209–21; and Zhonggong dangshi renwu zhuan (ZGDSRWZ) (Biographies of Personalities in CCP History), vol. 2 (Xi'an: Shaanxi renmin chubanshe, 1981), pp. 249–60.

[64] A possible exception is He's major role in the military competitions organized by Luo Ruiqing (see above, n. 48), but the materials on the Lin-He conflict make little reference to this issue.

Ye Qun's deep resentment went back to events in Yan'an days involving both He and his wife, Xue Ming. Ye and Xue were two of the young women drawn to Yan'an who became new wives of CCP leaders. They had also known each other previously in Nanjing where Ye had worked as a newsreader at a Guomindang radio station, a past Xue felt Ye should reveal to the Party. Ye refused to do this, but during the rectification campaign in 1942 Xue disclosed the matter to He Long who took it up with Lin Biao. The result was a longstanding enmity, with the two women reportedly not speaking over the next twenty years, although the events surrounding Luo Ruiqing's purge (see below) suggest that matters may not have been quite that bad.[65] In any case, Ye Qun was reportedly involved deeply in anti-He Long activities as events unfolded, with one of her secretaries implying that she rather than Lin took the lead.[66]

One of the major problems with the official account of He's fall is not only its link to Lin Biao but its dating from the summer of 1966. He Long had already been in trouble by the time Luo Ruiqing came under attack in December 1965. Following the December Shanghai conference He lost responsibility for the day-to-day work of the MAC, his most significant position within the military. During that meeting two interesting exchanges took place between the previously bitterly opposed wives, Ye Qun and Xue Ming. First, Ye visited He's residence at the conference to convey Lin's concern and goodwill to the old marshal, and talked with Xue who also served as head of He's office. Two days later Xue returned the visit, and Ye reminded her that Lin had recently taken the initiative to have He's name attached to a major Army Day article on PLA democracy because of his good reputation and good work in the army. Ye also said that she had not sought out He's family for many years because she was afraid of He Long's bad temper, and observed that although Xue had made false allegations against her in the past she would put

[65] See Salisbury, *New Emperors*, pp. 279–80.
[66] Guan Weixun, *Ye Qun*, p. 219.

the matter aside as long as Xue did not repeat them. More than half a year later, He's situation deteriorated further seemingly as a result of events at the Eleventh Plenum in August 1966, but here the link was to Mao and not to Lin Biao. On that occasion He held back during 'Party life meetings' (shenghuohui) where Liu Shaoqi and Deng Xiaoping came under sharp criticism. Mao asked He whether he had joined in and encouraged him to speak frankly, but He replied that he could not make such severe allegations as those offered by other leaders. Shortly afterwards He Long's situation seriously worsened.[67]

With his position increasingly shaky, further developments during the tension-filled early Cultural Revolution period in mid-1966 created new problems for He Long. Apart from the so-called 'February [1966] mutiny', which has been over-emphasised in some official accounts,[68] by late August He became entangled in the growing factionalism within the PLA which also drew in Lin Biao, now anointed as the successor. Following Mao's big character poster 'Bombard the headquarters', aimed at Liu Shaoqi, which appeared in early August, a poster entitled 'Bombard Yang Chengwu' was put up at the offices of the PLA General Staff. Yang Chengwu at the time was a close associate of Lin Biao, while the authors of the poster, Wang Shangrong and Lei Yingfu, had been part of He Long's old Second Red Army and were then serving as head and deputy head of the PLA Warfare Department. The poster was further supported by the staff of He Long's office, and all these factors led at least Ye Qun to interpret the

---

[67] See Guoshi yanjiu cankao ziliao (Reference Materials on National History), no. 2 (1993), pp. 79–81.

[68] This 'mutiny' was a fantastic distortion of routine military exercises in Beijing's northern suburbs which had been approved by He but in summer 1966 was painted as a plot to seize power. The issue had first been raised by radical students at Beijing University in July who assumed disgraced former Beijing Mayor Peng Zhen had been responsible, and at this time Peng bore the brunt of the blame. Subsequently, however, Kang Sheng linked the affair to He, as early as the end of July by some accounts (see Gao Gao and Yan Jiaqi, 'Wenhua dageming', pp. 214–16), but more likely toward the end of the year or even later. In any case, the most careful biographers of He Long conclude that this incident had little if any influence on his fall. See Guoshi yanjiu cankao ziliao, no. 2 (1993), p. 83.

affair as an attack on Lin. It was from this point that efforts to gather evidence against He began at Maojiawan.[69]

Lin Biao was clearly involved as events unfolded in September, but the question of initiative is open to modification. While materials may have been collected and sent to Mao on the orders of Lin Biao and/or Ye Qun, at this time a substantial quantity of letters addressed to Mao and Lin arrived at Maojiawan; according to the recollection of Zhang Yunsheng, these were supposedly documents that had been 'signed by Chairman Mao'. What is unclear is whether this was simply Mao passing on documents that originated with Maojiawan in the first place, or if the Chairman was independently providing new materials to stimulate Lin's interest in the case further. Moreover, Zhang also recalled, Mao asked Lin in early September, i.e. presumably *before* his consoling remarks to He Long, to convene a MAC Standing Committee meeting in order to 'issue a warning' concerning He, and it was with Mao's authorization that Lin touched on He's case at the meeting by saying that according to some evidence He had been grabbing power in the military. Also, contrary to the official version with its view of Mao's continuing confidence in He, the Chairman's guideline was a more ambiguous 'First struggle, then protect'. At the MAC meeting Lin declared that He had 'problems' while it was apparently on this occasion or somewhat later that Jiang Qing offered the harsher judgment that He was 'a bad man' and 'a big butcher'. Lin's subsequent reception of He, again from Zhang's account, had all the elements of farce rather than a tense meeting of enemies. While Ye Qun worried about the encounter and hid bodyguards behind the curtains of the reception hall, the meeting reportedly passed without incident. If Lin did ask He who he supported, Zhang did not record it, and in any case the most likely meaning

---

[69] Zhang Yunsheng, *Maojiawan*, p. 33, only gave the poster's title as 'Bombard XXX'. We are able to identify the names of individuals deleted in Zhang's account from contemporary Red-Guard materials. See also *Zhonggong dangshi jiaoxue cankao ziliao (ZGDSJXCKZL)* (CCP History Teaching Reference Materials), vols 25–6, ([Beijing]: Zhongguo Jiefangjun Guofang Daxue dangshi dangjian zhenggong jiaoyanshi, October 1988), vol. 26, p. 89.

of such a question in the context of the moment would be to demand support for Mao's line as against the so-called 'revisionist' line of Liu Shaoqi and Deng Xiaoping. A response of the Party and Chairman Mao would have been in full accord with the current atmosphere, not to mention Lin's own *modus operandi*.[70]

After September Lin Biao essentially drops out of the picture concerning He Long, although in mid-November he still approved of He addressing a large rally with other old marshals.[71] Significantly, Lin also gave prior approval to He's speech, which was the most conservative of all the marshals' statements since it contained the clearest message that the army should not get involved in local Cultural Revolution activities. And when He failed to appear at another rally two weeks later, it was undoubtedly the result of Jiang Qing's protest at his participation in the first rally, and not due to any action by Lin Biao. Finally, the decisive events leading to He's expulsion from Beijing also originated from Jiang Qing again taking up the case at the end of December; while Lin naturally added his voice to the denunciations which followed, he was clearly not the driving force.[72] Whatever ambiguous and possibly duplicitous signals Mao had given earlier, by early 1967 he had clearly abandoned He, notwithstanding a few favourable remarks during the subsequent year. While formal control of He passed to Huang Yongsheng's second special case group for military cadres by mid-1968, the direct responsibility for He's mistreatment and death is unclear, with some sources painting Kang Sheng as the principal villain.[73]

[70] Zhang Yunsheng, *Maojiawan*, pp. 33–9; and Wang Nianyi, *Dadongluan*, p. 383.
[71] Wang Nianyi, *Dadongluan*, p. 123; *Xu Xiangqian zhuan* (Biography of Xu Xiangqian) (Beijing: Dangdai Zhongguo chubanshe, 1991), p. 522; and below, pp. 67–8.
[72] See Gao Gao and Yan Jiaqi, '*Wenhua dageming*', pp. 216–17; and Quan Yanchi, *Tao Zhu*, pp. 185–6. According to the latter account, Jiang even challenged Mao by pressing He's case at a December 1966 meeting where it was not on the agenda.
[73] Wang Nianyi, *Dadongluan*, p. 297; *Dangshi tiandi* (The Party History Field), no. 1 (1993), pp. 7–11; and Zhong Kan, *Kang Sheng pingzhuan* (Critical Biography of Kang Sheng) (Beijing: Hongqi chubanshe, 1982), p. 191. For a serious if somewhat uncritical biography of Kang in English, see John Byron and Robert Pack, *The Claws of the Dragon: Kang Sheng – The Evil Genius behind Mao – and his Legacy of Terror in People's China* (New York: Simon & Schuster, 1992).

When the cases of Luo Ruiqing and He Long are considered together, some similarities emerge. While in both cases Lin Biao or perhaps his household took advantage of the situation to deal with, if not political opponents, then at least leading figures against whom he had grievances, in neither case did he act without reference to existing pressures. In both cases Mao's perceived wishes seem to have been paramount, although those wishes were less than totally clear to the parties concerned. In He Long's case Mao's attitude was perhaps more obscure given his conflicting signals, but even Luo Ruiqing, though aware of the Chairman's displeasure, was also ignorant of the depth of his animosity and felt he (Luo) could retreat to a lesser post.[74] Apart from the anticipation of, or reaction to Mao's wishes, another common feature of the two cases was that in both – especially that of He Long – much of the animus emerging from Maojiawan can be traced to Ye Qun, and to matters of personal pique rather than to national policy or political principle. But the differences in the two cases are also significant. In the Luo Ruiqing affair Lin Biao's role seems to have been closely linked to pressures arising within his defence portfolio, and at least initially his actions were consistent with accepted procedures. In He Long's case the dynamic was that of military factionalism growing out of fast-moving Cultural Revolution developments which resulted both in perceptions of an attack on Lin's personal position and in threats to PLA institutional cohesion. Finally, while other key Cultural Revolution figures appear to have had only a marginal role at best in the Luo Ruiqing case, both Kang Sheng and Jiang Qing took the initiative in attacking He Long. Given that they had access to Mao and seemed attuned to his thinking, it is unsurprising that a generally reactive politician such as Lin Biao would – albeit cautiously – follow their lead.

Regardless of the degree of Lin's involvement, the He Long

---

[74] Luo discussed with Shanghai leader Chen Pixian the possibility of taking up a position there; Zi Ping, *Hu Yaobang, Yang Chengwu, Li Desheng* (Hong Kong: Kehua dushu chubangongsi, 1982), p. 132. While we normally eschew the use of Hong Kong sources, this book appears highly knowledgeable about CCP politics and is likely to have been written by an informed source from the PRC.

case suggests the importance of factional strife during the Cultural Revolution, something emphasized both in the official charges against Lin and Western analyses. Lin was accused of seeking to get rid of people loyal to other marshals and placing his own men in key posts, while the importance of tensions between different field army systems which reflected ties to the various marshals has long been noted.[75] In particular, Lin allegedly developed an especially close-knit 'clique' at the apex of the PLA whose 'principal members' were Chief of Staff (as of 1968) Huang Yongsheng, Air Force Commander Wu Faxian (from 1965), Navy Political Commissar Li Zuopeng (promoted from second political commissar in 1967), and Logistics Department Director Qiu Huizuo (since 1959). All these leaders had revolutionary career ties to Lin – though not exclusively so – with Huang and Wu being able to trace their links to the late 1920s and early 1930s and Li and Qiu having identifiable ties to Lin since 1939 and 1948 respectively. Together they supposedly supported Lin not only in various persecutions of other military factions but also in his plans for 'seizing supreme power'.[76]

There is no doubt that strong professional and personal ties existed between Lin Biao and the four generals. Apart from the legacy of battlefield service and work in the defence establishment, additional personal ties had developed. Before the Cultural Revolution Ye Qun reportedly selected Wu Faxian to accompany her to the countryside in 1964 to participate in the Socialist Education Movement. And during the Cultural Revolution the generals became involved in social life at Maojiawan, frequently attending movies and other functions, a scene joined by civilian radical and CRG member Chen Boda from about 1969 as his estrangement from Jiang Qing's group intensified. In this the old army ties were clearly important, a fact reflected in Ye Qun's

[75] The standard account of field army factionalism is William Whitson, 'The field army in Chinese Communist military politics', *CQ*, no. 37 (1969).
[76] For a summary of their alleged criminal liability, see *A Great Trial*, pp. 227–31. For career links to Lin, see Xiao Sike, *Caoji shenpan*, vol. 1, pp. 246–7, 287; *Who's Who in Communist China* (Hong Kong: Union Research Institute, 1966), pp. 635–6; and Barnouin and Yu, *Ten Years of Turbulence*, p. 204. On the non-exclusive nature of career links, see below, pp. 93–4.

reported comment that someone was completely a Lin Biao man if he had served in the First Army Corps of the First Front Army, one of Lin's early commands – a designation that applied to Huang Yongsheng and Wu Faxian. In any case, the PLA structure did, by mid-1968, place people from Lin's Fourth Field Army system (named after his civil war command) in a dominant military position at the Centre while those with career links to He Long suffered disproportionately. This situation caused considerable resentment among veterans of other field armies.[77]

While there is clearly a case for military factionalism in the Lin Biao story, a case which will be further examined when we consider the purge of Yang Chengwu in March 1968, much of the picture as presented benefits from the wisdom of hindsight, while specific aspects are simply untrue. In particular, the effort to paint the generals as part of an attempt to seize power does not hold up. Despite the gloss put on their activities, the generals denied any awareness of the '571 coup plot' for a military takeover which Lin Liquo allegedly drafted on Lin Biao's orders, or any plan to assassinate Mao, a denial not really challenged by the official verdict at their trial and, as we shall see, supported by the lack of any convincing evidence concerning supportive activities on their part in the days and hours preceding Lin's death in 1971.[78] More broadly, the notion of the 'Lin Biao clique' as presented overlooks some important features of the Cultural Revolution context. First, at least before the 1970 Lushan plenum, despite claims that the generals were loyal to Lin Biao as an individual, there is no reason to believe that they would have conceived that loyalty to Lin would conflict with that owed to Mao. After all, Lin's position was based on the

---

[77] Gao Gao and Yan Jiaqi, 'Wenhua dageming', p. 321; Zhang Yunsheng, Maojiawan, pp. 167–70, 180–2, 378–81; and oral sources. At the provincial level, however, the Fourth Field Army did not gain disproportionate appointments to the revolutionary committees and new Party committees in 1967–71, although apparently veterans of the First Field Army associated with Peng Dehuai and He Long were significantly underrepresented. See Frederick C. Teiwes, Provincial Leadership in China: The Cultural Revolution and Its Aftermath (Ithaca: Cornell University East Asian Papers, 1974), pp. 62–3, 87, 106.
[78] See Xiao Sike, Caoji shenpan, vol. 1, p. 193; and below, p. 160, n. 116.

idea of *his* complete loyalty to Mao, and his political practice was
to re-emphasise that fact repeatedly, while historically if the
generals belonged to Lin's faction or 'mountaintop' (*shantou*),
they together with Lin himself were all part of Mao's mountaintop. Indeed, Mao himself in the summer of 1971 described Lin's
group as those who were attacking 'my mountaintop' from
within.[79] According to one close student of Lin Biao, a historian whose overall interpretation retains much of the official
viewpoint, when the generals were elected to the Politburo in
1969 they were not particularly thought of as Lin Biao's men since
they all had Mao's approval. In fact, we conclude, the promotion
of the four generals was probably much more a result of their
perceived higher loyalty to Mao than their obedience to Lin.

In addition, the positions of the four generals at the top of
the military hierarchy, while resulting in an unbalanced allocation of posts among veterans of the different field armies, were
not due to outrageous promotions. Wu and Qiu, in fact, held
their posts before the Cultural Revolution, while Li was also
highly placed as the navy vice commander in charge of day-to-day
operations. Huang Yongsheng was transferred from Guangzhou
to become Chief of Staff only as a result of the mysterious 1968
purge of Yang Chengwu, an event which, as we see subsequently, probably had more to do with other actors than with
Lin Biao, however much Lin may have contributed to Huang's
appointment to the vacant position. It is also instructive that
whatever degree of resentment various army leaders may have
harboured – and an authoritative oral source considers that conflict among field army groups was not a major factor in Cultural
Revolution military politics – in the view of another senior
historian, discontent remained 'deep in their hearts' and largely
unexpressed because of Mao's sanction of the arrangements and,
in contrast to attitudes toward Ye Qun and Jiang Qing, because
of the feeling that the status of the generals was not so objec-
tionable because of their contributions to the revolution. As for
Lin Biao, he articulated a cadre policy that emphasised loyalty to

[79] Mimeo of leadership speeches in 1968–71 available at the Sinological Institute,
University of Heidelberg, p. 71.

Mao above all else: 'Regardless of which mountaintop they come from, people will be protected completely as long as they side with the proletariat and Chairman Mao; some people will be over-thrown completely, some partly regardless of their mountaintop so long as they oppose the proletariat and Chairman Mao.'[80] In practical terms this meant that, whatever bias existed in appoint-ments favouring old Lin Biao associates, there were many cases of officers from other field armies being promoted to key posts during the Cultural Revolution at least with Lin's assent if not on his initiative.[81] Perhaps even more telling, Lin was not blindly committed to those with past career ties to him: Xiao Hua, the PLA GPD head who fell in 1967 after nearly a year of attacks on his department by Jiang Qing and her daughter, and Chief of Staff Yang Chengwu – a 'complete Lin Biao man' – are cases of men whose close historical links did not prevent their being discarded. While this has been officially interpreted as Lin deciding that such individuals did not have sufficient personal loyalty despite historical links, it more probably reflected his inability to withstand external pressures created by changing cir-cumstances.[82] Taken together, these developments point to the

---

[80] *ZGDSJXCKZL*, vol. 25, p. 367. Mao gave high praise to Lin's speech of 20 March 1967 which included this comment.

[81] While we cannot assume that Lin Biao played a leading role in such promotions, by the same token it cannot be demonstrated that he was behind the advancement of the four generals. What does seem clear is that while Mao would have had the decisive say in all key military appointments, Lin as Minister of Defence would also have been involved in the process. Cf. above, n. 77.

[82] On Xiao Hue's career links, see Donald W. Klein and Anne B. Clark, *Biographic Dictionary of Chinese Communism, 1921–1965* (2 vols, Cambridge: Harvard University Press, 1971), I, 330–2. On Yang Chengwu, see the discussion of his March 1968 purge, below, pp. 92–4. Cf. Barnouin and Yu, *Ten Years of Turbulence*, pp. 204–5, for further discussion of Lin's failure to protect his subordinates including Fourth Field Army veterans.

Regarding Xiao Hua and the GPD, the orthodox account claims joint pressure by Lin Biao and Jiang Qing from late 1966; see David Shambaugh, 'The soldier and the state in China: the political work system in the People's Liberation Army', *CQ*, no. 127 (1991), pp. 540–1. Zhang Yunsheng, however, reports that in January 1967 Lin refused to bow to Jiang's demands by holding that 'the head of the Political Department should not be knocked down lightly'. See *Maojiawan*, p. 65; and Wen Feng, *Shentanxia*, p. 69. On Xiao's subsequent fall and its relationship to the emergence of the four generals, see below.

unpredictable dynamic of the Cultural Revolution as the key factor shaping factional politics in the PLA.

The *Cultural* Revolution ironically meant that almost anyone holding *military* power could come under attack. Indeed, starting in the fall of 1966, all four generals and particularly Qiu Huizuo came under intense attack from rebel groups (*zaofanpai*) in the army which were supported by the CRG and particularly by Jiang Qing, who had become increasingly active on the question of how the PLA should carry out the Cultural Revolution since September 1966. This was in her new capacity as adviser to the PLA's Cultural Revolution Group (PLACRG). Qiu, however, was protected by the ostensibly unlikely quartet of Lin Biao, Zhou Enlai, Marshal Xu Xiangqian and Chen Boda. Such intervention by Lin, though allegedly delayed in order to let the pressure build up against them so that their gratitude would be all the greater, did have the effect of building up loyalty to the Defence Minister, but against this background his actions can be seen as part of an effort to uphold stability in the army. In fact, it reflected a broader consensus at this time involving various marshals who sought to insulate the military from mass struggle with special attention being given to protecting key central PLA organs – the General Staff (i.e. Yang Chengwu), the GPD (Xiao Hua), logistics (Qiu Huizuo), the navy (Li Zuopeng) and the air force (Wu Faxian). However, Lin's efforts were overrun by events which set some of those he backed against one another, in particular Xiao Hua against Wu, Li and Qiu. The key development was the so-called 13 May [1967] incident, a violent clash between rival PLA theatrical groups growing out of a dispute over the staging by an air force art troupe of a performance to celebrate the twenty-fifth anniversary of Mao's Yan'an talks on literature and art, an event which reflected a larger factional conflict within the Beijing military. In the judgment of the premier historian of the period, Wang Nianyi, this was the event when the 'clique' began to form.[83] While our own analysis must

[83] Wang Nianyi, *Dadongluan*, pp. 379–80; *ZGDSJXCKZL*, vol. 25, p. 250; Huang Zheng *et al.*, *Zai lishi de dang'anli – wenge fengyunlu* (In the Historical Archives – A Record of the Cultural Revolution Storm) (Shenyang: Liaoning Daxue chubanshe, 1988), p. 31; and above, n. 82.

necessarily remain tentative, we believe there are other more important aspects to this curious affair.

The unfolding of this matter involved key players in the Cultural Revolution drama, many of whom operated with an imperfect understanding of what was going on. Not surprisingly, Mao's role was pivotal albeit distant after his initial involvement. In April, with the dispute over the planned performance building up, three dancers from the group wishing to put on the performance, who had been Mao's dancing partners at functions organised for the top leaders in Zhongnanhai, approached the Chairman with their story. Their group supported Commander Wu Faxian and Political Commissar Yu Lijin in the internal factional struggles of the air force, and thus was *ipso facto* regarded as 'conservative' by the majority radical faction. Mao, fully aware of their support of Wu Faxian and Yu Lijin, was sympathetic and furthermore disclosed to the young dancers his intention to protect Wu, and finally referred them to Ye Qun – not Jiang Qing who supported the attacks on the performance. As a result Ye received the three girls in late April, reassured them that their support of Wu was correct, and endorsed their plans for a performance on 13 May. Meanwhile, the majority faction in the air force was joined by civilian Red Guards in attacks on Wu's minority faction, and were supported by Jiang Qing who was seemingly unaware of Mao's intervention. Recognizing the minority status of the air force group, Ye advised them to join other 'royalists' from the navy and logistics department, a union which intensified the opposition of the majority. At this stage Xiao Hua – also presumably unaware of the actions of Mao and Ye and apparently feeling constrained by pressure from Jiang Qing, who had been attacking Xiao's GPD over the previous months – decided to take a neutral stance by instructing the two factions to stage a joint show (a view reportedly endorsed by Zhou Enlai), only to have the suggestion rejected by both sides. Xiao's action, however, was said to have enraged Ye Qun, and Lin Biao could not have been happy with the resulting disturbances. In this situation, Lin indicated his support for the 'conservative' faction by attending a subsequent performance in early June – but in the company of Mao and clearly following his lead.[84] With a further hint from Mao,[85] Lin withdrew his support of Xiao by July (finally endorsing moves by Li Na, the daughter of Jiang Qing – and of Mao – to 'demolish' the GPD on the 25th) and gave his backing to the Wu-Li-Qiu faction. Meanwhile the latter faction had exchanged declarations of support with Jiang Qing despite her previous hostility towards its leaders. Obviously a key consideration for Lin Biao was to align himself with Mao's perceived wishes.[86]

Another consideration was the need to stabilise the Beijing military situation given the turmoil within the army in mid-1967 – a turmoil that is examined in greater detail later in the context of events from the 'February adverse current' to the July Wuhan incident. Briefly, the February developments alienated Mao not only from the old marshals who participated in the 'February current' but from lesser figures such as Xiao Hua who had backed the effort to set limits on the Cultural Revolution in the military. This, combined with Jiang Qing's ongoing vendetta against the GPD and dissatisfaction with the PLACRG (whose head, Xu Xiangqian, was one of the offending marshals in February), undermined the two organs responsible for army political work. Xiao's fall meant the disgrace or pushing aside under Jiang's pressure of the three leaders responsible for the PLACRG since it was formed in June 1966 – Liu Zhijian, Xu Xiangqian and now Xiao Hua. Given the chaos within the military such as that surrounding the 13 May incident and the inability

[84] Ye Yonglie, *Ye Yonglie caifang shouji* (Reporter's Notes of Ye Yonglie) (Shanghai: Shanghai shehui kexueyuan chubanshe, 1993), p. 120. While Ye dates this in May we believe this must be in error and the reference is to the 9 June performance. The aftermath of the event demonstrated Lin Biao's political style. After being embarrassed by shouts of 'Long live Vice Chairman Lin' from the audience, the next day Lin's office ordered the CRG to issue a circular stipulating that in the future only 'Long live Chairman Mao' should be used. See also Wang Nianyi, *Dadongluan*, p. 373.

[85] Wang Dongxing, presumably representing Mao, came to Maojiawan enquiring whether Xiao should attend another army art troupe performance; Zhang Yunsheng, *Maojiawan*, p. 119.

[86] For information on the 13 May incident, see Wang Nianyi, *Dadongluan*, pp. 287, 379–80; Ma Qibin, *Sishinian*, p. 292; Barnouin and Yu, *Ten Years of Turbulence*, pp. 132–4; and above, n. 82. The preceding paragraph is our best effort to reconstruct this still inadequatcly understood affair.

of the PLACRG and GPD to provide leadership, there was an obvious need to select army figures in Beijing who could form a new organ vested with PLA political authority. And since the Wu-Li-Qiu group had clashed with the by now discredited Xiao Hua, and in view of the four generals' presumed loyalty to Mao, it made some sense to settle on them. Thus in mid-August following the Wuhan incident, with the overall emphasis shifting to restoring order, a MAC Vigilance Small Group (*Junwei kanshou xiaozu*) was established directly under the CRG, with not only the Beijing military but also army units throughout the country expected to look to this organ for guidance concerning the conduct of the Cultural Revolution in the PLA. While some accounts attribute this organ to the efforts of both Lin Biao (or at least Ye Qun) and Jiang Qing, with one particularly questionable version having them reporting to Mao after the fact, the proposal for the new small group was actually made by Zhou Enlai. In any case, whatever personal benefit Lin may have gained from the placing of close supporters in this new key body, the arrangement also quickly stabilized the situation within the military in the capital and promoted figures who would work for PLA order while at the same time being acceptable to Zhou, Jiang and Mao. Moreover, in the whole process leading to the new small group, Zhou Enlai and Jiang Qing were at least as significant as Lin, while it is difficult to believe that Mao was anything other than in full accord with the result.[87]

Thus, while the four generals did form a close-knit group personally and professionally loyal to Lin, their emergence in key military and political positions could not be traced to Lin alone. A whole range of factors were crucial. These included their existing high PLA posts, the twists and turns of the Cultural

---

[87] Wang Nianyi, *Dadongluan*, pp. 287, 380; *Xu Xiangqian zhuan*, p. 535; *Xinqingyuan* (New Light Industry College) (Red Guard newspaper), no. 40 (19 September 1967), p. 4; and oral source. The term *kanshou* implies vigilance on behalf of someone who is away which, in the context of the latter half of August, would either refer to Lin Biao who had gone to Beidaihe for a rest, or to Yang Chengwu who accompanied Mao on his southern trip. The Small Group was reorganized in September, and made directly responsible to the MAC; see below, p. 88.

Revolution which placed Jiang Qing on 'their side' at a critical juncture, and not least the confidence of Mao who after all was to name Huang Yongsheng to the three-man group to vet the new Politburo in 1969.[88] Moreover, while actions such as ostensibly placing Lin Liguo in control of the air force (which in fact was highly exaggerated) betokened unusual slavishness, and, as will be examined, the generals became involved in the ill-fated 'state chairman' and 'genius' issues before and at the 1970 Lushan plenum, none of those acts would have been conceived of as opposing Mao. And even if the outcome at Lushan placed them in a similar predicament to that of Lin Biao, there is nothing to indicate participation in whatever desperate activities were initiated in the months immediately preceding September 1971. Overall, while the four generals behaved at times like a tightly organized purposeful clique, on other occasions and in the larger sense they were figures caught up in developments they could not fully understand or control – a situation ironically similar to that of Lin Biao himself.

Purposeful clique or not, the four generals clearly identified with Lin Biao at least where opposition to Mao was not involved. Lin's relations with other key actors – Zhou Enlai and the so-called 'Jiang Qing clique' – were necessarily of a different order. The conventional view of Zhou as a major antagonist of Lin's – a view much more strongly advanced in Western analyses than CCP claims[89] – does not stand up to scrutiny. There is a broad consensus of Chinese scholars interviewed, including

[88] See below, p. 105. Another sign of Mao's confidence was that Huang and Wen Yucheng had the right to attend Party Centre meetings since immediately after the 'February adverse current' (see Tan Zhongji, *Shinianhou*, p. 31), an arrangement that surely originated with Mao.

[89] For analyses emphasizing Lin-Zhou conflict as virtually more salient than even Lin-Mao conflict, see Domes, *China after the Cultural Revolution*, pp. 88, 100–2, 133–4; and van Ginneken, *Rise and Fall*, pp. 218–19, 230–4. Such analyses are primarily based on the logic of Lin's and Zhou's presumed policy positions and political interests, with very few concrete indications of conflict offered from CCP sources. Examples which do exist largely consist of alleged comments such as Lin's 'If Zhou can invite Nixon, I can invite Brezhnev', or such dubious *ex post facto* claims as Mao's assertion in 1972 that Lin opposed the opening to the United States. See Jonathan D. Pollack, 'The opening to America', in *CHOC*, vol. 15, pp. 414–15.

researchers specialising on both Lin and Zhou and several senior Party historians, that in the period from Lin's assuming the successor role in August 1966 to the Lushan plenum in the summer of 1970 when Mao first indicated serious dissatisfaction with Lin there is very little evidence of any Lin-Zhou conflict. This situation, of course, was facilitated by Lin's habitual practice of simply following Mao, having no major policy initiatives of his own, and not interfering in Zhou's administrative sphere. While some scholars speculated about submerged tensions over Zhou's efforts to moderate the Cultural Revolution and protect veteran cadres, no concrete instances were offered of direct clashes. Moreover, the overview of the Zhou-Lin relationship offered by oral sources did not merely focus on the absence of conflict but spoke of the Premier as subordinate to Lin, consistently treating him with great respect, and offering absolute support before Lushan.

The Zhou-Lin relationship must be seen against the background of history and the characters of both men. As analysed by one Zhou scholar, for the bulk of their careers the relationship had been one of the subordination of Lin to Zhou given Zhou's higher Party rank and greater seniority, a situation further deepened by the fact that a teacher-student relationship had existed at the Whampoa Academy in the 1920s when Zhou was the academy's political commissar and Lin was a cadet. Over their remaining revolutionary careers, the scholar continued, there was no question of serious conflict given their different roles, lack of much direct contact, and especially Zhou's higher status. The pattern continued after 1949 first during the period of Lin's inactivity, then after 1959 when he held the defence portfolio, and finally in 1965 when he was named the first Vice Premier; even in the latter stages there was little conflict between the two men as Lin demonstrated little interest in wider government work and continued to show Zhou respect. The situation underwent a radical change in August 1966 with the reversal of the two men's status in the hierarchy. However much the positions of Lin as number-two and Zhou as number-three made nonsense of their relative contributions in CCP history and especially their current work capabilities, there is nothing to indicate that Zhou did anything other than fully embrace the new arrangement whatever reservations he may have had deep in his mind. This, without doubt, was primarily a result of bowing to Mao's will, but it also reflected Party discipline since Lin's elevated status had been affirmed by the Central Committee, as well as a long-term propensity for the unambitious Zhou, who had declared on many occasions that he 'did not have the talent to be number-one', to follow his superiors loyally.[90] Whether or not the con-clusion of an authoritative oral source that Zhou would willingly have served Lin if Mao had died before the Lushan plenum is valid, what is beyond dispute from the testimony of these varied sources is that Zhou's political practice as well as the larger situa-tion made it impossible for him to lead opposition to Lin while Mao was alive and still retained confidence in his successor.

But what of Lin's attitude toward Zhou? Not only is there no evidence of explicit conflict – which might after all be explained by Mao's trust in Zhou's loyalty, if not his ideological orientation[91] – but the one known instance where tension emerged between Maojiawan and the Premier suggests a far from hostile under-lying attitude on Lin's part. In March 1967 Zhou suggested to Mao calling a meeting to deal with the PLA's role in the Cultural Revolution. The Chairman immediately agreed and issued a document. The next day Zhou phoned Maojiawan to report the decision and Lin added his own agreement. However, Kang Sheng and Jiang Qing seized upon the fact that Lin was only informed after the decision had been made as not showing proper respect

---

[90] See the discussion of Zhou's propensity in Teiwes, 'Mao and his lieutenants', pp. 57–8; and Quan Yanchi, *Zhou Enlai*, p. 9. Cf. Nie Rongzhen's reference to Mao's trust in Lin and Central Committee endorsement as explaining Lin's acceptance as the successor by the old marshals; *XHRB*, 18 October 1984, in *FBIS*, 5 November 1984, p. K18.

[91] A sign of both Mao's trust in Zhou and perhaps of mutual confidence between Zhou and Lin were events surrounding Mao's famous July 1966 letter to Jiang Qing (see Kau, *Lin Piao*, pp. 118–23) raising doubts about Lin's May 1966 speech on coups which will be discussed later in this study. Mao revealed the contents of this letter to Zhou who in turn informed Lin, leading to a show of repentance on the Defence Minister's part. Wang Nianyi, *Dadongluan*, p. 7.

to the Vice Chairman, and Ye Qun quickly took up the theme that Lin had been made a figurehead. She phoned Maojiawan from Diaoyutai, the site of the offices and residences of the CRG, where she had been discussing the matter with Kang and Jiang, and an annoyed Lin ordered her home. In the event Zhou wrote Lin a long letter of apology and promised that such a thing would never happen again; according to Zhang Yunsheng, this letter led Lin to draft one of his own stating: 'I am deeply moved by your comments [and] I should learn from your modest spirit.' Ye Qun, apparently appalled that the Vice Chairman should put such sentiments in writing to a subordinate, intervened and talked Lin into tearing the letter up.[92] This incident, apart from indicating Lin's attitude to Zhou and again pointing to the critical role of Ye Qun at Maojiawan, is also of interest for what it reveals of the relationship between the 'two cliques'.

Western interpretations, particularly those of the period itself and immediately following Lin Biao's demise, generally picture Lin and the civilian radicals of the CRG as allies during the active phase of the Cultural Revolution in 1966–8, and still potential allies after the Ninth Congress as manifested in the defection of Chen Boda to Lin's group, the alliance only breaking down with the desertion of the radicals as a dominant coalition formed against Lin in 1970.[93] The official Chinese view is broadly consistent with this, except that greater emphasis is placed on conflict in a relationship of 'cooperation and conflict'. In the CCP version, the 'two cliques' increasingly went their own ways after the Ninth Congress, both having lost their sense of common purpose with the destruction of the old order and becoming uncertain about their relative positions in the reorganized power structure. The

---

[92] Zhang Yunsheng, *Maojiawan*, pp. 98–9.
[93] E.g., Domes, *China after the Cultural Revolution*, pp. 67–8, 88. This was not a universal interpretation, however. For an analysis emphasising greater conflict between civilian radical and military perspectives in 1966–8, see Hong Yung Lee, *The Politics of the Chinese Cultural Revolution: A Case Study* (Berkeley: University of California Press, 1978), pp. 332–4, 336–9. Lee's analysis, however, is more concerned with the PLA as an institution than Lin Biao who is pictured as someone trying to satisfy both the radicals and his institutional base.

result was that each group jockeyed for power and the contradictions between them grew. According to one official source, after the Congress 'most ... power fell to Lin Biao and his followers [but] the possibility of losing out to Jiang Qing and Zhang Chunqiao put him on tenterhooks.'[94] And, as we see later, with Mao having raised the idea of CRG member and Shanghai leader Zhang Chunqiao as the successor to Lin sometime around the Ninth Congress,[95] major conflict broke out between the two groups over the state chairmanship issue in the summer of 1970. But while this version is closer to the truth, it hardly does justice to the complexity of the relationship.

Clearly there had been cooperation between the 'two cliques' early in the piece. A particular accusation levelled in the post-Mao period was that each group allegedly helped the other to cover up embarrassing episodes from the past. Thus Jiang Qing reportedly responded to Ye Qun's request for assistance in destroying evidence of Lin Biao's contacts with Gao Gang during the latter's alleged 'anti-Party activities' in 1953, while Ye and Wu Faxian organised a raid on the homes of artists in Shanghai and seized materials on Jiang's 1930s activities in the city.[96] While such actions would have furthered the specific interests of the two groups, it is essential to emphasise that their larger cooperation was fundamentally based on the positions in which both had been placed by Mao as leading forces required to carry out his Cultural Revolution line. In any case, it is also important to note that, at least in the first few years of the Cultural Revolution, the 'Jiang Qing clique' had not formed into a tightly-knit group and probably had less cohesion than Lin Biao's group.

[94] Zong Huaiwen (comp.), *Years of Trial, Turmoil and Triumph – China from 1949 to 1988* (Beijing: Foreign Languages Press, 1989), p. 151. MacFarquhar's study in *CHOC*, vol. 15, pp. 315–19, places greater weight on conflict between the two groups than earlier Western studies, and Barnouin and Yu, *Ten Years of Turbulence*, ch. 6, give even greater emphasis to this conflict.

[95] Wang Nianyi, *Dadongluan*, pp. 387–8; and below, p. 110.

[96] *A Great Trial*, p. 23; and Hei Yannan, *Shinian haojie* (*A Disastrous Decade*) (Hong Kong: Fengfu wenhua qiye gongsi, 1986), p. 93. Hei's book is an account by a PRC author published outside China.

Thus Zhang Chunqiao, though a leading figure of the CRG, came under strong attack in early 1968, and this was endorsed by Ye Qun but also supported by Jiang Qing. However, it was Jiang who saved Zhang's position at the last moment.[97] Nor was every clash with a member of the Lin Biao group a conflict with the group as such. For example, later in 1968 when Jiang vigorously opposed a trip abroad by Huang Yongsheng, the cause of the ruckus, according to a historian specialising in Lin Biao, was Jiang's strong personal distaste for Huang, who reportedly did not know how to please her. This apparently followed a sharp clash when Jiang bitterly complained over Huang's failure to inform her of the transfer of some troops to the CRG.[98] These instances suggest that many of the conflicts between 'Mao-jiawan' and 'Diaoyutai' (the respective residences which became shorthand for the two groups) were individual and idiosyncratic affairs rather than direct challenges to either Lin Biao or Jiang Qing, although that situation did not prevent a more collective distrust from developing between the two groups.

Despite all the idiosyncratic causes of tension, above all Jiang Qing's personality, the conflict between Maojiawan and Diaoyutai can be traced to some fundamental structural factors. First, there was the great difference in status between the two groups: as one official account put it, 'Lin Biao still had some "political capital" [while the Jiang Qing clique] were gamblers without capital.'[99] This, of course, reflected the vast difference between the revolutionary accomplishments of not only Lin Biao but also his senior generals in comparison with people such as Zhang Chunqiao whom Lin had not even heard of before the Cultural

[97] Wang Nianyi, *Dadongluan*, p. 385.
[98] Zhang Yunsheng, *Maojiawan*, pp. 201–2; Barnouin and Yu, *Ten Years of Turbulence*, p. 212; and oral source. Zhang, however, considers the trip issue the trigger which started the conflict between the two groups. For further trivial incidents creating tension between the two groups, see Guan Weixun's discussion of conflict between Ye Qun and Yao Wenyuan over the borrowing of a book, and Huang Yongsheng's annoyance with Jiang Qing forcing the Politburo to consider the details of her theatrical productions, in *Ye Qun*, pp. 101–2, 108.
[99] *Renmin Ribao (RMRB) (People's Daily)*, 18 May 1978, in *FBIS*, 24 May 1978, p. E8.

Revolution.[100] But at the same time it vastly understated the large if fragile 'capital' of Jiang Qing as Mao's wife who could always claim, as she did in attacking a senior cadre who had allegedly failed to vote for her as a Politburo member, that any negative reactions to her were signs of a 'lack of feeling for Chairman Mao'.[101] A second and closely related factor concerned Lin's institutional loyalties to the PLA, and the tension, long reflected in Chinese culture, between the pen and the gun. As we have already seen and will see in greater detail in the course of analysing events in 1967, a major concern of Lin Biao and his group was to minimize chaos in the army, which was frequently promoted by Jiang Qing's actions, and also to ward off Jiang's attempts to interfere in military affairs more generally. A case in point was her opposition to the appointment of Wang Hongkun as head of the military control group responsible for the GPD – a saga which caused the four generals considerable heartburn.[102] Finally, the respective roles of Lin and the CRG in the Cultural Revolution – leaving aside the military aspect – led to conflict. While Lin as the successor was certainly expected to give active support to the Cultural Revolution despite his reservations, he had a larger responsibility (however passively exercised) for overseeing all work, while the CRG's sole function was to push the movement forward. The more activist role fitted Jiang's personality and resulted in a performance aptly summed up by Lin in March 1968: 'On the one hand, [Comrade Jiang Qing] loyally executed Chairman Mao's instructions, and on the other, she has been very *creative* herself . . .'[103] Clearly, Jiang's *modus operandi* was quite different from Lin's and undoubtedly contributed to tensions between them. But while Jiang's actions could sometimes annoy Lin, not to mention Mao, the fact that she might at any

[100] Wang Nianyi, *Dadongluan*, p. 384.

[101] See Jiang's 1972 rebuke of Xiao Jingguang in *Xiao Jingguang huiyiluxuji*, pp. 299–301.

[102] See Zhang Yunsheng, *Maojiawan*, pp. 206–9.

[103] Kau, *Lin Piao*, p. 496 (emphasis added). This statement ostensibly praised Jiang's activities in the Yang Chengwu case, but it can be read as a more general description of her Cultural Revolution role without the praise implied.

time reflect the Chairman's wishes created a major problem for Maojiawan, a consideration partly explaining Ye Qun's compelling need to be a frequent visitor to Diaoyutai.

While there do not appear to have been any open political clashes between Lin and Jiang before 1970,[104] the Vice Chairman's personal attitude towards Mao's wife appears to have been one of distaste; he did not take her over-seriously, and tried to keep as much distance as feasible. Thus in late 1969 when Jiang Qing wished to visit Lin Biao in Suzhou, Lin was unwilling to receive her and attempted to move residences so as to avoid her. Shortly afterwards Jiang sent Lin a collection of materials claiming that, even around the time of the Ninth Congress when Lin was formally anointed as successor, literature and art remained as 'black' (i.e. revisionist) as before the Cultural Revolution, and sought Lin's backing for her position which Mao had already treated dismissively. Lin now simply instructed his secretary to ignore the collection. Even more dramatic was an encounter in early February 1967 on the eve of the 'February adverse current' when a meeting with Jiang discussing the Cultural Revolution in the military went so badly as to lead the normally undemonstrative Lin to shout to Ye Qun: 'Get Jiang Qing out of here!'[105]

If Lin Biao had difficulty in abiding Jiang Qing, Ye Qun normally adopted quite a different posture. This did not simply involve smoothing things over and keeping relations between Maojiawan and Diaoyutai on as even a keel as possible: it further consisted of a deeply deferential attitude on Ye's part. Ye realised that she had inferior status to that of Jiang and sought to cultivate the latter and advance her interests. A revealing episode occurred when Ye went to Beijing airport to receive a visiting dignitary, only to discover that unexpectedly Jiang was not there. Feeling very uneasy that a slight might be perceived if she upstaged the absent

---

[104] This could even be extended right up to September 1971 as far as direct public (in the inner-Party sense) conflict with Lin Biao personally is concerned, as opposed to clashes with his group as at Lushan or the type of private tension noted in the remainder of this paragraph.

[105] Wang Nianyi, *Dadongluan*, pp. 384, 387–8; and Zhang Yunsheng, *Maojiawan*, pp. 163–5, 222–4.

Jiang, Ye ignored the entreaties of Zhou Enlai to stay and left before the visitor arrived. Ye's efforts to ingratiate herself also involved attempts to repair Jiang's standing with Mao after family quarrels, and to avoid possible conflict with Lin. Thus when Mao was angry with Jiang, Ye reportedly made a point of singing her praises to the Chairman. And as far as her own husband was concerned, as we have already seen in at least one case, Ye sought to improve his relations with Mao's wife by having a secretary (one of several who could imitate Lin's calligraphy) write a sentence of praise on a document lauding Jiang while keeping the matter from Lin.[106]

Thus, in addition to the basic structural conflicts between the two groups, the difficult personality of Jiang Qing was crucial to many of Maojiawan's problems and to élite tensions generally. Indeed, as much as anything, it probably explains Chen Boda's defection to Lin Biao; not only did Jiang and Chen reportedly have utter contempt for each other, but Chen was isolated within Diaoyutai, where the other younger and lower-ranking civilian radicals showed Jiang respect but ignored him despite his formal status as head of the CRG, and he even had to suffer such indignities as her pulling the insignia off the military uniform which he, like most civilian leaders, wore in this period.[107] More broadly, Jiang generated continuous petty conflicts, such as the issue of Huang Yongsheng's trip abroad (although the underlying conflict with Huang was certainly based on her attempts to interfere in PLA affairs[108]), while her unrelenting radicalism grated on Lin and even on Mao. Yet for all her abrasiveness, Jiang was subordinate to Lin in the hierarchy and had to show respect. Indeed, even after the major tensions of 1970 she continued to demonstrate a certain wary regard, as was graphically

---

[106] Zhang Yunsheng, *Maojiawan*, pp. 171, 174; Wen Feng, *Shentanxia*, p. 190; and above, pp. 12–13.

[107] Zhang Yunsheng, *Maojiawan*, p. 130; Xiao Sike, *Caoji shenpan*, vol. 1, p. 103; Quan Yanchi, *Tao Zhu*, pp. 186–7; Barnouin and Yu, *Ten Years of Turbulence*, p. 213; and oral sources. Some historians, however, cite other factors such as the declining role of the CRG as crucial to Chen's defection.

[108] See especially the observation of Guan Weixun, *Ye Qun*, p. 212, that Jiang felt she was being blocked in the army and initially blamed Huang. After a while, however, she felt there must be someone behind Huang and concluded it was Ye Qun.

illustrated by the publication of a photo she had taken of Lin
as a sign of 'good will' as late as July 1971, and when she proudly
boasted of a gift of watermelon from Vice Chairman Lin on the
very eve of his fatal flight.[109] With Mao's ultimate intentions
towards Lin still uncertain, it behoved her to remain cautious.
This indeed was the situation in both 'camps' for, as Zhang Yunsheng observed, they each 'understood that they could only
manoeuvre within the limits set up by Mao, [and] once they sur-
passed that limit they would be in deep trouble'.[110] The
shadow of Mao also hung heavily over the major events involving Lin Biao during the Cultural Revolution to which we now
turn.

[109] RMRB, 18 May 1978, in FBIS, 24 May 1978, p. E6; Zhang Yunsheng, Maojiawan,
p. 389; and Jiao Ye, Ye Qun zhi mi – yige mishu yanzhongde Ye Qun yu Lin Biao (The
Riddle of Ye Qun – Ye Qun and Lin Biao in the Eyes of a Secretary) (Beijing: Zhongguo
wenlian chubangongsi, 1993), pp. 383–4.
[110] Zhang Yunsheng, Maojiawan, p. 383.

3

LIN BIAO DURING THE ACTIVE PHASE OF THE CULTURAL REVOLUTION, 1966–1968

After a brief period of élite purges, culminating in the formal dismissals of Peng Zhen, Lu Dingyi, Luo Ruiqing and Yang Shangkun in May 1966, the Cultural Revolution entered an active mass mobilization phase involving first student Red Guards and then 'revolutionary rebels' in factories, government offices and, to a lesser extent, villages. This phase lasted till the late summer and fall of 1968 when Mao, finally disillusioned with the widespread chaos in society, began to reimpose a harsh order. Before this state of affairs was reached, the movement had gone through a succession of upsurges and clampdowns, as well as a great number of perplexing particular events.[1] As number-two in the regime, notwithstanding his inclination simply to follow Mao, Lin Biao necessarily had to become involved in the key events of the period. What do Lin's actions and his role tell us about him? And what larger lessons do they have concerning Chinese élite politics during the Cultural Revolution at its most intense and chaotic? To answer these questions we will examine a number of major developments in distinct subperiods of the movement: (1) Lin's emergence as the successor with particular attention to the May 1966 expanded Politburo meeting and the August Central Committee plenum; (2) the extension of the Cultural Revolution into military institutions, industry and the countryside in October–December 1966; (3) the reaction in early 1967 to the disorder caused by 'power seizures' as the movement expanded, as seen in the eight-point military directive and the 'February adverse current'; (4) the upsurge of radicalism following the Wuhan incident in July 1967 and subsequent efforts to bring the situation under control; and (5) the mysterious purge

---

[1] See Harding in *CHOC*, vol. 15, for an overview of the fluctuating developments of the period.

in March 1968 of Yang Chengwu, Yu Lijin and Fu Chongbi which marked the start of a new radical upsurge.

The Making of a Successor, January–August 1966

Whatever precise role Lin Biao played in the Luo Ruiqing affair in late 1965, there is little to indicate that he had any prior knowledge of or was any better informed than most CCP leaders concerning the real meaning of other critical developments in this period. In particular, there is no solid evidence of his involvement in the initial criticism of the *Hai Rui* drama which ultimately led to the downfall of the Beijing mayor and Party leader, Peng Zhen.[2] In the first half of 1966, however, Lin began to appear on the national stage in non-military matters, matters which were closely linked to the themes and struggles of the Cultural Revolution. Notwithstanding his promotion of Mao's Thought and the holding up of the PLA as a model for the entire country in the 1964 'Learn from the PLA' campaign, Lin's activities before 1966 had been basically limited to the military. But now, in February 1966, he sponsored Jiang Qing's army literature and art forum which directly challenged the policies of Peng Zhen, Lu Dingyi and others. In March he became involved in industry and communications work with a letter emphasising the importance of Mao's Thought and putting 'Politics in command' in this system. Subsequently Lin's presence was felt in industry, agriculture and education through a report

[2] While Barnouin and Yu, *Ten Years of Turbulence*, p. 56, cite the harsh denunciation of *Hai Rui* in a *PLA Daily* editorial note in late November as evidence of Lin Biao's role in the affair, it is important to note that this eventuated nearly three weeks after the original publication of Yao Wenyuan's critique of the play and only after Mao's complaints concerning the disappointing media response to Yao's article. Moreover, it is unclear who orchestrated the *PLA Daily* editorial note. One version has Mao complaining to Lin about the inadequate response and Lin replying that he would stick by Mao and deal with anyone opposing the Chairman, and more extremely that a deal to oppose both Peng Zhen and Luo Ruiqing emerged; see Xiao Sike, *Caoji shenpan*, vol. 1, pp. 80–3. By contrast, in *Quzhe fazhan*, p. 618, the excellent historian Cong Jin reports Jiang Qing approaching Luo Ruiqing about the attitude of the army paper, with Luo responding by ordering publication of Yao's article which appeared together with the severe editorial comment.

that became the basis of Mao's 7 May directive on breaking down specialization so that soldiers, workers, peasants and students would become competent in and participate in all these and other areas. And at the expanded Politburo meeting in May he delivered his infamous speech warning against *coups d'état*, which raised the temperature of the meeting and led to Mao's July letter to Jiang Qing expressing disquiet with his 'friend'. Against this background Lin replaced Liu Shaoqi as the successor at the Eleventh Plenum less than three months later. From hindsight these events have appeared to some analysts as deliberate interventions by an ambitious Lin which culminated in his elevation.[3]

Nothing can be said with complete assurance as to what exactly Lin knew and when he knew it, but it is safe to say that in the period leading to the Eleventh Plenum he was aware that Mao was pushing for significant changes in personnel as well as policy but hardly knew the full extent of what was afoot. Lin's involvements from January till March appear to have been not only reactive but in most cases somewhat routine. The most significant step – his 'entrusting' Jiang Qing with the task of convening a literature and art forum within the PLA – was clearly a response to Mao's initiative. Apparently wishing to increase the pressure on Peng Zhen, Mao urged Jiang to seek Lin's support ('beseech a god') for framing an alternative policy to that of Peng. Jiang then visited Lin in Suzhou in late January 1966 to propose the army forum. According to Lin's daughter, with Ye Qun absent the meeting went badly and 'came close to fighting', with Lin approving her request only when she made it clear that the forum was Mao's idea, and even then he attempted to distance himself by stating 'My health is very poor'. He ordered the GPD to cooperate, and the concrete work for the forum was carried out under Liu Zhijian, the department's deputy head responsible for propaganda, who was to fall out with Jiang Qing before the end of the year. After Jiang Qing's complaints concerning the GPD's 'inadequate' summary of the forum, Mao asked Chen Boda, Kang Sheng, Zhang Chunqiao

---

[3] E.g. Harding in *CHOC*, vol. 15, pp. 118, 123–4, 130–2, 138–40.

and Yao Wenyuan to revise the document, and then himself revised their effort three times and added Lin Biao's name to the document's title. Aware of Mao's role, Lin forwarded the revised version to the MAC Standing Committee in March along with his own resounding words about the still undecided struggle against revisionism. In all this Lin was obviously taking his lead from Mao and Jiang, and delegated responsibility to others. His involvement overall was described by one historian who has worked on the period as passive.[4]

Lin's 'intervention' in the industry and communications sphere in March appears much more routine. His letter, written on 11 March and published in the *People's Daily* the following June, came shortly after the conclusion of a five-week national conference on industry and communications and political work in this area. Since part of the emphasis on learning from the PLA had been to set up army-style political work departments in civilian units,[5] a comment from the defence chief was only appropriate. Moreover, the content of Lin's letter, despite its mandatory praise of politics and the study of Mao, differed in an important sense from his harsh warning about sharp class struggle on the literature and art front. Indeed, it could be regarded as praise of Bo Yibo, the alternate Politburo member in charge of this area of work. Lin did not take the opportunity to challenge the conference remarks of Deng Xiaoping that while politics must command business affairs, 'Politics in command' must result in [increased] production – a serious 'revisionist'

---

[4] Cong Jin, *Quzhe fazhan*, pp. 620–2; Wang Nianyi, *Dadongluan*, p. 349; Zhang Yunsheng, *Maojiawan*, pp. 156–7; Guan Weixun, *Ye Qun*, p. 211; Barnouin and Yu, *Ten Years of Turbulence*, pp. 59–60; Kau, *Lin Piao*, pp. 323–4; and oral sources. The title given to the summary by Mao was 'Summary of the army forum on literature and art which Comrade Lin Biao entrusted Comrade Jiang Qing to convene'.

[5] For an account arguing a greater intrusion of the PLA into the civilian sphere in 1964–5 and suggesting that Lin proposed the formation of political departments, see Harding in *CHOC*, vol. 15, pp. 117–18. In fact, the 1963 proposal to strengthen political work in civilian units came not from the PLA but from Minister of Metallurgy Wang Heshou. *ZGDSJXCKZL*, vol. 24 (July 1986), p. 374; and interview with a former middle-level cadre in a political department who saw the relevant document.

view from a Cultural Revolution perspective. Moreover, in sharp contrast to Jiang's picture of the literature and art sphere, Lin declared that the industrial and communications system – a system led by Bo Yibo and other officials whom, as we see later, Lin was to denounce by the end of the year – was doing an 'excellent' job in promoting politics, and in recent years had been reforming the spiritual outlook of the working people. Lin's involvement, then, appeared not only routine but benign.[6]

Given that Mao's emphasis in his 7 May directive on the participation of soldiers, workers, peasants and students in production, military affairs, culture and politics introduced one of the large ideological themes of the Cultural Revolution, it is even more telling that there appears to be nothing remarkable in Lin Biao's role in the events which produced the directive. Mao's instruction came in response to a report by Qiu Huizuo's Logistics Department on improving the army's agricultural sideline production, which Lin had passed on to Mao for approval. The report apparently contained nothing unusual for the period and merely provided some concrete measures for carrying out the PLA's traditional role in agricultural production and upholding Mao's Thought. The same scholar who described Lin's involvement in the literature and art forum as passive also believes that any initiative in this case was minimal, and doubts that given his health Lin would have done more than read the report cursorily before forwarding it to Mao. Thus while the incident contributed to a further development of Mao's radical opinions, there is nothing to suggest that Lin or Qiu were doing more than carrying out their normal duties while reflecting the ideological climate in early 1966.[7]

By contrast, Lin's role at the expanded Politburo meeting in May, can hardly be described as routine. Indeed, the official view of Lin's speech on 18 May as pushing matters to leftist extremes

[6] Kau, Lin Piao, pp. 321–2; and Ma Qibin, Sishinian, pp. 264–5.
[7] Li Ke and Hao Shengzhang, 'Wenhua dageming' zhongde Renmin Jiefangjun (The PLA during the 'Cultural Revolution') (Beijing: Zhonggong dangshi ziliao chubanshe, 1989), p. 386; Ma Qibin, Sishinian, pp. 268–9; Jerome Ch'en, Mao Papers: Anthology and Bibliography (London: Oxford University Press, 1970), pp. 103–5; and oral source.

can hardly be faulted. But as with so much else concerning Lin's role, the situation was more complex. First, by the time Lin spoke the major political departures of the meeting had already occurred. On 6 May the activities of Peng Zhen and Lu Dingyi in 'opposing the revolutionary line in culture' had been exposed, and Peng, Lu, Luo Ruiqing and Yang Shangkun were labelled 'anti-Party, anti-socialist, anti-Mao Zedong Thought' elements. On the 16th the 'Centre' issued a report on Luo's mistakes, and – most importantly – the famous circular denouncing Peng's cultural policies, which already contained a passage inserted personally by Mao warning of the danger of a coup, was approved. These events, as well as the overall thrust of the meeting, were clearly based on the absent Mao's views as expressed at an April Politburo Standing Committee meeting in Hangzhou. In the early stages of the Politburo conference Kang Sheng, Zhang Chunqiao and Chen Boda conveyed Mao's opinions and developed the themes of the Cultural Revolution.[8]

Moreover, when Lin did address the meeting on the 18th, in many ways he simply echoed the emerging Cultural Revolution rhetoric, arguing the importance of quashing the revisionist threat to proletarian political power, the importance of rebuffing the bourgeois agents in the propaganda sphere, the danger of Khrushchev-like people in the upper echelons of the Party, and the brilliance of Mao and his ideas. But what made the speech remarkable was, as he noted in one passage, 'the smell of gunpowder'. Lin devoted a great portion of the speech to military coups; he not only included the recent spate of such events in Asia, Africa and Latin America and examples from Chinese history where dynasties were challenged even before they had lasted one or several decades in power, but also applied the label to the recent activities of Peng, Luo, Lu and Yang with blood-curdling talk of killings and seizures of power.[9] Yet signifi-

---

[8] Wang Nianyi, *Dadongluan*, pp. 9–16; Ma Qibin, *Sishinian*, pp. 267–8; and Ye Yonglie, *Chen Boda* (Chen Boda) (Hong Kong: Wenhua jiaoyu chubanshe youxian gongsi, 1990), p. 261. Again (see above, p. 27, n. 45), this is a foreign edition of Ye's work.

[9] Kau, *Lin Piao*, pp. 328–33.

cantly the impetus for such talk does not appear to have come
from the military man. Certainly Lin was not alone in formulat-
ing the speech,[10] but it is more important that the real source
of the attention to coups was Mao, who had raised the issue as
early as a December 1965 conversation with General Xu Shiyou.
In the speech itself Lin noted that he 'ha[d] not thought much
about this problem' but that Chairman Mao, who had 'not
slept well for many days', had noticed the issue and several times
called in responsible comrades to discuss ways of preventing
counterrevolutionary coups.[11] According to Lin:

> In recent months Chairman Mao has paid particular attention to the adop-
> tion of many measures toward preventing a counterrevolutionary *coup
> d'état*. After the [Luo Ruiqing] problem he talked about it. Now that the
> [Peng Zhen] problem has been exposed, he has again summoned several
> persons and talked about it, dispatched personnel and had them stationed
> in the radio broadcasting stations, the armed forces, and the public security
> systems in order to prevent a . . . *coup d'état* and the occupation of our
> crucial points.[12]

Thus in dwelling on the issue Lin was addressing a preoccupation of Mao's, a preoccupation which possibly explains the Chairman's eventual abandonment of the alleged coup plotter He Long,
and arguably contributed to Lin's involvement in anti-He
activities in the late summer of 1966. But what of the disquiet
expressed in Mao's letter to Jiang Qing following Lin's speech?
The Chairman's reservations only briefly mentioned Lin's
emphasis on coups, but did not focus on this question. Instead,
most of Mao's doubts were to do with the claims concerning

[10] According to *RMRB*, 18 May 1978, in *FBIS*, 24 May 1978, p. E3, Zhang Chunqiao worked on the *coup d'état* formula and collected the information which went into
the speech. This claim is dubious given that Lin Biao was not even aware of Zhang's
existence before the Cultural Revolution (see above, pp. 51–2), but is conceivable in
view of Mao's involvement with the Shanghai radicals in 1965.
[11] Kau, *Lin Piao*, pp. 328, 329, 332; and Cong Jin, *Quzhe fazhan*, p. 635.
[12] Kau, *Lin Piao*, p. 328. Regarding radio and television stations, a further sign of
Mao's concern was the activities in April–May 1966 of Zhou Enlai who visited such
stations in Beijing, warning that they could not be allowed to fall into enemy hands
and had to run normally if chaos developed; Cheng Hua, *Zhou Enlai he tade mishumen*
(Zhou Enlai and his Secretaries) (Beijing: Zhongguo guangbo dianshi chubanshe,
1992), p. 444.

his genius and supernatural powers.[13] Such reservations by the Chairman, however, were by now familiar,[14] and people in the inner circle who took them seriously did so at their own peril, even if completely ignoring them, as Lin was to discover in 1970, could also be fraught with danger. In any case, Mao put aside whatever concerns he may have had and approved the circulation of the speech within the Party and subsequently had it reprinted and distributed at the Eleventh Plenum.[15]

The period between the May Politburo conference and the Eleventh Plenum saw the emergence of the Cultural Revolution as a mass movement on university campuses in urban China, particularly in Beijing. The major élite actors in this drama were the CRG, which had been formed at the May meeting and which encouraged the activities of radical students, and the Party apparatus under Liu Shaoqi which attempted to bring some order to the unfolding campaign through the long-tested device of work teams. Watching from Hunan was Mao who after the so-called 'fifty days' of clashes on campus returned to Beijing in late July and declared that the activities of the work teams had wrongly suppressed revolutionary students.[16] Through all this there is no evidence of any action by Lin Biao who was on sick leave in Dalian from at least early July until he was called to the plenum by Mao in early August,[17] nor concerning whether he even had an opinion on what was happening.

When the Eleventh Plenum convened on 1 August, Lin was apparently unaware of the momentous decisions which were about to take place. Various oral sources, including a close student of the case who initially thought that Lin must have had some inkling of the fate of Liu Shaoqi and still regards Lin as

---

[13] Kau, *Lin Piao*, pp. 119–20. Mao's reservations on coups, moreover, had more to do with the theoretical inadequacy of Lin's presentation than the subject itself.

[14] Cf. Mao's contradictory views on the powers of his 'Thought' in 1964–5 in Teiwes, *Leadership*, pp. 67–8.

[15] Wang Nianyi, *Dadongluan*, p. 17. Wang does not attribute these decisions to Mao, but that surely was the case.

[16] For an overview, see Harding in *CHOC*, vol. 15, pp. 134–7.

[17] Guan Weixun, *Ye Qun*, p. 215; and *Xiao Jingguang huiyiluxuji*, p. 263.

an ambitious politician, believe that he had no idea he would soon replace Liu as the successor nor even a sense that any major developments would take place at the plenum, which he had no intention of attending. As events unfolded, it was only after writing his 'Bombard the headquarters' wall-poster on 5 August that the Chairman summoned Lin to the plenum and sent Wu Faxian and a plane to Dalian to pick him up. Lin was not happy about having to go to the hot weather of the capital, and – oral sources believe – it was only after arriving in Beijing and reading Mao's wall-poster that he began to understand what was going on. Mao then called in Lin and informed him that he would be the successor. Lin's reaction was to try and back away from the position; he wrote a report to the Chairman saying he could not accept, but Mao insisted and the Defence Minister gave in.[18] Shortly tkereafter the organizational changes were made which elevated Lin to the position of sole Vice Chairman and Mao's heir apparent.

Lin's new position was perhaps the one clear outcome of the Eleventh Plenum. But even the organizational changes of the plenum deserve further comment because many of those promoted at this key juncture did not stay the course. Of particular note was Tao Zhu, a 'leftist' figure in the context of the early 1960s who had just become the Party's propaganda chief and now ranked number-four in the hierarchy, and Marshal Ye Jianying, who had already been prominent in heading the investigation of Luo Ruiqing and had been elevated to the Party Secretariat and the position of MAC Secretary-General in May; now, together with two other marshals, Xu Xiangqian and Nie Rongzhen, he was further promoted to the Politburo. In addition, the status of the main losers, Liu Shaoqi and Deng Xiaoping, remained unclear since they retained high rank – though not function – and their self-criticisms to the plenum were approved by Mao. In policy terms, the sixteen-point directive on the Cultural Revolution

---

[18] Guan Weixun, *Ye Qun*, p. 215; and oral sources. Other signs of Lin's reluctance reported by a military Party historian are that Zhou Enlai had visited Lin in Dalian at the end of July to urge him to be more active, while after his arrival in Beijing Mao chided Lin by comparing him to a Ming dynasty ruler who engaged in Daoist pursuits.

produced contradictory demands by calling for pushing forward the movement even where some disturbances were likely, and for affirming the aim of sweeping 'capitalist roaders' out of high office; at the same time it stipulated overall Party leadership of the process, called for relatively lenient treatment for erring cadres, excluded various groups in society from the campaign, and forbade any disruption of production. Moreover, the PLA was particularly insulated from outside radical interference under this decision, with Cultural Revolution activities in the army placed under the MAC rather than the CRG. Finally, there were many anxious questions from the participants at the plenum concerning how long the movement would last. This apparently led to assurances that it would be over in three months.[19]

Thus not only had Lin Biao been thrust into the role of successor at the Eleventh Plenum without forewarning, and without major initiative on his part or even any evident desire for the role; but he had also been thrust into the midst of a fundamentally ambiguous situation where there were few indications of what was to come. Over the next month and a half Lin's known activities were basically limited to appearing at mass rallies, sometimes only after considerable nagging by Ye Qun, and dutifully propounding the rhetoric of the Cultural Revolution. Soon, however, he was to be faced with the problem of how far the movement should go.

Extending the Cultural Revolution, October–December 1966

In the immediate post-Eleventh Plenum period the expectations of a short movement mostly restricted to non-productive urban organs continued to prevail. In late August Mao told a central work conference that he was prepared to allow chaos to continue for several months but that the Cultural Revolution would not affect the military, and he approved Zhou Enlai's request that

[19] Harding in *CHOC*, vol. 15, pp. 138–41, 174; Zhou Ming (ed.), *Lishi zai zheli chensi – 1966–1976 nian jishi* (Contemplating History – A True Record of 1966–1976) (vols 1–3, Beijing: Huaxia chubanshe, 1986), vol. 1, p. 167; and oral source.

it be wound up in Party and government units by the middle of October.[20] Before mid-November even the CRG leaders had no idea of how the Cultural Revolution should be conducted in factories and villages and merely followed existing Socialist Education Movement practices in these areas.[21] Nevertheless, over the last three months of 1966 several major steps in the extension of the Cultural Revolution took place – the 'urgent directive' of 5 October which endorsed Lin Biao's proposal to abolish restrictions on the campaign in PLA academies and schools, and undermined the Party committee system in these units (and by extension in various non-military institutions), and the December decisions of expanded Politburo meetings chaired by Lin for the movement to enter China's factories and villages. Thus Lin was clearly involved in the extension of the movement but, as throughout the Cultural Revolution, other actors played key roles and Mao's wishes were decisive.

The story of the 5 October directive which reversed the restrictions of the Eleventh Plenum on the Cultural Revolution in the army began on the rostrum of Tiananmen at the National Day celebrations on 1 October. On that occasion a representative of a mass organization within military educational institutions, perhaps Tao Zhu's daughter,[22] approached Mao and Lin to complain of the suppression of mass activities in these institutions. On this or another occasion at about the same time, a young petitioner presented Lin with a bloodstained coat, and Lin was reportedly moved by the courage it symbolised. He ordered the PLACRG to draft an urgent directive on the conduct of the

[20] Ma Qibin, *Sishinian*, p. 274; and Li Ping *et al.*, *'Wenhua dageming' zhongde Zhou Enlai* (Zhou Enlai during the 'Cultural Revolution') (Beijing: Zhonggong zhongyang dangxiao chubanshe, 1991), pp. 120–1.

[21] This is our conclusion based on a reading of their contemporary speeches.

[22] In a version of events at Tiananmen reported in an interview by a Party historian in the military, the daughters of Tao and Mao were engaged in a conversation in which Tao Shiliang was critical of suppression within army institutions. Lin Doudou was also present and reported the conversation to her mother, Ye Qun. Ye interpreted this as indicating a new direction in the Cultural Revolution and urged Doudou to 'blow wind in Lin Biao's ear' on the matter and, more important, to present the message as if it were Mao's view.

movement in military schools, and this produced a document with various proposals but one which basically affirmed leadership by Party committees. Lin then sent this draft to the CRG for review with the result that Chen Boda, Jiang Qing, Kang Sheng and Zhang Chunqiao objected that various points could not be allowed. They made many revisions and added a stipulation abolishing Party committee leadership of the campaign. This led to a sharp exchange with Liu Zhijian, then the head of the PLACRG, who argued that there was no precedent for such a step. When Zhang Chunqiao stated that Party leadership was equivalent to leadership by Mao and Mao's Thought, Liu retorted that such leadership was all very fine, but that the lower levels still needed concrete individuals to lead them.[23]

In the event, the 5 October directive reflected the position of the CRG in abolishing Party committee leadership in PLA educational units (though not within the larger military structure), attacking constraints on the masses, and declaring invalid all labels placed earlier on rebellious students. However, it also stipulated that military schools were not to get involved in the Cultural Revolution activities of the localities. The 'Centre' completely agreed with the revised directive, both Mao and Lin approved of its being issued, and Mao reportedly attached great importance to the document. A broad spectrum of the leadership then participated in mass rallies propagating the directive, including Zhou Enlai, Tao Zhu, Ye Jianying and others in addition to the CRG. The effect of all this within army schools was to increase the legitimacy of 'rebellion' and undercut the response of PLA authorities. A major development was a siege of the Defence Ministry in late October–early November by military students, a matter which Lin Biao tried to avoid and which was only defused by Zhou Enlai's political skills. Later in November the GPD sponsored two mass rallies at which several old marshals addressed the students in an effort to persuade them to eschew excessive slogans and violence. While these speeches had

---

[23] Wang Nianyi, *Dadongluan*, p. 96; Zhang Yunsheng, *Maojiawan*, pp. 42–3; and oral sources.

Lin's backing, they were still denounced by radical student factions. Meanwhile, the broader result flowing from the directive
was a chain reaction in which its abolition of Party organization
leadership within army schools was applied to many non-military
units and especially to universities and middle schools. The
by product was considerable anarchy. As part of this process, the
view was advanced that if Party leadership could be laid aside
in military academies, then the same situation should apply in
factories and the countryside.[24]

This pressure to extend the movement further clashed head-on
with the injunction of the Eleventh Plenum not to disrupt production and with the interests of those officials and organizations
responsible for the economy. The matter came to a head at a
November–December industry and communications seminar.
One of the leading planning officials, Yu Qiuli, proposed to Li
Fuchun, the nominal State Planning Commission (SPC) head and
a newly-elected member of the Politburo Standing Committee,
that such a meeting be held to handle the question of the Cultural
Revolution and production needs, and the seminar began in mid-
November after Li informed Mao, Lin, Zhou Enlai and others. The
discussion centred on a twelve-article CRG draft which led to
extended discussion and basic rejection by the assembled economic
officials. This was followed by the drafting of a counter-position,
a fifteen-article document by Yu Qiuli and another economic
official, Gu Mu, under the direction of Tao Zhu. This document,
however, was rejected by Mao on 22 November who instructed
that the workers' right to establish mass organizations must be
supported. A final document, Chen Boda's ten articles reflecting
the Chairman's views, was then passed by the meeting.[25]

[24] Wang Nianyi, *Dadongluan*, pp. 96–9; Zhang Yunsheng, *Maojiawan*, pp. 56–8,
61–2; Ma Qibin, *Sishinian*, pp. 277–8; *ZGDSJXCKZL*, vol. 25, p. 161; *Zhongguo
Renmin Jiefangjun liushinian dashiji (1927–1987)* (PLA 60 Years Chronology,
1927–1987) (Beijing: Junshi kexue chubanshe, 1988), p. 627; Barnouin and Yu, *Ten
Years of Turbulence*, pp. 126–32; above, p. 36; and oral source.
[25] Wang Nianyi, *Dadongluan*, pp. 134–7; Tan Zhongji, *Shinianhou*, pp. 47–52; and Li
Ping, *'Wenhua dageming' de Zhou*, p. 122. Yu Qiuli was in fact the person responsible
for the SPC, while Li Fuchun's duties were to assist Zhou Enlai with overall responsibility for the economy.

It was at this stage in early December that Lin convened an enlarged Politburo meeting. At this meeting Gu Mu continued to articulate the concerns raised at the seminar which produced attacks on him by Jiang Qing and other CRG members. The political stakes were raised further with an attack on Tao Zhu by one of the junior CRG figures, Wang Li, for allegedly using production to suppress revolution, and Tao was forced to make a self-criticism. On 6 December Lin Biao summed up the meeting with a speech endorsing the radical position, reflecting that a complete about-turn had taken place during the conference, and attacking the revisionist bourgeois line imposed for the past ten or twenty years [sic] on industry and communications by the same officials whose work he had praised in March. Clearly Lin's role was significant, but as Wang Nianyi has observed, his speech was obviously not merely an individual opinion but reflected Mao's intention and, as Wang further suggested, was in substance 'passive and perfunctory'. Similarly, on 15 December another expanded Politburo meeting passed a resolution on extending the movement to the villages, a measure which the agricultural chief, Tan Zhenlin, commented had come from the CRG but which Lin noted he had been asked by Mao to have passed. Thus we see again the importance of the CRG in pushing the campaign forward, as well as Mao's ultimate authority. The events of November–December also reflect on Zhou Enlai, who on 24 November, two days after Mao declared his position, despairingly commented that one could not avoid the inferno, there was no escape, and all one could hope for was to ride the situation out and not be swept away. If Lin Biao played an important role in the about-turn of early December, Zhou, who was in a difficult position himself due to allegations of contradictions between 'the new CRG and the old government', did nothing to prevent it. Both men would have to face the consequences of the new radicalization of the movement early in 1967.[26]

[26] Wang Nianyi, *Dadongluan*, pp. 137–43; Tan Zhongji, *Shinianhou*, pp. 52–6; Li Ping, *'Wenhua dageming' de Zhou*, pp. 9, 126; and Kau, *Lin Piao*, p. 413.

But between mid-December and the new upsurge of January 1967 'a final act in the extension of the Cultural Revolution was played out – the fall of one of Lin Biao's most favoured leadership colleagues, Tao Zhu. In addition to his involvement in the industry and communications question, he was particularly vulnerable – as both official and Western analyses have emphasised – for his efforts to contain the movement by protecting leading cadres from Red Guard attacks.[27] In the official version, however, both Lin Biao and Jiang Qing are seen as villains in bringing Tao down, a version in serious conflict with the facts. Although Jiang and her CRG colleagues were in the forefront of attacks on Tao, Lin tried to counsel his friend as the storm raged, while – as with so many events in this period – Mao's shifting attitudes determined Tao's fate. Clearly Mao became disappointed with Tao's relatively restrictive interpretation of the Cultural Revolution, but at the same time he was at first well disposed toward the new number-four in the regime who had struck a 'leftist' posture in the years immediately preceding the Cultural Revolution. As for Tao, the evidence suggests that he thought he was doing what Mao wanted, particularly in shielding his old Central-South colleague and a particular Mao favourite, Wang Renzhong, who had come under attack from the CRG. When the pressure on Wang increased, Tao, feeling he could not abandon an old colleague who had been placed in such a terrible situation, rejected an approach made on 26 December by Kang Sheng who urged him to stop protecting large numbers of 'royalists' before it was too late. On the next day the CRG shifted its attack to Tao Zhu himself.[28]

During this period of escalating attacks extending into the new year, Mao expressed his concern for Tao and criticised Jiang Qing's actions, steps which produced a great sense of relief and a feeling on Tao's part that 'my problem is not so serious'. The Chairman's actions, however, contained an ominous message for Tao, who had advocated handling the cases of Liu Shaoqi

[27] See Harding in *CHOC*, vol. 15, p. 152; Gao Gao and Yan Jiaqi, '*Wenhua dageming*', pp. 126–31; and Huang Zheng, *Zai lishi dang'anli*, pp. 12ff.
[28] Quan Yanchi, *Tao Zhu*, pp. 197–8, 201–6.

and Deng Xiaoping as 'contradictions among the people': Mao criticised Tao's claim that 'at the present stage contradictions among the people should figure prominently' and warned him that serious 'matters of principle' were involved. Both Zhou Enlai and Lin Biao offered Tao encouragement during this difficult time, with Lin providing the advice that he should adopt a passive posture to avoid errors and overcome his difficulties. The CRG leaders, however, pressed their attack on Tao with Jiang Qing, Kang Sheng and Chen Boda all playing prominent roles in raising charges that ranged from not consulting the CRG and not carrying out Mao's line to being a spy and a traitor during the revolutionary period. At some point during the first week of January they apparently succeeded in altering Mao's attitude by arguing that the hot-tempered Tao, who had refused to be questioned by Red Guards, had 'oppressed the masses'. Tao reportedly was not only surprised by the charges against him but bewildered by the emerging signs that the Chairman was siding with his accusers. Tao's wife, not believing a report that Mao had said that Tao was 'dishonest' (*bu laoshi*) and thinking he must have used the similar, (Chinese) term 'unsophisticated' (*bu laocheng*), wrote to her old friend seeking clarification, only to receive her letter back without comment but with the word 'dishonest' underlined by the Chairman and a question-mark added, a response that left Tao numb and in tears. A final twist to this story saw Mao express his continuing dissatisfaction with the excesses committed by Jiang Qing and Chen Boda in bringing down Tao, especially in a rebuke in February critical of 'one Standing Committee member [Chen] knocking over another [Tao]' and by requiring them both to engage in self-criticism. But through all this neither Lin Biao nor Zhou Enlai, despite their sympathy for Tao's plight, did anything effective to protect him. The inferno had truly been entered, not only by China's factories and to a lesser degree villages, but ever more threateningly by the CCP's top leadership.[29]

[29] *Ibid.*, pp. 207–11, 214–16, 224–6, 229–34; and Ye Yonglie, *Chen Boda*, pp. 348–9, 366.

Coping with Anarchy, January–March 1967

In January 1967 the Cultural Revolution reached an even more disruptive stage with the 'seizure of power' by radical mass organizations from established Party bodies, violent clashes among different 'rebel' groups, and rough treatment of disgraced officials at the hands of the 'masses'. The PLA was not immune to this process: military organizations were attacked and army cadres abused. In the official view, while Zhou Enlai strove to restrain the escalating violence and protect various leaders, both Lin Biao and the CRG encouraged the destructive activities. A particular subtheme, echoed to a considerable extent in the conventional Western view, pictures Lin inciting attacks on the remaining old marshals, even to the point of sanctioning disruption of the PLA while seeking to eliminate his 'opposition' within the army. In contrast, the major efforts to curb the chaos in this period – the eight-point directive which allowed the PLA to defend itself against mass attacks and gave the army authority to restore a degree of order in society, and the 'February adverse current' where four old marshals in conjunction with three Vice Premiers engaged (fruitlessly) in a more wide-ranging attack on Cultural Revolution excesses – are credited to the old marshals. Lin, together with Jiang Qing's group, allegedly sought to sabotage these efforts; they were unsuccessful in the case of the eight points but effective in the case of the 'February current', with the result that a new radical upsurge emerged by late March and the PLA's powers were limited by a new ten-point directive issued by Lin in early April.[30]

A variety of sources indicate that the above picture of Lin's role is seriously distorted. In Zhang Yunsheng's account, rather than utilizing the instability of early 1967 to further his political ambitions, Lin felt profoundly threatened by the chaos, especially in so far as it affected the PLA. A meticulous PLA Party historian of the period, moreover, has concluded that Lin may actually

[30] See Gao Gao and Yan Jiaqi, 'Wenhua dageming', pp. 135–45, 258; RMRB, 26 February 1979, in FBIS, 28 February 1979, pp. E7, E9–15; and Harding in CHOC, vol. 15, pp. 175–9.

have organised the other marshals to check the Cultural Revolution in the military. More broadly, on a number of occasions in February–March 1967 Lin emphasised the importance of production, arguing that, while revolution had priority, engaging in production was the primary task in terms of allocation of time, revolution could not be grasped at the expense of promoting production, and if production was not grasped tightly it would cause very great danger that would damage revolution.[31]

In connection with the eight-point directive issued in late January, Lin played a more important and positive role than standard accounts acknowledge, albeit one that accorded close attention to cues from Mao. The initiative in the first instance appears to have been taken by Marshal Xu Xiangqian, who had just replaced the by then discredited Liu Zhijian as head of the PLACRG. With reports streaming in from local commands about officers being assaulted and tortured by students and disruption to military training and war preparations, Xu and other PLA leaders felt the need for restrictions on mass activities. In this they gained some initial support from Mao, who would certainly have approved the Party Centre circular of 14 January which prohibited 'directing the spearhead of struggle against the armed forces'. Mao's attitude at this point was apparently influenced by several factors. First, apart from Lin Biao, he seems to have been counting on Marshals Xu Xiangqian, Ye Jianjing and Nie Rongzhen for support against what he perceived as the 'Liu-Deng line', with Xu nominated by none other than Jiang Qing as PLACRG head and Ye continuing in his key role as MAC Secretary-General. Also, while clearly wanting to see the Cultural Revolution pushed forward, the Chairman was also concerned with containing disruptions to social and political order, and sought some way to balance these contradictory desires. Thus Mao at least went along with the 14 January circular, but when faced with a request from the Anhui military authorities for instructions as to whether they could send troops

---

[31] Zhang Yunsheng, *Maojiawan*, p. 76; *ZGDSJXCKZL*, vol. 25, pp. 324, 369; and oral source.

to guard a meeting called by mass organizations to criticise the provincial Party leader, he responded on the 21st with his famous instruction that 'the PLA should support the broad masses of the revolutionary left'. When issued formally on the 23rd, this instruction countermanded all past directives limiting army involvement in the Cultural Revolution in local areas, directives which Lin seemingly supported strongly.[32]

At this critical juncture Mao received, on the 22nd, a delegation of participants in an ongoing MAC meeting which undoubtedly included Lin Biao.[33] With Xu Xiangqian providing a briefing, the meeting saw emotional complaints about the treatment of army veterans at the hands of 'revolutionary rebels'. The Chairman was seemingly moved by the distress of men who had loyally served him for decades and declared that such destructive behaviour should not be allowed, but at the same time he urged the assembled generals not to rest on their achievements during the revolutionary period but to play a positive role in the current movement. With Mao having shown a willingness to protect the military, at least to some degree, the MAC meeting continued even as the 'Support the left' directive was issued on the 23rd, with proposals for a new document containing some regulations that would guarantee that army leaders would not be hauled out for public struggle. In this context Xu then went to see Lin on the evening of 24 January to report on the escalating chaos within the PLA. Lin declared that 'disorder can't be allowed in the army', and sanctioned the drafting of a MAC document. Based on seven points orally conveyed by Lin himself, a nine-point instruction was drafted which, interestingly, gained the blessing of the CRG head, Chen Boda. But given the power set-up at the time, approval by the full CRG was also necessary. After a heated debate at a joint meeting of the MAC and CRG, reservations by the civilian radicals led to the

---

[32] Wang Nianyi, *Dadongluan*, p. 195; Zhang Yunsheng, *Maojiawan*, p. 176; *Xu Xiangqian zhuan*, p. 523; Li Ke and Hao Shengzhang, *'Wenhua dageming' de Jiefangjun*, p. 39; and Barnouin and Yu, *Ten Years of Turbulence*, pp. 135–7, 227.

[33] There is no direct evidence of Lin's attendance, but given his role and his presence at the MAC meeting the next day this is surely the case.

dropping of two points to produce a seven-point document. Xu then reported the outcome to Lin by letter, emphasising that the Cultural Revolution should be conducted prudently in the army. Ye Jianying and Yang Chengwu also submitted separate reports to Lin. On receiving the seven-point document, Lin sent it to Mao, together with a letter elaborating how it had been drawn up and five supporting documents demonstrating how military organs had been attacked and officers dragged away. Mao was particularly interested in these accounts, approved the seven points and asked that an eighth point on the need for cadres to pay attention to their children be added. The Chairman also noted that if military organs were attacked by 'rightists' they should resist, but they should welcome attacks by 'leftists'. However, with an eight-point document now ready for review by Mao and Zhou Enlai on the 28th, the Chairman made a last change banning attacks on the army from any source. When Lin and Xu Xiangqian visited Mao for final approval that afternoon, an uncharacteristically emotional Lin burst out into three cheers of 'Long live [Chairman Mao]' in apparent gratitude that the Chairman had approved a document that ostensibly protected the PLA from further disruption.[34]

The broad outlines of the 'February adverse current', one of the epochal events of the Cultural Revolution, are well known. Still angry at the disruption caused by the movement but arguably encouraged by Mao's approval of the eight points and Lin's support for their concerns as well as by the Chairman's demand that Chen Boda and Jiang Qing undergo self-criticism for their excesses in the purge of Tao Zhu, a number of senior leaders – including Marshals Ye Jianying, Xu Xiangqian, Chen Yi and Nie Rongzhen and Vice Premiers Li Fuchun, Li Xiannian

---

[34] Wang Nianyi, *Dadongluan*, pp. 195–8; Zhang Yunsheng, *Maojiawan*, pp. 77–8; Li Ke and Hao Shengzhang, *'Wenhua dageming' de Jiefangjun*, pp. 40–2; and *Zhonggong dangshi yanjiu* (*ZGDSYJ*) (Research on CCP History), no. 6 (1991), pp. 53–9. Since the details in these sources differ somewhat, we have attempted to provide the most likely account of the events. Zhang Yunsheng, p. 77, presents an even more active Lin who assertedly took the initiative to call in the old marshals to discuss the urgent situation, a view similar to that expressed in interviews with a leading Party historian (see above, pp. 72–3).

and Tan Zhenlin – articulated their discontent in a series of *ad hoc* meetings in early and mid-February. These so-called 'putting heads together meetings' (*pengtouhui*), which brought together Politburo and CRG members as well as other high-ranking officials, were chaired by Zhou Enlai because Lin Biao was not present, and their confrontational nature was indicated by the seating arrangement which placed the marshals and Vice Premiers on one side of the table and the CRG representatives on the other. With Zhou largely performing a procedural role, the marshals and their civilian allies expressed great emotion, pounding the table, admitting to having wept over the current state of affairs, and, in the case of Tan, even threatening to walk out. They harshly attacked the radicals for causing chaos in the Party and society, completely negating Party leadership, and wanting to overthrow all veteran cadres, and accused them of now trying to extend disorder into the PLA. Privately, they also concluded that the ultimate objective of the radicals was to overthrow Zhou Enlai. The radicals, however, allegedly produced a distorted record of the marshals' comments which greatly angered Mao, led him to demand their self-criticisms and removal from authority, and resulted in the suspension of the Politburo as a policy-making body. Significantly, the Chairman had interpreted the actions of the veteran leaders as directed at *his* Cultural Revolution, and declared that 'whoever opposes the CRG will meet my resolute opposition'.[35]

There is little sign of Lin Biao in official accounts of these events, although various remarks of the old marshals are unconvincingly portrayed as being directed at Lin.[36] More concretely, Lin is accused of playing a provocative role in the case of Tan Zhenlin. Apparently the most hot-headed of all the participants, Tan not only expressed distaste for Jiang Qing at the meetings but also wrote a letter to Lin alone which criticised her and her CRG associates in an angry tone. Lin, even in a recent account

---

[35] See *RMRB*, 26 February 1979, in *FBIS*, 28 February 1979, pp. E10–15; *XHRB*, 21–22 October 1984, in *FBIS*, 6 November 1984, pp. K22–24; Dong Baochun, *Tan Zhenlin waizhuan* (Unofficial Biography of Tan Zhenlin) (Beijing: Zuojia chubanshe, 1992), p. 128; and above, p. 71.

[36] E.g. *RMRB*, 26 February 1979, in *FBIS*, 28 February 1979, p. E13.

by serious scholars, is reported to have passed on his copy to
Mao with derogatory comments about Tan, thus attempting to
pour oil on the flames.[37] Such accounts, however, are at odds
with various pieces of evidence indicating a common perspective
shared by Lin and the old marshals, and that any negative role
he played came only after Mao's attitude was clear.

One sign of Lin's sympathy with the marshals' position came
when he received an instruction from Mao in the first half of
February asserting that 'attacks on troops should not be tol-
erated' and sanctioning (at least after persuasion failed) the
shooting of the leaders of such assaults. Lin immediately ordered
Zhang Yunsheng to deliver the instruction to Marshal Ye Jianying, and Ye's remarks to both Zhang and to Ye Qun by phone
indicated great relief on his part. Ye Jianying then had Zhang
accompany him to a meeting with other marshals where the
same sentiment was conveyed: that previously they had been
given instructions by the radicals that they thought were from
Mao but now they could see that they were fabricated, and that
the Chairman really cared about stability in the military. The
clear presumption on the marshals' part was that Lin Biao was
on their side.[38] An even more explicit example of this occurred
during a private meeting after one of the heated 'putting heads
together meetings'. Gathering at Li Fuchun's home, the marshals
and Vice Premiers discussed what to do given the impasse at the
pengtouhui. Tan Zhenlin suggested that they talk to Lin Biao,
and everyone agreed that Lin was the person to win over and
that he was likely to be sympathetic to their views.[39]

But what of Tan Zhenlin's letter which had been written on
16 February after a particularly bitter meeting with the radicals.[40]
A careful reconstruction demonstrates that Lin received the letter
the following day, and initially did nothing. In fact, according

[37] Liao Gailong (ed.), *Xin Zhongguo biannianshi* (Chronological History of New
China) (Beijing: Renmin chubanshe, 1989), p. 296. Cf. below, n. 50.

[38] Zhang Yunsheng, *Maojiawan*, pp. 86–90.

[39] Dong Baochun, *Tan Zhenlin*, p. 108.

[40] Some confusion is caused because Tan apparently wrote at least three similar letters, one to Lin, another addressed to 'the Chairman, Vice Chairman Lin and all Politburo comrades', and a third to Chen Boda. See Dong Baochun, *Tan Zhenlin*,
pp. 124–6; and Ye Yonglie, *Chen Boda*, pp. 376–7.

to his secretary's account, Lin ordered that the letter be kept secret, thus having the effect of protecting Tan. Mao convened a meeting on the evening of the 18th, which Ye Qun attended since Lin had begged off on grounds of ill-health – a meeting at which a furious Chairman lambasted the marshals and Vice Premiers for their comments and demanded that they step aside and engage in self-criticism. It was only on the 19th, after this meeting had taken place, that Lin forwarded Tan's letter with a comment expressing amazement at the degraded state of Tan's mind. When Mao returned the letter to Lin without comment, Lin was apparently upset and reportedly threw it in a spittoon – an action normally taken by official historians as evidence of his anger that his plot to destroy Tan had been foiled.[41] In our view, however, Lin's reaction can be explained rather as embarrassment that his effort to please Mao had produced no sign of the Chairman's appreciation. In fact, it is likely that Mao was somewhat annoyed by the slowness of Lin's response – much as he apparently had been over his successor's performance concerning Tao Zhu.[42] In the present case, on the 17th before receiving Tan's letter, Lin was briefed by Jiang Qing and junior CRG member Wang Li on the fierce debate of the previous evening and, more important, concerning Mao's initial critical response to the comments of Chen Yi in particular (although it was considerably less harsh than his subsequent explosion on the evening of the 18th).[43] Thus whatever the reason for Lin's seeming annoyance at his returned letter, he had only acted after Mao had made it un-equivocally clear that Tan was in trouble. His role in criticizing the old marshals and their civilian allies at ongoing meetings

---

[41] Zhang Yunsheng, *Maojiawan*, pp. 95–6; Wen Feng, *Shentanzia*, p. 106; and *RMRB*, 26 February 1979, in *FBIS*, 28 February 1979, p. E14.

[42] In early February on the same occasion that Mao criticised Jiang Qing and Chen Boda for their role in Tao's fall he reportedly complained to Lin that 'You kept me in the dark like you have always done in the past'; see *Dangshi ziliao tongxun* (Party History Materials Bulletin), no. 10 (1978), p. 5. While this report interprets the incident as a rebuke to Lin for his 'plot' against Tao, given Lin's longstanding relationship with Tao and his behaviour at the turn of 1966–7 it is more likely Mao was upset with Lin's private sympathy for Tao.

[43] Dong Baochun, *Tan Zhenlin*, p. 122.

lasting into March must be seen in the same light, and in fact was apparently less severe than that of Zhou Enlai. Thus when both addressed a mass rally on 20 March, Lin emphasised the importance of economic production and made no mention of the February events, while Zhou declared: 'At present there is an adverse current of bourgeois restoration coming from the top.'[44]

These events reveal again the familiar pattern of Mao determining the major turns of the Cultural Revolution, whether in a moderating or more radical direction, the CRG – and not Lin Biao – being the critical force pushing for radicalization, and Lin operating in a largely reactive mode. Yet in the case of the eight-point directive Lin appears, in a highly unusual posture for him, to be doing more than just following Mao and instead to be participating in a process attempting to influence the Chairman even though his major role seemingly developed only after Mao had revealed his inclination to protect the PLA. This very fact, together with his untypical emotional outburst when Mao approved the document, suggests an underlying 'moderate' policy preference – or at least a desire to protect the institutional interests of the military. This apparently was how the old marshals and others saw it during the 'February adverse current', and if Lin's actions – particularly his apparent failure, similar to that of Zhou Enlai, to lend tangible support during the crisis – would have disappointed them, his performance was a far cry from the disruptive role officially portrayed. A similar picture of Lin was to emerge from the next major attempt to curb turmoil in the wake of the Wuhan incident that summer.

---

[44] See the two-volume Cultural Revolution publication, *Mao Zhuxi de wuchanjieji geming luxian shengli wansui* (Long Live the Victory of Chairman Mao's Proletarian Revolutionary Line) (n.p.: n. pub., n.d.), p. 514; and *ZGDSJXCKZL*, vol. 25, pp. 363–71.

The Wuhan Incident and its Aftermath, July–September 1967

The dramatic 20 July Wuhan incident – the seizure and roughing up of high-ranking leaders of a central delegation by a 'conservative' mass organization with the passive support of the local military command – initially led to a radical upsurge, violent 'civil wars' and direct attacks on the PLA, and then, by late August and early September, to a reaction involving the reining in of the 'extreme left' and a reaffirmation of military authority. The sharp fluctuation in the fortunes of individuals and institutions during this period is encapsulated in the person of Wang Li, a junior member of the CRG who was seized in Wuhan, returned to Beijing a few days later to a hero's welcome, played a prominent role in the escalating attacks against established authority, and was then purged at the end of August apparently as a scapegoat for the excesses of the previous month.[45] How did Lin Biao fit into this volatile situation? According to the official version, Lin played a leading role in bringing pressure to bear on the Wuhan military authorities before the incident and then in orchestrating the radical upsurge following 20 July.[46] Western sources, however, present a more subtle picture of Lin as vacillating between the radical impetus provided by the CRG and the need to provide some stability in the military.[47] While

[45] Wang was purged together with another prominent CRG radical, Guan Feng, while Qi Benyu who was also involved in the disruptive activities of the period fell in January 1968; see Wang Nianyi, *Dadongluan*, p. 267. For the sake of convenience we use the conventional designation of a 'Wang-Guan-Qi affair' even though in fact Qi survived another half year.

[46] See Gao Gao and Yan Jiaqi, '*Wenhua dageming*', pp. 257–67.

[47] See Joffe, 'Chinese army', pp. 461–2; Lee, *Chinese Cultural Revolution*, pp. 248, 338; and Harding in *CHOC*, vol. 15, pp. 180, 182, for variations on this theme. For an analysis positing open Lin-CRG conflict over the incident, see Thomas W. Robinson, 'The Wuhan incident: local strife and provincial rebellion during the Cultural Revolution', *CQ*, no. 47 (1971), pp. 436–7. Ironically in view of their frequently sophisticated treatment of events, Barnouin and Yu, *Ten Years of Turbulence*, pp. 148–50, are close to the official line in arguing that Lin Biao in addition to Jiang Qing wanted a deep purge of the Wuhan military and in attributing the protection of the PLA to Mao with no mention of Lin's role.

this view is closer to the truth, a re-examination of the case is necessary for a fuller understanding of the complexities of his role and the situation generally.

The Wuhan incident occurred against the background of the increasing radicalization since March following the criticism of the 'February adverse current'. Mao's discontent with both the old marshals over the 'February current' and with local military commanders who cracked down on 'rebel' activities under the eight-point directive led, in early April, to the new ten-point directive which restricted the authority of the PLA to respond to attacks from mass organizations.[48] Local army leaders were now under increasing pressure since they were required to 'support the left', but many self-proclaimed 'leftists' attacked them. In this situation, with almost all leaders of large military regions in trouble for 'failing to support the left', Wuhan Commander Chen Zaidao and Political Commissar Zhong Hanhua who had taken a relatively firm line in handling disruptive 'rebels' were especially vulnerable and came under Jiang Qing's direct attack in mid-April at a conference in Beijing to which they had been summoned.[49] This apparently also reflected Mao's displeasure with their performance, and when the meeting concluded in late April, Chen and Zhong were dispatched home rather than invited like other participants to join the Chairman for May Day celebrations. In this conflict there is little indication of a direct role by Lin Biao, although about this time Lin reportedly commented privately to Wu Faxian concerning the need to 'drag out a small handful of bad people in the army', while Wu made a number of phone calls to air force units in Wuhan advising them to distance themselves from the regional military authorities who were now perceived as 'conservatives'. The most likely reason

---

[48] While Lin Biao played a prominent role in drafting the ten-point directive, as on other occasions he was clearly following Mao's lead. See Zhang Yunsheng, *Maojiawan*, pp. 106–7; and Li Ke and Hao Shengzhang, *'Wenhua dageming' de Jiefangjun*, pp. 233–4.
[49] Jiang also singled out the Chengdu Military Region. Arguably her choice of these regions had less to do with the actual behaviour of the local military than with their leaders' historical ties to He Long (in the case of Chengdu) and Xu Xiangqian (Wuhan).

for these activities is simply following the dominant trend of the period, but it is possible that some trivial personal matters were also involved. According to Chen Zaidao's recollections, Lin may have been upset by Chen's failure to return to Wuhan in 1965 to greet him when he visited on an inspection trip. An even more likely source of tension was an old grudge which Ye Qun bore against Zhong Hanhua for his part in dealing with her involvement in the Nationalist youth movement during cadre screening in Yan'an. In any case, in the lead-up to 20 July Maojiawan's role in bringing pressure on the Wuhan leaders seems to have been relatively peripheral.[50]

Mao had been in Wuhan for about a week before 20 July as part of an inspection tour that was to last into September. He arrived with the preconceived idea that the military region had 'committed very serious mistakes in failing to support the left', a view that was conveyed to Chen Zaidao by Zhou Enlai on the 18th although Chen refused to admit 'errors in direction'. While subsequent official and Western accounts depicted the central delegation led by Public Security Minister Xie Fuzhi, and in particular a member of the delegation, Wang Li, as taking a more provocative position than Mao, in fact all of Wang's activities strictly reflected the Chairman's orders.[51] In any case, in passing on the verdict that the military region was mistaken in direction and line Wang outraged the 'conservative' faction,

---

[50] Wang Nianyi, *Dadongluan*, pp. 259–61; *ZGDSJXCKZL*, vol. 25, pp. 508–24; and Barnouin and Yu, *Ten Years of Turbulence*, pp. 138–43. The perceived link between the 'February adverse current' and the local military suppressions is seen in the labelling of Chen Zaidao as 'Wuhan's Tan [Zhenlin]' (*Wu lao Tan*). Interestingly, 'Lin Biao clique member' Huang Yongsheng, then commander of the Guangzhou Military Region, was labelled 'Guangzhou's Tan' (*Guang lao Tan*).

[51] For the standard view of the delegation's role, see Gao Gao and Yan Jiaqi, '*Wenhua dageming*', pp. 261–3; and Harding in *CHOC*, vol. 15, pp. 181–2. Evidence that Wang was simply carrying out Mao's wishes includes the Chairman's comments as recorded in Wang's notebook which he showed to radical groups in Wuhan, and the conclusion of the Party Centre after fifteen years of investigation exonerating Wang from any wrongdoing. See Ye Yonglie, *Shenmi zhangquanzhe*, p. 242; and Chen Zaidao, *Huodong zhongde yimu – Wuhan qierling shijian qinliji* (A Scene in the Movement – Personal Historical Notes on the Wuhan 20 July Incident) (Beijing: Jiefangjun chubanshe, 1989), p. 61.

with the result that on 20 July it stormed the delegation's hotel, briefly seized other delegation leaders, and kidnapped Wang; the local leadership did nothing. This was seen as a major challenge to the regime's authority and produced a swift response. An urgent meeting including Lin Biao, Jiang Qing and other leading CRG figures, and Zhou Enlai was held in Beijing that afternoon and decided to send reliable troops to Wuhan, ordered the local military to ensure the safety of the delegation, and dispatched Zhou to oversee the Chairman's safe passage to Shanghai. Whatever the differences among the leaders in Beijing, the initial response to bring the situation in Wuhan under control was seemingly a unanimous one, and it quickly achieved the release of Wang Li.[52] One further development during this sequence of events requires comment. On the 18th Mao remarked to Wang Li that 'if Lin Biao's health is not good enough we can bring back Deng Xiaoping', a striking statement interpreted by Wang as showing dissatisfaction with Lin and which we speculate may have been related to Lin's partiality to military interests. Thus however active Lin became after the crisis broke, this gives further support to the impression that he did as little as possible to inconvenience local commanders before the 20th.[53]

Not surprisingly the Wuhan incident received huge national publicity, and radical views encouraging attacks on 'conservative' mass organizations and denigrating local PLA authority were widely propagated. In this process the CRG was in the forefront, promoting actions disruptive of society and threatening to the army. On 22 July Jiang Qing urged Red Guards to 'defend with weapons, attack with words', a slogan which had the effect of legitimizing violent confrontations. About the same time another

[52] Wen Feng, *Shentanxia*, pp. 148-9; Zhang Yunsheng, *Maojiawan*, pp. 124-5; and Lee, *Chinese Cultural Revolution*, pp. 246-7.
[53] Ye Yonglie, *Shenmi zhangquanzhe*, p. 242. Further evidence suggesting Lin's support of local commanders is a secretary's report that he received Nanjing Commander Xu Shiyou who complained of radical activities, and Lin indicated that any attacks on Xu was the equivalent of attacks on him. Unfortunately the precise timing of this event was not given, but it appears to have taken place between May and August 1967, i.e. the period in question. Guan Weixun, *Ye Qun*, p. 212.

slogan, 'Drag out the small handful in the army', gained wide currency. Kang Sheng authorised its use by the New China News Agency on 25 July, and it had a prominent place in the editorial of the 1 August issue of *Red Flag* drafted by Lin Jie, read by Wang Li and Guan Feng, and approved by Chen Boda, which called on the proletariat to 'seize control of the gun'.[54] Lin Biao clearly played a role as events unfolded. He chaired the 22 July meeting attended by all CRG members which heard Xie Fuzhi's briefing on the Wuhan events, labeled those events a 'counterrevolutionary riot', and immediately recalled Chen Zaidao and Zhong Hanhua to Beijing. He also accepted CRG demands for a million-strong welcome for Wang Li and his associates and was prominent at the ensuing rally on 25 July. In addition, soon after the 20th Lin Liguo, writing under a pseudonym, used the 'Drag out the small handful' slogan in an article, while Ye Qun too was reportedly active in stirring up demonstrations against the Wuhan leaders who had been brought to Beijing. Most significantly, Lin approved (as did Mao[55]) the open letter of 27 July to the Wuhan masses declaring that they had successfully defeated a small group of bourgeois powerholders in the Party and army. The net result of all these activities involving Lin and others was to exacerbate the serious fighting that had already broken out in at least half a dozen provinces.[56]

The initial harsh rhetoric had the backing of Mao, who was undoubtedly the true source of the 'Drag out the small handful' slogan,[57] but as evidence of the escalating violence mounted, both the Chairman and Lin Biao began to have second thoughts. Mao was still touring provinces in East and Central-South China

[54] Wang Nianyi, *Dadongluan*, pp. 266–7; Zhang Yunsheng, *Maojiawan*, pp. 126, 128–9; and Ye Yonglie, *Shenmi zhangquanzhe*, p. 246.

[55] Mao and Lin actually approved two letters, the harsh open letter issued on the 27th and a milder one dated the 26th to the Party committee of the Wuhan Military Region which referred to 'Comrade Chen Zaidao'. *ZGDSJXCKZL*, vol. 25, pp. 503–6; and Wang Nianyi, *Dadongluan*, p. 264.

[56] Wen Feng, *Shentanxia*, pp. 149–51, 154; and Zhang Yunsheng, *Maojiawan*, pp. 126–9.

[57] The sentiment if not the exact words can be traced to the 16 May 1966 circular that was one of the early measures initiating the Cultural Revolution. The slogan itself was coined by Guan Feng in January 1967 (see *RMRB*, 18 May 1978, in *FBIS*, 24 May 1978, p. E6). During the Wuhan crisis Mao explicitly approved its use at least twice on 24 or 25 July and 27 July; see *ZGDSJXCKZL*, vol. 25, pp. 505, 524.

and thus able to get a comparatively realistic picture of the growing chaos, even if this was not necessarily reflected in his rhetoric.[58] In mid-August the Chairman indicated his unhappiness with developments by declaring the 1 August *Red Flag* editorial a 'poisonous weed', and by circling references to 'Drag out the small handful' with the notation 'Do not use' on another document from the military which had been endorsed by the CRG members Guan Feng and Qi Benyu and forwarded to Mao by Lin's office.[59] While the timing is not completely clear,[60] it seems that Lin was showing concern even before the Chairman and initially took a more serious view of the deteriorating situation. In particular, Lin was alarmed by the seizure of weapons from PLA armouries and made this a key point of a letter reporting the situation to Mao, apparently in early August. After noting that the Chen Zaidao problem had been handled according to the Chairman's instructions and that new personnel had been sent to take over the Wuhan Military Region, Lin uncharacteristically took the initiative to state that the confrontation of mass factions and especially the seizure of weapons required immediate attention. Since Mao himself had clearly authorised the arming of 'leftists' about the time of the Wuhan incident,[61] this move, which again indicated Lin's deep concern for the

[58] During and after his provincial tour Mao repeatedly praised the national situation as 'not just OK but really wonderful'. See Wang Nianyi, *Dadongluan*, p. 269.

[59] Wen Feng, *Shentanxia*, pp. 153-4; *Mao Zedong dazidian* (Mao Zedong Dictionary) (Guangzhou: Guangxi renmin chubanshe, 1992), p. 1232; and *ZGDSJXCKZL*, vol. 25, p. 524.

[60] This is based on the tenor of Zhang Yunsheng's recollections rather than specific dates. See Wen Feng, *Shentanxia*, pp. 152-4. 'Mid-August' (*Bayue zhongxun*) refers to 11–20 August, while the second document referred to was prepared by the new MAC Vigilance Small Group which had been set up on the 17th. Apparently the first occasion when Mao reacted negatively to the slogan occurred when he viewed a struggle session against local leaders on television while in Shanghai, again probably in mid-August; see the Red Guard publication, *Dongfanghong kuaibao* (The East is Red Bulletin), no. 102 (October 1967), p. 12.

Note that the military document discussed is the case mentioned previously (see above, p. 12) where Ye Qun had a secretary imitate Lin's signature rather than bother the Vice Chairman. This further demonstrates both Lin's limited personal involvement in the 'Drag out' slogan and Ye's enormous influence at Maojiawan.

[61] Wang Nianyi, *Dadongluan*, p. 266. As late as 16 August Kang Sheng and Guan Feng still declared guns could be issued to radicals if necessary. *Ibid.*, p. 268.

integrity of the PLA, was all the more significant. More characteristically, Lin cautiously had CRG leaders vet the letter before dispatching it to the Chairman, a process which produced some textual changes but apparently no alteration of the basic message. In the event Mao, notwithstanding his own concerns in the same period, was more sanguine and returned the letter with the comment that there was no need to worry now, and that the arms seizures could be dealt with at the proper moment.[62]

Whatever the precise rethinking at the highest levels in early August, concrete steps soon began to be taken. One of the earliest was a talk given on 9 August by Lin Biao to leaders of the large military regions, notably the new Wuhan leaders Zeng Siyu and Liu Feng. This, under the circumstances, was clearly a moderate statement. Lin declared that Party and government cadres who reformed themselves would be welcome, and that while every military region had comrades who had made mistakes, efforts should be made to save all who could be saved; he believed that a majority could be won over. However, he also expressed some continuing radical sentiments, including permission for the 'masses' to seize the leaders of 'conservative' organizations, the assertion that 'revolutionary rebels' should be the teachers of err-ing army cadres, and – perhaps most telling of all – the injunction that 'You absolutely cannot use the fact of whether or not they have attacked military regions as a criterion for delineating leftists and rightists'. This last stipulation points to another feature of the speech, that it did not provide any concrete remedies for military commanders finding themselves under attack by rebels. Instead, Lin's concern seemed more with protecting local leaders from possible political missteps with higher authority. The fundamen-tal message of his talk was to avoid rash action and report all matters including minor questions to the Centre for decision. This, of course, reflected his own personal method of following Mao closely, but it concretely meant reporting everything to the Premier *and* the CRG. As Lin put it, 'The Premier and Comrades Chen Boda, Kang Sheng and Jiang Qing are working day and

[62] Wen Feng, *Shentanxia*, pp. 152–3; and Zhang Yunsheng, *Maojiawan*, pp. 129–31.

night', so commanders should phone, telegraph or even come by plane with their problems.[63]

Not surprisingly the CRG as well as army commanders responded favourably to Lin's statement, but – perhaps more surprising – on 11 August Jiang Qing and Chen Boda were more forceful in pushing for moderation by denouncing the purported 'ultra-left' 16 May Group for aiming the spearhead at Zhou Enlai.[64] Moreover, the 20 August issue of Chen Boda's *Red Flag* reversed the journal's earlier 'poisonous' position with an editorial hailing the PLA as the 'reliable pillar' of the Cultural Revolution. In the meantime disruptive activities continued in Beijing as well as the provinces with government offices coming under heavy mass attack. Most serious was the seizure of the Ministry of Foreign Affairs by 'rebels' as the culmination of a month of turmoil in that institution, a process which also saw the burning of the British diplomatic mission on 22 August. This apparently was the last straw for Mao, and with Zhou Enlai making what was for him an uncharacteristically strong call for action, on 25 August a notice launching a 'Support the army and love the people' movement signalled the intention to use the PLA to restore order. Wang Li and Guan Feng were arrested at the end of the month, and on 5 September Jiang Qing repudiated her 'Defend with weapons and attack with words' slogan and a central directive was issued which finally forbade the seizure of PLA weapons.[65] This major shift toward asserting military control and curbing radical mass organizations surely corresponded to Lin Biao's preferences, but he apparently played little or no role in the events that unfolded in the latter half of August, particularly in connection with the so-called 'Wang-Guan-Qi affair'. This may be inferred from a comment

[63] Kau, *Lin Piao*, pp. 432, 435–7, 439, 441; and *ZGDSJXCKZL*, vol. 25, pp. 595–7.

[64] This initial step by the CRG leaders can be regarded as part of the process of moderation but distinct in focus from the effort to curb attacks on the PLA. Here Jiang Qing *et al.* were largely concerned with rebuffing radical attacks on Zhou which had been a common feature of wall posters in early August and became an aspect of rebel activities in the Foreign Ministry.

[65] See Wang Nianyi, *Dadongluan*, pp. 266–8, 271; *RMRB*, 26 February 1979, in *FBIS*, 28 February 1979, p. E16; and Lee, *Chinese Cultural Revolution*, pp. 252–4.

by Lin, made at the time of the purge of Yang Chengwu in March 1968, that when Mao had asked Yang during the previous summer to visit Lin (who was ill in Beidaihe) to discuss the case of Wang Li, Guan Feng and Qi Benyu, Yang was hesitant to go – an account which places Lin on the periphery of events.[66] But considering Lin's performance during the Wuhan incident and its aftermath as a whole, we find a rare case of initiative in the effort he made in early August to alert Mao to the dangers of the situation, notwithstanding his general pattern of reactive and even passive behaviour.

In one area, the reshaping of the military leadership structure, Lin seemingly obtained some narrow political gains. The new leaders of the Wuhan military, Commander Zeng Siyu and Political Commissar Liu Feng, seemingly had close relations with Lin – although the full situation is more complicated.[67] And as we saw earlier, in the same period the MAC Vigilance Small Group – including Wu Faxian, Ye Qun and Qiu Huizuo – was established on 17 August to guide the Cultural Revolution in the army. However, this particular institution was created in conjunction with Jiang Qing on the proposal of Zhou Enlai and placed under the direct leadership of the CRG; on the military side Ye Qun, rather than Lin Biao recuperating in Beidaihe, took the lead. Furthermore, it had more to do with the final collapse of the GPD than the Wuhan incident.[68] In any case, the small group was reorganised in September as the MAC Office (*Junwei banshizu*), but was no longer responsible to the CRG; it was headed, ironically in view of future events, by yet another historical associate of Lin Biao, Yang Chengwu. While these developments concerning personnel have been regarded as conscious clique-building, in all likelihood they are better under-

---

[66] Kau, *Lin Piao*, p. 495.

[67] Zeng had served under Lin in the 115th Division during the Anti-Japanese War, and personal ties can be seen in Ye Qun entrusting him to find a new secretary for Lin's office (see Wen Feng, *Shentanxia*, p. 4). However, Zeng's career also involved important links with Marshal Nie Rongzhen, and he did not suffer in the purge following Lin's demise. Liu Feng was regarded as a particularly close follower of Lin and did suffer in that purge, but no career data are available to determine whether he had served under Lin during the revolutionary period.

[68] Wang Nianyi, *Dadongluan*, p. 380; and above, pp. 42–5.

stood as *ad hoc* responses to the chaotic conditions of the time, with Lin Biao less involved than appeared on the surface.

As for other actors in events following the Wuhan incident, Zhou Enlai did perform his officially lauded moderating role, particularly over the foreign affairs sector, and the Premier clearly benefitted from the dénouement in late August-early September, but there is little sign of any moderating effort on his part during the initial radicalization after 20 July. Meanwhile, Jiang Qing and other CRG leaders played true to type by spreading inflammatory slogans in this early period, but they appear to have quickly taken the hint from Mao by mid-August and played a major part in bringing the situation under control. In terms of overall direction, there seems to be little essential difference in the postures of Lin Biao and the CRG during either the early post-20 July period or from about 9 August. What difference there was appears to be not only in Lin's early perception of the need to cool things down, but also in his caution in carrying through that view and his considerably lower profile by comparison to the civilian radicals in pushing for moderation from mid-August on. This is perhaps partly explained by his poor health and absence from Beijing for most of August, and also by the possibility that Mao assigned the task of bringing the excesses under control to the CRG leaders, given both their responsibility for those excesses and their credibility with radical mass organizations. In any case, the outcome of the whole affair was a setback for the CRG leadership.

By September, then, a new situation of enhanced PLA institutional power had emerged in conjunction with the clampdown on the mass movement. Notionally these developments would also have enhanced Lin Biao's personal position, but another PLA figure who exercised great clout throughout the whole sequence of events and subsequently was Yang Chengwu.[69] The various

---

[69] Yang's importance was demonstrated by his carrying key messages for Mao during this period and by the Chairman entrusting him with hosting the Army Day celebrations on 1 August. See Dong Baocun, *Yang-Yu-Fu shijian zhenxiang* (The True Account of the Yang-Yu-Fu Affair) (Beijing: Jiefangjun chubanshe, 1987), pp. 46–7; and *Zhonggong dangshi ziliao* (CCP History Materials), June 1993, p. 148. Of course, Yang's power was based on his closeness to Mao before the Wuhan incident, a

factors in this situation, along with a number of petty and idiosyncratic matters, were to come together in the next and most peculiar turning point of the Cultural Revolution – the purge of Yang together with Yu Lijin and Fu Chongbi in early 1968.

The Purge of Yang Chengwu, Yu Lijin and Fu Chongbi, March 1968

The purge of the Acting PLA Chief of Staff Yang Chengwu, the Air Force Political Commissar Yu Lijin and the Beijing Garrison Commander Fu Chongbi seemingly came out of the blue in late March 1968 and, as Wang Nianyi has noted, many interested people still remained confused by the affair twenty years later.[70] Nevertheless, an official interpretation of the event did emerge which has been generally echoed in Western scholarship. This interpretation places great weight on the role of Lin Biao and his factional objectives, particularly his alleged ongoing struggle to eliminate the influence of his fellow marshals. In addition, another key factor was said to be the continuing conflict between 'radical' and 'conservative' mass organizations in the provinces, a process in which, since the aftermath of the Wuhan incident, the PLA and Yang Chengwu in particular had increasingly sided with the 'conservatives'. Finally, the affair is said to reflect tensions between Zhou Enlai and the CRG, with Zhou – assisted by Yang and Fu – having attempted to protect various civilian and military leaders whom Jiang Qing wished to overthrow.[71] While these factors were all involved, the overall story was inevitably more complex, with personal grievances and

---

closeness demonstrated by the Chairman's choice of Yang to accompany him on his provicial tour in the first place.

[70] Wang Nianyi, *Dadongluan*, p. 285.

[71] See Gao Gao and Yan Jiaqi, '*Wenhua dageming*', pp. 267–6; Harding in *CHOC*, vol. 15, pp. 185–7; and Barnouin and Yu, *Ten Years of Turbulence*, pp. 164–71. As these diverse factors suggest, the case was not really a single 'affair' but instead a number of distinct issues which, in typical Cultural Revolution fashion, were simply lumped together.

Mao's peculiar and vexing theoretical concerns also playing significant parts. While a re-examination of the case cannot clear up all of its complexities, it can dispel some misconceptions and provide a more realistic picture of Lin's comparatively limited role.

The Yang-Yu-Fu case erupted against the background of not only the enforcement of military control in China's localities, but also the creation of provincial revolutionary committees, the new organs of local power which were increasingly dominated by the PLA and included representatives of 'conservative' mass organizations. In late 1967 and early 1968 Yang Chengwu had been responsible for resolving a number of provincial disputes which seemingly favoured 'conservative' elements although, as we shall see, his overall performance of this delicate task was more complicated. In Shanxi, where a revolutionary committee had been set up previously in March 1967 under a radical civilian chairman, Yang refused to back the chairman against local military officers. Also, in Hebei during the process leading to the establishment of the provincial revolutionary committee in February 1968, Yang supported a 'conservative' coalition of military units and mass organizations. It is important to note in this context that Yang, apparently assigned a leading role in dealing with conflicts within the local military personally by Mao,[72] carried out the Chairman's new anti-'ultra left' emphasis as reflected in the handling of the 'Wang-Guan-Qi affair' in the aftermath of the Wuhan incident which was only wound up with the arrest of Qi Benyu in January 1968. But such activities inevitably led to conflict with Cultural Revolution goals and caused CRG leaders to fear a 'rightist wind of verdict reversals', and Jiang Qing and her associates reported their concerns to Mao

---

[72] According to Zi Ping, *Hu Yaobang, Yang Chengwu, Li Desheng*, p. 136, Mao appointed Yang, Yu Lijin and others to a seven-man small group to handle 'Support the left' activities in the PLA immediately after the Wuhan incident. Whether this account is strictly accurate (see above, p. 37n), Yang clearly did perform the function of sorting out conflicts within the military and military-dominated political structures in various localties over the following months which resulted in local grievances against him. See below, pp. 95–6.

who by the time of the Yang-Yu-Fu purge backed their view. This issue predominated leadership concerns in the week preceding the purge with key CRG leaders and Zhou Enlai – but not Lin Biao – warning of the danger of the 'rightist wind', and the purge itself was used to launch an attack on an alleged second 'February adverse current'. While this theme was linked to the three victims in the campaign following the purge, this was not universally the case when Party leaders attempted to explain the reasons for the dismissals to puzzled military leaders on 24 March. Although nearly all speakers that evening – including Zhou Enlai – addressed the issue, the odd man out was again Lin Biao. Speaking from an outline provided by Mao, Lin mentioned a number of factors – but not any 'rightist wind'. This puzzling fact notwithstanding, what we do know, as indicated by the testimony of key speakers at the 24 March meeting, is that the purge was *solely* Mao's decision, and that the 'rightist wind' provided a crucial context for his decision, but the precise relationship of this context to the fall of Yang and his associates remains unclear.[73]

What Lin Biao did emphasise on 24 March was Yang Chengwu's 'mountaintopism', i.e. his alleged factional mentality. According to Lin, Yang only trusted a 'small gang' of people with whom he had been intimate since the revolutionary period, particularly people from one district of the Jin-Cha-Ji (Shanxi-Chahar-Hebei) base area; such an attitude ignored the contributions to the revolution of the main field armies, and tried to place these favoured people in key positions while ousting everyone else.[74] This, of course, was not only the same charge as that laid against Lin Biao after his death in general terms, but also the specific accusation concerning his behaviour in the Yang-Yu-Fu case. While Yang assertedly sought to place veterans of

---

[73] Wang Nianyi, *Dadongluan*, pp. 273–84, 286, 293; Harding in *CHOC*, vol. 15, p. 186; Teiwes, *Provincial Leadership* pp. 12, 22–4, 31; Kau, *Lin Piao*, pp. 488–500; and Barnouin and Yu, *Ten Years of Turbulence*, pp. 165, 167.

[74] Kau, *Lin Piao*, pp. 489–90, 494. Interestingly, Lin did not refer to the Jin-Cha-Ji area as falling under the North China Field Army but instead treated it as part of the sphere of his own forces. On the implications of this, see below, pp. 94–5.

the North China Field Army in key positions, Lin allegedly moved against cadres from that army and its main leaders, Marshals Xu Xiangqian and (especially) Nie Rongzhen.[75] By examining these similar if opposite charges we may be able to shed light not only on this case but on the general question of military factionalism during the Cultural Revolution.

The significance, but also the limitations, of 'mountaintops' in military politics is illustrated by one minor matter recollected by Zhang Yunsheng. According to Zhang, Lin received in early 1968 a report signed by Yang Chengwu and Wu Faxian concerning the promotion of a vice commander in one army to the position of full commander of another army. Lin wanted to know the background of the officer, and when told that he had served in the North China Field Army instructed that the report be filed away, commenting 'What's the point of promoting him into another army instead of filling the vacancy from within the same army?'[76] This account suggests not only the relevance of field army ties in making appointments, but it also gives some weight to the claim that Yang was seeking to extend the influence of old subordinates.[77] Yet at the same time it indicates that the salience of field army tensions may be overrated in that the report had gained the assent of the Fourth Field Army's Wu Faxian who was alleged to be not only a 'principal member of the Lin Biao clique', but also the target of Yang's and Yu Lijin's effort to usurp power within the air force.[78]

More broadly, career patterns at the top of the PLA, while indicating the importance of revolutionary ties, also suggest that few leaders simply stood on the top of isolated 'mountaintops' given the substantial intermingling of revolutionary careers. This is apparent from the background of the principals involved here.

[75] *XHRB*, 19 October 1984, in *FBIS*, 5 November 1984, p. K19; and *Beijing wanbao* (Beijing Evening News), 12 April 1985, in *FBIS*, 1 May 1985, p. K9.
[76] Zhang Yunsheng, *Maojiawan*, pp. 135–6.
[77] For a Western analysis also suggesting that there may have been some validity in this charge against Yang, see William L. Parish, Jr., 'Factions in Chinese military politics', *CQ*, no. 56 (1973), pp. 679–89.
[78] Kau, *Lin Piao*, p. 488.

Most significantly Yang Chengwu had important career links to Lin Biao at various stages during the revolution. He served in the First Army Corps of the First Front Army in the early 1930s, thus making him a 'complete Lin Biao man' according to Ye Qun's definition, then served as a commander in Lin's 115th Division during the Anti-Japanese war, and in 1948 led his army into battle in the decisive victory guided by Lin in the Northeast. Yet in this process Yang developed even closer ties to Nie Rongzhen, Lin's deputy in the 115th Division and commander of the North China Field Army which Yang's forces belonged to after 1945. Moreover, in the decisive battles of 1948 Yang's army worked in conjunction with that of another North China Field Army leader, Luo Ruiqing, himself a 'complete Lin Biao man' in Ye's terms. Thus there were several ironies when, in his 24 March speech, Lin accused Yang of another major error, namely 'double dealing', and claimed that he was a 'Luo Ruiqing element' despite his show of opposition during the struggle against Luo.[79] And especially striking is the similarity between the careers of Yang and the man who replaced him as PLA Chief of Staff, 'principal Lin Biao clique member' Huang Yongsheng. Huang too served under both Lin Biao and Nie Rongzhen at different periods of time, with Huang later declaring: 'During my career I worked under Marshal Nie for the longest period of time, [11 years] under his direct leadership.'[80] In none of these cases is the relationship of the concerned generals to Lin Biao and the other marshals as clear-cut as has frequently been claimed.

This points to an even more relevant relationship, that of Lin Biao and Nie Rongzhen, Lin's purported target and the alleged ultimate 'behind-the-scenes backer' of the 'North China mountain

[79] *Ibid.*, pp. 493–4; Wang Jianying (ed.), *Zhongguo Gongchandang zuzhishi ziliao huibian* (Compilation of Materials on CCP Organizational History) (Beijing: Hongqi chubanshe, 1983), p. 167; Klein and Clark, *Biographic Dictionary*, II, 642–3, 968–9; and above, p. 30.

[80] Xiao Sike, *Caoji shenpan*, vol. 2, p. 537. According to one of Lin's secretaries, moreover, the relationship between Huang and Lin was not particularly close from 1949 to the Cultural Revolution. Jiao Ye, *Ye Qun zhi mi*, p. 210.

stronghold mentality'. Nie's ties to Lin went back a long way and were quite close. In the early 1930s Nie was political commissar in Lin's First Army Corps, and he again was Lin's chief political officer oil the Long March. After the conclusion of the March the close relationship continued for several years, as is seen in Nie's deputy post in the 115th Division until their careers began to diverge with Nie's involvement in the Jin-Cha-Ji area and eventually the North China Field Army.[81] Thus the revolutionary past gives little reason for any vendetta on Lin's part; indeed, it makes some sense to regard Nie's North China Field Army as part of Lin's extended 'mountaintop'. Moreover, official charges against Lin in this regard – including Nie's own aspersions in his biased memoirs – contain little of substance. In any case, if Nie can be believed, there was no reason for Lin to be concerned since, Nie claimed, while he maintained social contact with his old North China subordinates he never instructed them on how to do their work. Nie's problems in early 1968 would appear to be more related to his so-called 'multi-centre theory' (*duo zhongxin lun*), an obscure matter which seems to have been interpreted as opposing 'Mao's centre' and to have drawn the Chairman's displeasure.[82] In any case, Mao does not appear to have taken the factional issue too seriously, disingenuously telling Nie after Yang's fall that 'Speaking of Yang Chengwu's behind-the-scenes backer, I am the first one, and you are only the second.' Interestingly, on 24 March Lin made no mention of any 'behind-the-scenes backer', but directly following the Vice Chairman's speech Zhou Enlai called for the pursuit of such a backer of Yang Chengwu.[83]

In the context of charges concerning Yang's 'factionalism', a more telling indicator of what was really involved in his fall may have come in Lin Biao's claim on the 24th that Yang wanted to remove Wu Faxian, Xie Fuzhi, Xu Shiyou, Han Xianchu, Huang Yongsheng, Chen Xilian and Yang Dezhi from power.

[81] Klein and Clark, *Biographic Dictionary*, II, 696–8.
[82] See Wang Nianyi, *Dadongluan*, pp. 278, 287, 312, 317, on the 'multi-centre' issue.
[83] *XHRB*, 20 October 1984, in *FBIS*, 6 November 1984, pp. K20–21; Wang Nianyi, *Dadongluan*, p. 312; and oral source.

While Wu, of course, was a 'principal clique member' in the PLA central command, the others were a diverse lot. Minister of Public Security Xie was a well-known civilian radical and head of the Beijing Municipal Revolutionary Committee, and the remaining 'targets' were all local military commanders with past connections to all field armies except the First; they had largely acted in a 'conservative' manner which frequently produced clashes with 'revolutionary rebels'. Here, it can be argued, the key is the role which Yang had been assigned since mid-1967, apparently by Mao, of dealing with local military and political structures over a period encompassing both the radical 'Support the left' phase and the anti-Wang-Guan-Qi stage of oppoting the 'ultra left', a situation which would inevitably have involved conflict whatever Yang's personal inclinations might have been. This also makes some sense of the otherwise incomprehensible accusation that Yang was responsible for both the 'Wang-Guan-Qi affair' and the 'rightist wind'.[84] In addition Yang, together with Fu Chongbi, appears to have been involved in a power struggle with Xie Fuzhi for local dominance in the capital – as reflected in wall posters attacking Xie in February-March. These circumstances made Yang and Fu vulnerable given the concern with the 'rightist wind' and the status of revolutionary committees as 'new-born things of the Cultural Revolution'.[85]

In terms of personal relations, any falling out between Lin Biao and Yang Chengwu during the Cultural Revolution appears to have been limited and to have had more to do with trivial matters and a loss of personal trust than any large issue of field army factions or policy direction. When Nie Rongzhen, his access apparently intact, visited Lin in April 1968 to seek an explanation for Yang's disgrace, Lin could only offer a weak response: 'He did not come to see me'. In this, of course,

---

[84] See Kau, *Lin Piao*, pp. 490, 495; *ZGDSJXCKZL*, vol. 26, pp. 88, 90; and above, pp. 87–8. Lin's further comment that Yang was the minority and others were the majority, and that the decision was taken to knock down the minority, undoubtedly reflects the tensions between Yang and local leaders, but it should not be taken literally that one side or the other had to be knocked over.

[85] Wang Nianyi, *Dadongluan*, p. 280.

Lin echoed the complaint he made on 24 March against Yang's hesitation to visit Beidaihe in connection with the Wang-Guan-Qi case the previous summer. It may also have reflected tension from the same period when Yang, while accompanying Mao on his southern trip, heard some critical comments by the Chairman concerning Lin but was instructed not to repeat them. Yang reportedly did disclose something to Zhou Enlai and several old marshals but adhered to Mao's instruction as far as Maojiawan was concerned despite Ye Qun's efforts to find out what had been said. This, in the view of one leading military Party historian, was largely because Ye was a chatterbox who could not be trusted with confidential information.[86] It is asserted that other personal annoyances included Yang sending MAC documents to the old marshals despite Lin's request to stop or modify the practice, and Yang's reluctance to vouch for Ye Qun's behaviour during the revolutionary period.[87]

Another petty matter apparently of greater significance in causing Yang Chengwu difficulty with Maojiawan concerned a power struggle within the air force Party organization between Lin Liguo's protégés and the 'clan of secretaries', which became an open clash through an alleged love affair between Yang's daughter and Yu Lijin's secretary. When the scandal became known seemingly only days before the dramatic dismissals of Yang and Yu, Lin Liguo's followers wanted Wu Faxian, in his capacity as air force commander, to arrest the secretary but Wu, who had recommended Yu's appointment, declined to do so until he came under pressure from Ye Qun. The arrest reportedly angered Yu, who sought Yang's help in trying to gain the

[86] *XHRB*, 20 October 1984, in *FBIS*, 6 November 1984, p. K20; Wang Nianyi, *Dadongluan*, p. 288; and oral source. Similarly, Wu Faxian reportedly on three occasions visited Yu Lijin who had also accompanied Mao on his provincial tour in order to learn of the Chairman's comments, but Yu was reluctant to talk; see *ZGDSJXCKZL*, vol. 26, pp. 61–3.

[87] Tan Zhongji, *Shinianhou*, pp. 81–2; *ZGDSJXCKZL*, vol. 26, p. 83; and Barnouin and Yu, *Ten Tears of Turbulence*, p. 169. A senior Party historian, however, discounts allegations against Lin concerning documents sent to the old marshals, claiming that a decision to stop the practice was Mao's idea and was passed at a Party Centre meeting chaired by Mao.

secretary's release, but Wu refused. Yang then tried to gain Lin Biao's support, but while Lin expressed agreement when meeting Yang, he allegedly actually encouraged Wu to hold firm, which led to a major confrontation between Yang and Wu – a confrontation which was perhaps the basis of the distorted claim Lin made on 24 March that Yang sought to usurp power in the air force from Wu.[88] While Lin himself was clearly involved in this last instance at least, in the view of the same military historian who reported Yang Chengwu's unwillingness to confide in the chatterbox Ye, the main conflict resulting from such incidents was between Yang and Ye Qun rather than between Yang and Lin Biao. This claim, and the general view of limited tension between Lin and Yang, gains authority from the fact that – unlike the Luo Ruiqing case – there is *no* evidence of Lin taking any initiative against Yang, and that Lin was still praising Yang in early or mid-March 1968; during the purge itself his comments were restrained in comparison not only to those of CRG leaders but also to those of Zhou Enlai.[89]

If petty concerns and general personality tensions marred relations between Yang Chengwu and Maojiawan, they seem to have been even more crucial in the relationship between Yang and Jiang Qing and also to have affected Jiang's attitude toward Fu Chongbi. This is not to say that political issues were not also involved as the CRG's early 1968 concern with the 'rightist wind of verdict reversals' suggests. In particular, umbrage appears to have been taken at Fu Chongbi's efforts in carrying out Zhou Enlai's instructions to protect various civilian and military cadres during the conflicts of the summer of 1967, instructions which Mao subsequently approved. When Jiang's group pressed Fu concerning the whereabouts of certain protected leaders, Fu refused to reveal the information and said that they should ask the Chairman, a remark which made them afraid to pursue the matter further but undoubtedly left a residue of bitterness.

---

[88] Wang Nianyi, *Dadongluan*, pp. 288–9; Zhang Yunsheng, *Maojiawan*, pp. 138–41; and *ZGDSJXCKZL*, vol. 26, p. 36. We have attempted to provide a reasonable synthesis of these accounts which differ in detail.

[89] See Wang Nianyi, *Dadongluan*, pp. 292, 389–90; oral source; and above, pp. 24ff.

Meanwhile, when Yang Chengwu followed regulations and continued to send documents to the old marshals as MAC members over their objections, it reportedly earned the hatred of 'Jiang Qing and company' in addition to whatever displeasure it may have caused Lin Biao. For his part, Yang increasingly became intolerant of what they were doing. Yet, as Wang Nianyi has concluded, it is important to emphasise that, personal feelings aside, there was no political opposition on the part of Yang, Yu and Fu to Jiang Qing – a posture which was simply impossible under the conditions of the time.[90]

Against this background two events of no intrinsic importance occurred in early March 1968 which sharpened tensions between Jiang Qing and Fu Chongbi, and resulted in grossly distorted charges being levelled by the end of the month. In one instance Jiang decided that she wanted to read a letter from Beijing University rebels to the Central Committee, and personnel from the Beijing Garrison Command went to the University to get it. Several visits failed to secure it, and the radical leader, Nie Yuanzi, phoned Jiang Qing to complain about forced searches. While Jiang admitted asking for the letter, she said she had nothing to do with the heavy-handed tactics, and within weeks the affair was used against Fu as an example of suppressing the masses. Even more bizarre, and more significant, was the so-called break-in at the CRG headquarters at Diaoyutai. In this case an original manuscript by the famous writer Lu Xun was missing from the Lu Xun museum in Shanghai, apparently as a result of actions by the recently purged Qi Benyu the previous year acting on the orders of Jiang Qing. Now, with Lu Xun's widow having just died, Zhou Enlai ordered an effort to recover the manuscript for the museum. Jiang asked Fu to investigate, and his investigations suggested that it was probably at Diaoyutai. When Fu turned up to report, Jiang demanded to know what he was doing there without permission, and she denied that the document could possibly be in CRG files. But when she opened the files to prove her point, the draft was found there to her

[90] Wang Nianyi, *Dadongluan*, pp. 288–90.

great embarrassment. By the end of the month this farcical situation was transformed into a case of Fu – allegedly backed by Yang despite the lack of any concrete evidence of his role in the matter[91] – arriving at Diaoyutai with armed vehicles, breaking in, and attempting to arrest people as part of a conspiracy of the 'rightists' Yang, Yu and Fu joining forces with the 'ultra-leftists' Wang, Guan and Qi to attack the CRG.[92]

The final issue which Lin raised against Yang Chengwu, assertedly one of his 'principal errors' along with 'mountaintopism' and 'double dealing', was the 'distortion of Marxism'. Specifically, this referred to Yang's alleged theory of Mao's 'absolute authority', a theory which a philosophical Chairman had criticised the previous December on the grounds that according to Marxism everything was in a process of development and all authority was relative.[93] While this was clearly the most arbitrary of all the charges against Yang *et al.*, it is significant for what it says about the overall problem of being a CCP leader during the Cultural Revolution. Nearly two years earlier Lin Biao had similarly gone overboard in his May 1966 speech, and Mao had expressed private disquiet about this in his letter to Jiang Qing, yet Lin, Jiang, Zhou Enlai and all other leaders continued to engage in such extravagances over the intervening period in the obvious belief that such a posture was *de rigueur* for political survival.[94] The case at hand was all the more poignant because while Mao had objected to the 'absolute authority' concept on several occasions in the latter half of 1967, he explicitly absolved Yang from blame since Yang had merely supplied his name to the article propounding the theory (in the Chairman's eyes Chen Boda was the chief culprit), only now to

[91] Yang, however, reportedly refused to get involved in the matter when called to Daiyutai by Jiang Qing. During this period Jiang and Ye Qun engaged in a mutual gripe session about Yang which assertedly contributed to action against him. See Dong Baocun, *Yang-Yu-Fu shijian*, pp. 111, 126–8.

[92] Gao Gao and Yan Jiaqi, '*Wenhua dageming*', pp. 270–6; and Kau, *Lin Piao*, pp. 494–5.

[93] Kau, *Lin Piao*, pp. 489, 497–9.

[94] For examples of such statements by Lin and Zhang Chunqiao in 1966–7, see *RMRB*, 18 May 1978, in *FBIS*, 24 May 1978, p. E4.

sanction the issue as one of Yang's 'principal mistakes'.[95] Yang's setback would not alter the calculation within the élite of the necessity of lavishing praise on Mao, but in 1970 Lin Biao's supporters were to find themselves under attack ostensibly for continuing in this vein.

How all these factors came together remains obscure but it happened extremely rapidly. On 20 March Yang Chengwu attended an important central meeting in apparent good political health,[96] yet on the 22nd he and Yu were arrested and Fu was transferred, and all three were denounced at the meeting of military cadres on the 24th. Presumably the various specific incidents in March which angered Jiang Qing and annoyed Maojiawan triggered action against the background of festering resentments and the new major concern with the 'rightist wind'. Who took the initiative in bringing matters to a head is not known, but the decisive role of Mao in determining the outcome is beyond question. According to Lin's speech of 24 March, the top leadership met Mao four times to reach its decision, while Lin reportedly did not know what he would say as late as the afternoon of the 24th, and his text, when he finally appeared at the meeting two hours late, reflected the Chairman's outline. Even after the fact Lin apparently had little idea of what was really at issue. Apart from his vague response to Nie Rongzhen's enquiry, he also expressed ignorance to his own daughter of why it was necessary to get rid of Yang.[97] Whatever Lin's exact role in the affair, it seems clear that Jiang Qing had more significant axes to grind, and in any case it was she and her CRG colleagues – not Lin Biao – who voiced concern about the 'rightist' trend.

Ultimately the answer lies in the unusually opaque views of Mao, who certainly was not 'listening to Lin Biao's one-sided rhetoric' as he falsely claimed in 1973; undoubtedly he did not take seriously some of the charges as they applied to individuals,

[95] Dong Baocun, *Yang-Yu-Fu shijian*, pp. 95–7.
[96] Cheng Hua, *Zhou he tade mishumen*, p. 372.
[97] Kau, *Lin Piao*, pp. 488–9; Zhang Yunsheng, *Maojiawan*, p. 151; Guan Weixun, *Ye Qun*, p. 225; Wang Nianyi, *Dadongluan*, p. 290; above, p. 96; and oral source.

but he was certainly concerned with the new 'rightist' current. Perhaps the fate of Yang, Yu and Fu is best seen as dealing with various leadership tensions while at the same time the unfortunate trio were made scapegoats for the conservative trend. In any case, in policy terms the CRG was the main winner as the Cultural Revolution entered a final radical phase before renewed violence led Mao to opt for a decisive clampdown in the summer of 1968. But in organizational terms, at least nominally, the purge of Yang further ebhanced Lin's control over the military through the appointment of Huang Yongsheng as the new Chief of Staff,[98] through Mao's order for the MAC Standing Committee to cease all work, and through the denial of PLA documents to the old marshals.[99] While the latter developments apparently reflected Mao's dissatisfaction with the marshals, Lin's enhanced position in the PLA was to become a major aspect of the new situation once the mass mobilization phase of the Cultural Revolution had finally run its course and the leadership faced up to the task of building a new order.

[98] However, as argued previously, Huang's rise should be seen as primarily reflecting *Mao's* confidence in him; see above, p. 46. Nevertheless, the evidence suggests greater closeness and less tension between Lin and Huang than existed in the Lin-Yang relationship.

[99] Wang Nianyi, *Dadongluan*, pp. 285, 288, 297, 397; *XHRB*, 19 October 1984, in *FBIS*, 5 November 1984, p. K19; and Barnouin and Yu, *Ten Years of Turbulence*, pp. 167, 171, 320.

1. The young Lin Biao, aged nearly 30, in the fall of 1937 when he was appointed commander of the 115th Division of the Eighth Route Army, the renamed Red Army after the second united front was formed with the Guomindang following the outbreak of the Anti-Japanese war. By this time Lin had already established an extraordinarily high military reputation. He was still in good health before his serious wounding in the spring of 1938.

2. Lin Biao in Guangzhou about 1960 as Vice Chairman in charge of daily affairs of the Military Affairs Committee, together with other MAC Standing Committee leaders. *From the left*, Luo Ruiqing, Chen Yi, Nie Rongzhen, Liu Bocheng, Xu Xiangqian, Lin Biao, Tao Zhu, He Long, Ye Jianying, Luo Ronghuan. Tao Zhu was not a MAC member, and was undoubtedly present as the host local leader.

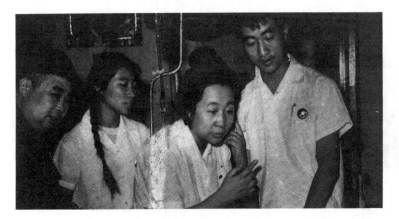

3. Lin Biao's family together with Air Force Commander Wu Faxian probably during the early Cultural Revolution period. Wu was one of the so-called 'four generals' who were close to Lin politically and personally during the Cultural Revolution, and who were officially charged with forming the 'Lin Biao clique' together with Lin and his wife, Ye Qun. *From the left*, Wu, daughter Lin Doudou, Ye and son Lin Liguo. Note that Ye and her children are wearing the Mao badges which proliferated during the Cultural Revolution.

4. The classic Cultural Revolution era photo of the Great Leader and his 'best student' and successor, Lin Biao. Lin typically carries an ever-present copy of the 'little red book' of Mao's quotations and wears a Mao badge.

5. Lin Biao together with Mao and Zhou Enlai at the August 1966 Eleventh Plenum which raised Lin, against his expectations and wishes, to the status of number two in the Party and Mao's designated successor.

6. Lin Biao reading his speech to the second mass reception of Red Guards at Tiananmen on 31 August 1966 with Mao peering over his shoulder. *From left*, Kang Sheng, Jiang Qing, Zhou Enlai, Lin, Mao.

7. A vivid portrait of Cultural Revolution political relationships with the emperor imperiously observing his dutiful subordinates, Zhou Enlai and Lin Biao, in a waiting room behind the Tiananmen rostrum during a Red Guard reception in 1966.

8. Mao and Lin Biao on the rostrum at the Ninth Party Congress in April 1969 when Lin was confirmed as Mao's successor and his status was written into the new Party constitution.

9. Lin Biao together with the 'four generals' about to return to Beijing in September 1970 following the Lushan plenum when Lin's relations with Mao began to unravel as a result of the activities of his group concerning the state chairmanship and Mao's 'genius' issues. *From the left*, Li Zuopeng, Wu Faxian, Lin Biao, Huang Yongsheng, Qiu Huizuo.

10. Mao receives American author Edgar Snow shortly after the Lushan plenum during 1970 National Day celebrations at Tiananmen. On this occasion Mao indicated his impatience with manifestations of his personality cult that Lin had so assiduously promoted. While Lin was present, at the end of 1970 he declined to meet Snow on the grounds that, as an old friend from Yan'an days, Snow would raise difficult questions which he (Lin) could not afford to answer, and he did not want to deceive Snow. *From the left*, Snow, interpreter Ji Chaozhu, Mao, Lin (still with the 'little red book' in hand)

11. On the rostrum of Tiananmen during evening May Day celebrations in 1971 when the Mao-Lin relationship was under serious strain. *Clockwise from the top*, Mao, Lin Biao, Mme. Sihanouk, Dong Biwu, interpreter, Prince Sihanouk. On this occasion Lin only appeared reluctantly, uncharacteristically arriving after Mao, was ignored by Mao and in turn failed to greet him, and left abruptly without excusing himself.

12. Lin Biao's last public appearance, at a reception for the Romanian leader Ceauşescu on 3 June 1971. Lin had initially refused to attend despite Mao's request, and only consented to go following Ye Qun's tearful pleas that he should think of his family. *From the left*, Zhou Enlai, Mme Ceauşescu, Lin, Ceauşescu, Mao.

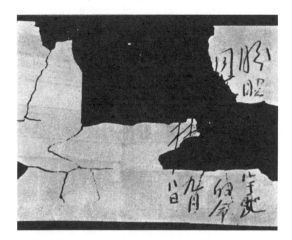

13. One of the few pieces of 'evidence' of Lin Biao's alleged order to assassinate Mao. This unaddressed note dated 8 September without any year (although 1971 was asserted by the authorities) allegedly said, '[I] hope you will act according to [the orders] of [Lin] Liguo and Zhou Yuchi.' Its fragments were reportedly pieced together after being torn up by Lin Liguo's 'co-conspirator' Zhou Yuchi as he attempted to flee on 13 September 1971. There is no way of knowing whether the message actually referred to an assassination attempt, or whether it was genuine in the first place, and several senior Chinese scholars believe the whole matter was fabricated. One such scholar, who claims to have seen the original note, states that it contained no date whatsoever.

14. Lin Biao's *Trident* no. 256 after crashing in Mongolia on 13 September 1971. Recent investigations have proved beyond any reasonable doubt that Lin, Ye Qun and Lin Liquo died on this flight. There are two versions of Lin's flight. The official version is that he fled after the discovery of his plot to assassinate Mao, while his daughter Lin Doudou claims he was virtually kidnapped from his bed by Ye Qun and Lin Liquo, who had panicked over signs that Mao planned to purge Lin.

4

LIN BIAO DURING THE CONSTRUCTION OF
THE NEW ORDER, 1969–1971

In the second half of 1968, with the student Red Guards being dispatched to the countryside and the military given a stronger writ to restore order than at any time since 1966, the overall emphasis of Chinese politics shifted from 'destruction' to 'construction'. The tasks in this stage included selecting a new CCP leadership, reviving the damaged state structure, rehabilitating cadres who had been criticised and pushed aside during the movement, reconstituting the shattered Party organization, and developing a policy programme to deal with the national and international agenda. This period up to the death of Lin Biao has been seen by both official sources and Western analyses as a time of sharpening political conflict given the uncertainties of the new redistribution of power beginning with the Ninth Party Congress in the spring of 1969, a conflict centering on Lin's supposed moves to strengthen his position. While official sources emphasise conspiratorial activities and specific conflicts, Western views tend to place individual disputes in the context of an alleged effort by Lin to shore up his fragile power-base by developing a policy programme aimed at securing broad support. Above all, taking up an element of the official version, these interpretations emphasize Lin's alleged efforts to perpetuate military dominance of civilian affairs as the core of political conflict during the last three years of his life.[1]

To assess the adequacy of the above claims and offer our own alternative interpretation of the 1969–71 period, we will examine a number of specific developments and several broad issues: (1) the personnel and programme issues surrounding the Ninth Congress; (2) Lin Biao's 'notorious' 'Order Number One' in October

---

[1] See especially the essays by Harding and MacFarquhar in *CHOC*, vol. 15, pp. 199, 214, 306, 311ff.

1969 which removed the old marshals and other leaders from Beijing in the name of defence preparations at a time of high Sino-Soviet tension; (3) the major domestic and foreign policy issues of 1969–71 where Lin allegedly had his own programme; (4) Lin's alleged attempt to create a military dictatorship; (5) the issue of the state chairmanship culminating in the summer 1970 Lushan plenum; and (6) Lin's political dilemma following Lushan until his death a year later.

The Ninth Party Congress, April 1969

The Ninth Congress has been seen, paradoxically, as a time of both great strength and vulnerability for Lin Biao. While he was formally named Mao's successor in the new CCP constitution and bolstered by the election of Huang Yongsheng, Wu Faxian, Qiu Huizuo, Li Zuopeng and Ye Qun to the Politburo, Party histories and outside analyses suggest a fragility in his position. The fact that other elements of the élite, including Zhou Enlai and other veteran cadres as well as the leaders of the CRG, were also represented on the Politburo to produce a far from united leadership, together with doubts about Lin's suitability for a new phase emphasising construction, has caused analysts to highlight such purported fragility.[2] Official sources, moreover, point to an alleged difference over the content of the political report to the Congress as one of the earliest signs of Mao's disenchantment with Lin, and to the emergence of direct competition for power and position with the Jiang Qing group as a further sign of vulnerability.[3] New information, however, provides an opportunity to gain a more accurate sense of both Lin's political health at the time of the Congress and his activities in the key events of the period. To this end we examine next the selection of the new Politburo, the differences over the political report, and a

---

[2] E.g. Harding in *CHOC*, vol. 15, p. 199; and Teiwes, *Leadership*, pp. 107–8.

[3] See Zhou Enlai's report to the 1973 Tenth Congress in Kau, *Lin Piao*, pp. 203–4; and Zong Huaiwen, *Years of Trial*, pp. 147–8, 150–1. Cf. Wang Nianyi, *Dadongluan*, pp. 387–8.

less vital issue at the time but one which would be crucial in 1970: the question of Mao's genius.

Apart from the machinations of the wives – Jiang Qing and Ye Qun – to obtain seats on the top body, conflict over the new Politburo revolved around the representation of the three main segments of the Cultural Revolution élite – the PLA, the civilian radicals and the surviving veteran cadres. This was reflected in the make-up of the personnel small group (*renshi xiaozu*) appointed by Mao, in the absence of a functioning Party organization department, solely to draw up a Politburo list and make other personnel arrangements at the Congress. This consisted of Premier Zhou Enlai, Chief of Staff Huang Yongsheng and the CRG's Kang Sheng. The main issue facing the group, in addition to the actual names on the list, was the size of the body. In outlining the task Mao said that three alternatives were possible – a big team, a middle-sized group or a small body. The implications of the two extreme possibilities seem clear. A large Politburo would provide an opportunity for Zhou to include old cadres of Politburo rank who had been criticised but not dismissed during the campaign – people such as Marshal Chen Yi and economic specialist Chen Yun. A small body, presumably favoured by the radicals, would have facilitated kicking out all or most 'conservatives', figures such as Ye Jianying and Li Xiannian. There is no indication of the position of Lin Biao or Huang Yongsheng on these matters; in Lin's case as revealed in the earlier discussion of Ye Qun's manoeuvres, he apparently only reviewed the list after it had been drawn up by the small group and vetted by Mao. In the event, Mao opted for a medium-sized twenty-one person Politburo which included Ye Jianying, Li Xiannian, Zhu De, Liu Bocheng and Dong Biwu from the moderate camp (but excluded Chen Yi and other old marshals), five CRG members, the five close supporters of Lin in the central military apparatus, and two regional military commanders.[4] The final outcome was inevitably a diverse top policy-making body, but

---

[4] Oral Source. Cf. above, p. 13. Minister of Public Security Xie Fuzhi, a radical but not a CRG member, held the final seat on the body. For the full Politburo list see Teiwes, *Leadership*, p. 107.

Lin Biao arguably came out of it better than either Zhou Enlai or the CRG, despite his seemingly minimal input. While the civilian radical representation matched that of Lin's military group, the fact that the CRG virtually ceased to function after the Congress left the radicals almost without operational posts. Also, by this time Chen Boda was fully alienated from his CRG colleagues. Finally, Zhu De, Liu Bocheng and Dong Biwu, who could be expected to be sympathetic to Zhou, were too old and/or ill to play effective roles.

On the second issue the official version claims that Chen Boda, in conjunction with Lin Biao, prepared a draft political report emphasising the productive forces rather than class struggle, a view rejected by Mao who had a new report drawn up that was read by Lin who only reluctantly accepted it. Even more subtle Party history accounts see both a different perspective between Mao and Lin on the question of production, and a sense of mutual dissatisfaction over how matters unfolded.[5] The actual story was much more complicated, however. It began in late 1968 with Mao appointing a group consisting of Chen, Zhang Chunqiao and Yao Wenyuan to draft the report. At the end of February 1969 a meeting called by Lin Biao decided that Chen would begin the actual drafting, a decision which, as one Party historian remarked, was quite natural given his position as head of the CRG – and, we might add, given his involvement in preparing many of Mao's most significant writings over the years. Nevertheless, it also reflected Chen's unwillingness to cooperate with Zhang and Yao. In any case, Chen was very slow in making progress and had only produced a part of a draft by mid-March. Mao commented on Chen's initial submission that the report should distinguish between Deng Xiaoping and Liu Shaoqi, a comment Chen allegedly disclosed to Zhou Enlai but not to Jiang Qing, while Zhang and Yao became impatient with the slow progress and criticised the incomplete draft for allegedly advocating the 'theory of productive forces'. At this point Mao decided that Zhang and Yao, together with Kang Sheng, should prepare

[5] See Wang Nianyi, *Dadongluan*, pp. 387, 396. Cf. below, p. 108.

their own draft. They completed the task in a week and sent their draft to Mao.[6]

At the meeting convened to discuss the draft prepared by Zhang and Yao, Chen raised heated objections to their version, particularly attacking it as a document that was all about movement but had no objective in the manner of the German revisionist Bernstein, and because it contained nothing about production (presumably as one legitimate Marxist goal). Mao was present and after initially saying nothing went to the lavatory, but on his return said that Chen's opinion should be incorporated among a significant number of other corrections that would be required. This account suggests that the whole issue of 'productive forces' raised after Lin's demise, while not groundless, was grossly exaggerated, as far as Mao-Lin conflict is concerned. A scholar who read Chen's draft could not recall any unusual emphasis on production, and he went on to comment that at the time no one dared to imply any easing of class struggle. But the differences which did exist in the opposing drafts apparently inflamed the egos and mutual dislikes of the intellectuals concerned. Personal dislikes also figured in another incident in late March when Jiang Qing, now angry after learning that Chen withheld Mao's comment concerning Deng and Liu from her, reportedly convened a meeting to demand his self-criticism and the removal of the insignia from his uniform. But if Chen was humiliated by Jiang's actions, he was soon devastated by the Chairman's reaction to his final draft. Mao inexplicably did not even bother to read his version, and returned it unopened. Chen later claimed that he wept, having never been so hurt in his entire life, and feeling that he had completely lost Mao's trust. He incorrectly concluded that he would be dropped from the new Politburo.[7]

[6] Ibid., p. 387; Ye Yonglie, Chen Boda, pp. 458-9; and oral sources. See also Zhang Yunsheng, Maojiawan, pp. 210-12.

[7] Wang Nianyi, Dadongluan, p. 387; Ye Yonglie, Chen Boda, pp. 458, 460-3; and oral sources. As for Jiang Qing's reported anger over not being briefed on Mao's comment, if true it reflects an uncalled for overreaction in that the Chairman's opinion distinguishing Deng from Liu had been made clear at the 12th Plenum in October 1968. See Wang Nianyi, Dadongluan, pp. 311, 315.

Chen's eventual election not simply to the Politburo but to its Standing Committee also suggests that the whole question of the political report was a storm in a teacup. As for Lin Biao, apart from the obviously distorted accusations after his death, there is little to indicate any deep involvement on his part. Ye Qun had turned up at the criticism session organised by Jiang Qing and added her voice against Chen, but she later explained to him privately that she had no choice under the circumstances. Moreover, when the two drafts reached Maojiawan, Lin apparently did not bother to look at either but only asked to see the changes made by Mao himself.[8] Whatever mutual dissatisfaction existed between Mao and Lin over the whole affair, it would seem largely related to the feelings each had for the intellectuals who were the real protagonists in the conflict; Mao was clearly unimpressed with Chen on this as on earlier occasions, while Lin had little regard for Zhang and Yao. This is not to say that Lin's (private) opinions on the emphasis that should be given to production were not different from Mao's. Lin, given fragmentary evidence of his attitude toward the importance of economic construction, was probably sympathetic to Chen's views on production, and in any case Ye Qun felt it necessary to take the precaution of warning his secretaries to guard against any revival of whatever interest Lin had in Chen's draft. But there is nothing to suggest any challenge to Mao which would have been the very opposite of Lin's *modus operandi*. Yet it is claimed by official sources that he resented the way that things had worked out. Lin abandoned plans to make an extemporaneous oral report to the Congress and merely went through the motions of reading the official document after refusing to look at it in detail beforehand. This tension notwithstanding, there is little to indicate that anything more serious was involved, or that it had a lasting effect on the Mao-Lin relationship.[9]

The third issue to arise out of the Ninth Congress, one that

---

[8] Zhang Yunsheng, *Maojiawan*, p. 214; and Ye Yonglie, *Chen Boda*, p. 460.
[9] Zhang Yunsheng, *Maojiawan*, pp. 212, 214, 215; and above, p. 73. This significantly revises the argument in Teiwes, 'Mao and his lieutenants', p. 66.

would be far more significant at the 1970 Lushan plenum, concerned the proper ideological treatment of Mao's 'genius'. The specific question was how Mao and his Thought should be characterised in the new Party Constitution. When the draft of the new Constitution was being discussed in the fall of 1968, Mao deleted from the draft the three adverbs in the statement that he had 'inherited, defended and developed Marxism-Leninism *with genius, creatively and comprehensively*' (*tiancaide, chuangzaode, quanmiande*), something he had also done on other occasions in this period.[10] This amended version then became the official formulation adopted at the Ninth Congress, one that had the effect of discarding the previous formulation of the Eleventh Plenum in August 1966 at which Lin Biao had been raised to the position of successor. It did not, however, mean that there was any diminution of the personality cult at the Congress or that the full range of leaders did not heap lavish praise on Mao. Yet the deleted words did not appear in Lin's report or the speeches of other leaders including Chen Boda, Kang Sheng and Huang Yongsheng with one exception – Zhou Enlai. In Zhou's speech on the very day the Constitution was approved, a speech also notable for its extreme praise of Lin Biao, Zhou used two of the three adverbs, 'with genius' and 'creatively', when lauding Mao's development of Marxist-Leninist theory.[11] Thus the leading moderate of the regime, someone who surely was aware of Mao's wishes, saw no political risk in emphasising the Chairman's genius, a fact that must surely have added to Lin's perplexity at Lushan.

In retrospect, Lin Biao appears to have emerged from the Ninth Congress in a very strong position. His position as successor had been reaffirmed in the most official way possible, the new Politburo line-up was more supportive of his position than

[10] Kau, *Lin Piao*, p. 60; Zong Huaiwen, *Years of Trial*, p. 151; and ZGDSJXCKZL, vol. 26, p. 516.
[11] 'Speech by Zhou Enlai at plenary session of the Ninth National Congress of the CCP on 14 April 1969', in *The Stockholm Journal of East Asian Studies*, vol. 2 (1990), p. 95; and Chinese texts of Ninth Congress speeches available at the Fairbank Center Library, Harvard University.

of any other leader or group, and he was extensively lauded in a way second only to the treatment of Mao, notwithstanding his own extremely humble remarks.[12] Moreover, his control of the PLA leadership, subject to Mao of course, was still very firm though not absolute,[13] Zhou Enlai remained punctiliously subordinate, and the CRG leaders emerged with status but with a diminishing concrete role since the body hardly functioned in the post-Congress period.[14] Whether or not Lin was the ideal person for the reconstruction of the system, there was no intrinsic reason why he could not play the same reactive, quasi-passive and Mao-centred role as he had throughout the tumultuous period of the Cultural Revolution. Yet his position was fragile because of Mao, but not because of any serious differences with the Chairman at the Congress. According to the available evidence, Lin had done little to obtain the ostensibly favourable personnel outcome which placed the four generals (and Ye Qun) on the Politburo, nor had he played a substantial part in shaping the CCP's programmatic statement for the period ahead. What he gained from the Congress was presented to him by Mao, but it was also apparently about this time that the Chairman first raised the question of a successor to Lin which reportedly caused the Vice Chairman concern.[15] What the Chairman giveth the Chairman might take away.

[12] See 'Impromptu remarks by Lin Biao', pp. 101–2.

[13] While the operational heads of the central PLA organs were largely members of Lin's 'clique', local military leadership remained far more diverse. In addition, the MAC Vice Chairmen newly elected at the Congress consisted of Marshals Liu Bocheng, Chen Yi, Nie Rongzhen, Xu Xiangqian and Ye Jianying as well as Lin Biao; *Dang zheng jun qun renminglu*, pp. 13–14.

[14] During the Ninth Congress Chen Boda reportedly engaged in secret discussions with Huang Yongsheng concerning whether the CRG would be needed after the Congress; Wang Nianyi, *Dadongluan*, p. 387. Chen, although nominally CRG head, did not suffer from that outcome since he became the Politburo Standing Committee member with overall responsibility for propaganda work.

[15] See Wang Nianyi, *Dadongluan*, p. 388. Wang does not specify the date of this occasion when Mao suggested Zhang Chunqiao as a possible future successor, but from the context it seemingly was not long after the Ninth Congress. Also, at some unknown point, Mao raised the need to cultivate a successor younger than sixty; see mimeo of leadership speeches in 1968–71 available at the Sinological Institute, University of Heidelberg, p. 71.

Lin Biao's 'Order Number One' October 1969

If the Ninth Congress has been – exaggeratedly we believe –
regarded as one source of tension between Mao and Lin, Lin's
'Order Number One' in the following fall has been identified
as the next step in the alleged deterioration of their relationship.
While this order issued in mid-October, which put the whole
army on combat readiness at a time of fears of a Soviet attack,
has received relatively little attention in the West, in Chinese
accounts – especially the memoirs of several old marshals – it has
been singled out as a prime example of Lin Biao's evil activities.
In various broadsides it has been attacked as a trial run for Lin's
alleged failed coup attempt in 1971, and especially as a case of
persecution of the old marshals who were dispatched from Beijing
along with various civilian leaders to different locations in China
as part of the war preparations.[16] In more moderate versions both
inside and outside China the event is seen as an effort to consolidate
Lin's power, or at least as an effort to test how much authority Mao
was actually willing to grant him.[17] And crucially, drawing on
Mao's reported reaction that the order should be burned, various
existing interpretations see the Chairman as critical of Lin's
action, perhaps more for its asserted unilateral character than for
its substance.[18] Once again, a careful review of new evidence
indicates that such interpretations are seriously flawed.

Tension in Sino-Soviet relations had been building up since the
Soviet-led invasion of Czechoslovakia in August 1968 and
reached open hostilities during the border clash at Zhenbao Island
on the Ussuri River in March 1969. By the fall there had been
further clashes on several sectors of the border as well as troop
build-ups and extensive war preparations on both sides. While
there were also diplomatic efforts to defuse the situation with
Zhou Enlai and the Soviet Prime Minister, Kosygin, meeting at

[16] E.g., Zong Huaiwen, *Years of Trial*, pp. 152–3; and Nie Rongzhen's memoirs as
serialized in *XHRB*, 24–25 October 1984, in *FBIS*, 7 November 1984, pp. K22–24.
[17] Pollack in *CHOC*, vol. 15, p. 413; and interview with a high ranking Party
historian.
[18] See the account in Teiwes, 'Mao and his lieutenant', pp. 66–7, which is based on
both written sources and interviews with Party historians.

Beijing airport on 11 September followed by an agreement in early October to revive border negotiations that had been broken off in 1964,[19] considerable suspicion of Soviet motives remained on the Chinese side. There indeed appeared to be an overreaction, as was indicated by a an instruction on 30 September to water conservancy units to open dams in order to prevent damage that would result from flooding caused by anticipated Soviet bombing. This order was strongly argued against by the professionals in those units; the latter gained the backing of Zhou Enlai who went to see Lin Biao and persuaded him to cancel the directive. Lin seemed particularly suspicious of Soviet intentions, reportedly believing that the scheduled arrival of the delegation to resume border talks on 20 October was cover for a full-scale attack. On the eve of the National Day celebrations on 1 October he ordered the immediate redeployment of all military planes from Beijing in what Wu Faxian described as 'the largest exercise since the formation of the PLA air force', and immediately thereafter he made a secret inspection of the route to be taken by the Soviet delegation, informing no one but Mao. However, there was good reason for concern, with Chinese intelligence reporting Soviet intentions to launch a surgical strike against PRC nuclear facilities following China's first successful underground nuclear test on 23 September, and Lin's bleak view was at one with Mao who hammered home the danger of war throughout the period and instructed the army to go on alert on 26 September. In mid-October a Politburo meeting acted according to Mao's concerns, took the decision to heighten vigilance immediately, and endorsed the Chairman's decision that all senior Party leaders except Zhou Enlai should retreat to other places outside Beijing before the Soviets arrived on the 20th.[20] This was the immediate context of 'Order Number One'.

[19] For an overview of these developments, see Robinson, 'China confronts the Soviet Union: warfare and diplomacy on China's inner Asian frontiers', in CHOC, vol. 15, pp. 254–78. Robinson, p. 278, argues that Lin led opposition to resuming the negotiations, but no convincing evidence is presented.

[20] Zhang Yunsheng, Maojiawan, pp. 106, 308; Wang Nianyi, Dadongluan, p. 362; Li Ke and Hao Shengzhang, 'Wenhua dageming' de Jiefangjun, pp. 125–6; ZGDSYJ, no. 5 (1989), p. 79; Wen Feng, Shentanxia, p. 245; and MacFarquhar in CHOC, vol. 15, p. 322.

While the dispersal of the old marshals was clearly linked to war preparations, it was not a direct consequence of 'Order Number One'. Measures for the removal of Party leaders and whole government offices from Beijing which would have been exposed to a lightning Soviet strike had been underway for some time in the context of a preoccupation with war preparations that can be traced to Mao at the time of the Ninth Congress. These measures involved a June seminar on war preparations, a September warfare conference of the three north China regions, and administrative arrangements assigning various high-ranking leaders special responsibilities in this area. 'Order Number One', moreover, produced truly massive activities on the ground involving the redeployment of one million troops and a transport burden greater than that of the Korean War, hardly an undertaking that could have been initiated behind Mao's back as officially claimed. Finally, as for the movement of Party leaders, this applied to Lin and to Mao himself as well as the marshals and senior CCP figures such as Deng Xiaoping and Chen Yun. Indeed, it was Zhou Enlai, with the assistance of Mao's chief bodyguard Wang Dongxing and not Lin Biao, who was in charge of the arrangements for moving personnel. Moreover, to the extent that there was a punitive element in the cases of the marshals, there is no reason to believe that this would have been solely or even primarily Lin's doing. According to an authoritative oral source, Mao was displeased with the attitude of the old marshals, who reportedly phoned one another to gossip about the Cultural Revolution, and happy to see them scattered. Indeed, Nie Rongzhen subsequently indicated that at the time he originally thought the order came from Mao, and only later decided that Lin must be responsible.[21]

In any case, once the Politburo decision to heighten vigilance was taken, Lin Biao departed for Suzhou on 17 October as part

[21] *ZGDSYJ*, No. 5 (1989), p. 79; Zhang Yunsheng, *Maojiawan*, p. 106; Ma Qibin, *Sishinian*, pp. 320, 322; *XHRB*, 25 October 1984, in *FBIS*, 7 November 1984, p. K24; Wang Nianyi, *Dadongluan*, p. 362; Li Ke and Hao Shengzhang, *'Wenhua dageming' de Jiefangjun*, pp. 125, 252; and oral source. On Zhou's role in moving veteran leaders, see *Chen Yi zhuan* (Biography of Chen Yi) (Beijing: Dangdai Zhongguo chubanshe, 1991), p. 615.

of the evacuation of senior leaders from the capital. After arriving he issued oral instructions to disperse military units and camouflage vital equipment among other steps to implement the Politburo decision. Secretary Zhang Yunsheng then relayed the instructions by phone to Huang Yongsheng, who issued them the next day under the grandiose title 'Number One War Order' of Vice Commander Lin', which in fact was one of four orders on war preparations issued to different institutions on that day. In the meantime Zhang suggested in a discussion with Ye Qun that Mao's confirmation should be sought, and Ye (and subsequently Lin) agreed after musing over the fact that during the revolutionary war Lin often acted first on military tactics and reported to Mao later. Zhang described Lin's overall role as not involving much effort, and his account pictures Lin as rather casual about the matter rather than taking deliberate action unilaterally. Still, if Lin did act without consulting Mao over the actual order, it was a careless departure from his general practice of checking everything closely with Mao before acting, a departure perhaps explained by the urgency of the situation with the Soviets arriving three days later.[22] As for Mao's comment 'Burn it', Ye Qun claimed what Mao actually said was '*Very good*, burn it', although there is doubt whether Ye invented the 'very good' comment. In any case, several senior Party historians regard the statement 'Burn it' as a typical ambiguous remark by Mao and interpret it as meaning 'There's no big deal about this, no particular need to report it, just carry on.' In this view, the whole affair is seen as Lin providing concrete measures to carry out the Politburo decision under emergency conditions and then providing Mao with a courtesy copy.[23]

Overall, the case of 'Order Number One' seems even more of an exaggeration of any Mao-Lin conflict than that of the Ninth Congress political report. The reason it apparently became a *cause célèbre* after Lin's fall was the bitterness of the old

[22] Another possible explanation is that Zhang's account is not fully accurate and exaggerates his own role.
[23] Zhang Yunsheng, *Maojiawan*, pp. 316–19; Wen Feng, *Shentanxia*, p. 248; and oral sources.

marshals. While not all were treated badly when they were removed from the capital,[24] they were under certain restraints and some suffered from inadequate medical treatment. The possibility that Lin Biao was to some degree responsible for the harsher aspects of their situation cannot be ruled out, yet there is an obvious wish on the part of the marshals not only to glorify Zhou Enlai, who played a key role in securing the return of some of them to Beijing for medical treatment, but also to absolve Mao of any responsibility.[25] But whatever the actual responsibility for any hardships suffered, 'Order Number One' itself is best understood as a response to the Mao-driven Politburo interpretation of the international situation.

Domestic and Foreign Policy, 1969–1971

The decisions of the Ninth Congress and the view of the international situation reflected in 'Order Number One' both related to the new policy agenda facing the CCP as the tasks of construction took centre stage following the conclusion of the active phase of the Cultural Revolution. This agenda included the appropriate strategy for economic development, reforms in the cultural and educational sphere, and foreign policy in a period where China was faced by two hostile superpowers – all issues which had to address the fundamental question of how to reconcile the 'revolutionary' aims of the Cultural Revolution with the practical concerns of policy. Where did Lin Biao fit into the resulting policy debates? Official sources, first in the year after Lin's death when he was referred to anonymously as a 'Liu Shaoqi-type swindler' and later in Party histories, paint Lin as pushing for an 'ultra-leftist' policy line in very broad strokes and

[24] The relaxed situation of civilian Party leader Chen Yun is discussed in Ye Yonglie, *Shenmi zhangquanzhe*, pp. 23ff.
[25] E.g., see Nie Rongzhen's memoirs in *XHRB*, 24–25 October 1984, in *FBIS*, 7 November 1984, pp. K22–24. MacFarquhar in *CHOC*, vol. 15, p. 322, argues that another factor in the *ex post facto* denunciation of Lin's order was because of the sharp reaction it produced from not only the Soviets but from the United States and Taiwan as well.

provide only sparse concrete evidence to sustain this view. The essential feature of this alleged policy orientation was a reckless economic programme reminiscent of the Great Leap Forward, and there have also been Chinese claims that Lin opposed the foreign policy of rapprochement with the United States.[26]

Western interpretations have essentially adopted this picture of Lin's policy preferences but have set it in a more elaborate interpretive framework. In this view Lin attempted to build a broad coalition whose core element was China's military-industrial complex. This meant in the first instance a high and substantially increasing rate of defence spending, an outcome which was spectacularly achieved and which fitted well with a foreign policy of confrontation with both superpowers. Beyond this it involved increased resource allocation to the industrial sector generally, thus limiting the funds available for agriculture. Lin's purported answer to the problem of agricultural growth was to adopt mass mobilization measures akin to those of the Great Leap, while at the same time cracking down on the private plots which were anathema to both the Leap Forward and the Cultural Revolution. Such a programme notionally had the benefits of appealing to China's most powerful institutional interests, limiting resource allocations to other areas, and being politically pure. A competing moderate coalition led by Zhou Enlai and including provincial military leaders as well as many central administrators allegedly contested Lin's programme, and gained the upper hand by the end of 1970.[27]

This study cannot resolve many questions surrounding the very sketchily documented policy process during this period. It can, however, call into question key aspects of the official view and Western interpretations, and offer some necessarily general

---

[26] See the press criticisms in 1971–2 collected in Kau, *Lin Piao*, pp. 127–71; Fang Weizhong (ed.), *Zhonghuarenmingongheguo jingji dashiji (1949–1980 nian)* (Chronology of Economic Events in the PRC, 1949–1980) (Beijing: Zhongguo shehui kexue chubanshe, 1984), p. 461; and below, p. 123.

[27] The most thoroughly researched study broadly advancing this perspective is Domes, *China after the Cultural Revolution*, chs 4–5, 7. Overviews include Harding, 'Political trends', pp. 71, 74–75; and Teiwes, *Leadership*, pp. 108–11.

conclusions concerning a more likely scenario for Lin's role in CCP policy-making during this period. First, in the vast majority of official accounts concerning domestic policy the accusations of 'leftist' errors are impersonal – 'Lin Biao and company' or 'Lin Biao, Jiang Qing and company' are attacked, but the number of times Lin or indeed anyone from his group is cited for *specific actions* can literally be counted on the fingers of one hand. Similarly, in Western analyses the overwhelming basis for the conclusions reached is to impute the radical phenomena which clearly did take place to Lin Biao on the basis of some assumed political interest. Against this stands the evidence of Zhang Yunsheng concerning Lin's general lack of interest in policy concerns, or at least his unwillingness to become actively involved, and the testimony of a wide range of Party historians that they are unable to locate evidence of policy advocacy on his part. In addition, there are fragmentary indications that Lin's personal preferences, rather than favouring a mass mobilization approach to growth as during the Great Leap, were for a more moderate programme. For example, after listening to a tape-recording of a speech by his son Lin Liguo in which the latter said 'We are not leftists' and advocated industrial modernization, Lin remarked that this reflected not only his thoughts but even his words.[28] But beyond these general considerations, a better sense of both Lin Biao's role and the overall policy process can be gained by examining first economic strategy and then foreign policy.

Even before the Ninth Congress, CCP economic policy took on a radical cast which, despite some moderating currents after the Lushan plenum, continued even past Lin Biao's death. In February 1969, Zhou Enlai's State Council – not Lin Biao – announced that a 'new leap forward' was emerging in the country's industrial and agricultural production.[29] This involved not only the rhetorical features of the Great Leap such as the slogan 'more, faster, better, more economically', but also substantial

[28] Wang Nianyi, *Dadongluan*, p. 391. For further evidence of Lin's attitude in this regard, see Guan Weixun, *Ye Qun*, p. 203; and above, pp. 18, 73, 108.
[29] Wang Nianyi, *Dadongluan*, p. 355.

mass mobilization of labour, stringently enforced restrictions on private economic activity especially before late 1970, and high growth-rates and massive investments in the heavy industrial and military sectors. As with the original Great Leap, this involved a rejection of the policies of balanced growth which had been advanced by Zhou Enlai and Chen Yun in 1956–7 in their efforts to 'oppose rash advance',[30] and then restored in the early 1960s after the failure of the Leap Forward. But it is important to examine the origins of the new policies. While clearly reflecting the ideological concerns of the Cultural Revolution in its hostility to private economic activity, the most potent factor behind the mobilizational approach and the investment pattern was the assessment of the international situation. In the wake of the Zhenbao Island incident at the time of the Ninth Congress, Mao declared 'We must be prepared for war', which led to the military measures preceding 'Order Number One'. This sentiment and its implications for economic construction were not new, particularly with regard to the huge investments in the Third Five-Year Plan which had been made on the so-called 'third front' in the interior since the mid-1960s on Mao's personal insistence – a massive effort in anticipation of foreign attack concerning which there is yet little concrete evidence of any input by Lin Biao. What was new were moves to place all national defence industry under a 'national defence industry leadership small group' (guofang gongye lingdao xiaozu) headed by Qiu Huizuo, which in turn was under the direct control of the MAC Office staffed by Lin's close supporters. This situation was formalized in December 1969, but the actual control exercised by the office was surely overstated. Moreover, that this small group was not the creation of Lin Biao is strongly suggested by its

[30] See Frederick C. Teiwes with Warren Sun, 'The politics of an "un-Maoist" interlude: the case of opposing rash advance, 1956–1957', in Timothy Cheek and Tony Saich (eds), New Perspectives on State Socialism in China (Armonk, NY: M.E. Sharpe, forthcoming).

persistence till September 1973, two years after his death.[31] But it was in this context that Lin Biao made one of his rare appearances on the policy stage in the summer of 1969.

Under the strategic direction set by Mao, the MAC Office convened a seminar to consider defence construction issues in June 1969. This meeting endorsed an ambitious programme to bring about a massive increase in the production of military equipment based on Lin Biao's general guideline of 'Observe everything, inspect everything, implement everything according to the viewpoint of preparing for war'. In addition, at the seminar Qiu Huizuo advocated building up a more independent and comprehensive defence industry system while declaring that everyone should forget about proportional development as war preparations were the only standard to consider. What should be noted here is that Lin's guideline, as well as Qiu's proposal concerning the defence industry, came at a conference solely concerned with military and military-related questions. It was only later, in January 1970, when the 'CCP Centre' – i.e. Mao – endorsed Lin's 'Everything according to preparing for war' criterion virtually word for word, that its application was extended to the entire economy as in fact was already the case. It was this extension, as was argued in the 1980s, that caused great disruption to the national economy, resulting in a 34 per cent increase in defence spending for 1969 and further increases of 15 and 16 per

---

[31] Wang Nianyi, *Dadongluan*, pp. 362–3; Ma Qibin, *Sishinian*, pp. 318, 324; 'Dangdai Zhongguo de jihua gongzuo' bangongshi (General Office of 'Contemporary China Planning Work') (ed.), *Zhonghuarenmingongheguo guomin jingji he shehui fazhan jihua dashi jiyao 1949–1985* (Outline of Events in PRC National Economic and Social Development, 1949–1985) (Beijing: Hongqi chubanshe, 1987), p. 294; Barry Naughton, 'The third front: defence industrialization in the Chinese interior', *CQ*, no. 115 (1988); Teiwes, *Politics and Purges*, pp. xxxvii–xxxviii, 503; and above, pp. 111–12.

With regard to the actual control of the small group and MAC office, the likelihood is that both Zhou Enlai and newly re-elected MAC Vice Chairman Nie Rongzhen played major roles in defence industry matters, an area where they had been deeply involved before the Cultural Revolution. Bureaucratically the small group was equivalent to the SPC which ultimately answered to Zhou (and of course Mao), and the 1970 defence industry plan was issued *jointly* by the small group and SPC. See *Jingji he shehui fazhan jihua dashi jiyao*, p. 298.

cent in 1970 and 1971 respectively. Thus while the enhanced emphasis on war preparations in economic planning was an important development, it was not only in accord with Mao's priorities but also involved transplanting his Defence Minister's slogan for military matters to national economic strategy.[32]

While Lin Biao's personal involvement is obscure, the continuing role of army leaders in both central ministries and the provinces was significant for the new bout of 'rash advance' as economic development speeded up under conditions of international tension in 1970-1. The excesses and mistakes of this process clearly owed much to both the unfamiliarity and the determination of the provincial military in particular; as Chen Yun observed many years later, these generals 'didn't have experience but they had a lot of guts'.[33] This large military role notwithstanding, it must be emphasized that the concept of a 'new leap forward' can be traced to Mao with many concrete details of the Fourth Five-Year Plan drafted in early 1970 and the results of subsequent economic meetings echoing the ideas so beloved by the Chairman – and not Lin Biao – in 1958, including doubling steel output, overtaking Britain and fufilling the targets of the 40-article draft agricultural programme. Implementation of economic policy, moreover, was under the leadership of Zhou Enlai's State Council. Planning conferences under the State Council's leadership in February-March 1970 and December 1970–February 1971 (i.e. after Lin's setback at Lushan) are held responsible for producing the 'leftist tendency' and a 'new flying leap' respectively, and even after Lin's death the State Council approved further capital construction increases in November 1971. In this process there was inevitably some tension involving the demands of the military representatives for

[32] Fang Weizhong, *Jingji dashiji*, pp. 454–5, 461; and Ma Qibin, *Sishinian*, p. 326. The slight differences in formulations were the 'Centre's' more formal use of *zhanbei* for 'war preparations' compared to Lin's more colloquial *dazhang*, literally 'make war'.

The transplanting of policies initially advanced by Lin for the military sphere to the larger national stage can also be seen in the pre-Cultural Revolution case of establishing PLA style political work departments in the civilian bureaucracy; see above, p. 59, n. 5.

[33] Wang Nianyi, *Dadongluan*, pp. 355, 363, 366.

more funds and faster growth; at the February-March 1970 conference which prepared the Fourth Five-Year Plan in particular, this appears to have contributed to the high targets set. But overall Zhou, under Mao's direction or with his blessing, presided over the new 'leap', and notwithstanding some moderation of rhetoric and especially policy toward the rural private economy, high-speed growth continued. Indeed, it was not till the end of 1971 that Zhou began to raise more general questions concerning the economic dislocations allegedly caused by 'Lin Biao's empty politics' – presumably on the calculation that Mao was now willing to reassess overall policy following the discrediting of Lin and his military followers and given the more favourable international situation due to the opening to the United States.[34]

Zhou Enlai's critical importance in implementing economic policy as well as a better sense of the military's role can be gained from an examination of administrative and personnel arrangements. Although PLA cadres had assumed leadership in various economic ministries in 1967–8 in response to Mao's demands for such takeovers to restore order, economic leadership before the Ninth Congress still rested with Zhou and Li Fuchun, the latter as a Politburo Standing Committee member with economic responsibilities and head of the State Council's Professional Work Office (*yewuzu*), a body with the same bureaucratic status as the MAC Office. Other key economic officials including Li Xiannian, Yu Qiuli and Gu Mu remained active throughout the period before and after the Ninth Congress, while Li Fuchun, in spite of having suffered a major setback at the end of 1968 (he was placed under house arrest according to one report), still issued orders in the summer of 1969. But significant changes did occur with a military representative, Su Jing, sent to the SPC in August 1968, and in December representing the SPC in the

---

[34] Wang Nianyi, *Dadongluan*, pp. 360–8; Fang Weizhong, *Jingji dashiji*, pp. 460–3, 470–1, 485–6; Zhao Desheng, *Zhonghuarenmingongheguo jingji zhuanti dashiji* (Chronology of PRC Special Economic Topics) (Henan: Henan renmin chubanshe, 1989), vol. 3 (1967–76), p. 41; and Domes, *China after the Cultural Revolution*, pp. 84ff, 104–19.

preparation of the 1969 budget under the instructions of Zhou Enlai, Li Xiannian, Yu Qiuli and General Su Yu. Not long after the Ninth Congress Zhou ordered the reorganization of an expanded National Capital Construction Commission in June 1969 with specific responsibility for speeding up 'third front' construction under the guideline of 'Stay close to the mountains, dispersed and hidden' – a guideline often condemned by orthodox accounts and simplistically attributed to Lin Biao. And the reorganization of the SPC and State Council in 1970 strengthened the institutional capabilities of economic organs while making them directly responsible to the Party Centre, i.e. to Mao through Zhou without an MAC role. Thus while PLA representatives in economic ministries and figures such as Su Jing and Su Yu at higher levels undoubtedly had significant influence in this period, the revived economic organs also provided major scope for the activities of civilian economic officials. This mixture of officials carried out Mao's line of a 'new leap forward', while administratively they answered to Zhou Enlai.[35]

As for Lin Biao who played such a limited role in economic affairs throughout the Cultural Revolution,[36] there is nothing concrete to link him to these developments. In fact, as already noted, significant steps in the 'rash advance' policies took place after both Lin's critical political setback at the Lushan plenum in the summer of 1970 and his death a year later. The Lushan meeting itself approved the high-speed, high-target 1970 budget, while shortly after the plenum the SPC and State Council further increased the already large increase in capital construction investment. Then in early 1971 the National Planning Conference approved another expansion of investment. Thus not withstanding some easing in rural policy, it is difficult to see a dominant

---

[35] *Jingji he shehui fazhan jihua dashi jiyao*, pp. 276–7, 284–6; *ZGDSRWZ*, vol. 44 (Xi'an: Shaanxi renmin chubanshe, 1990), p. 108; Zhao Desheng, *Jingji wenti dashiji*, vol. 3, p. 45; Fang Weizhong, *Jingji dashiji*, pp. 460–3; and Bo Yibo, *Ruogan zhongda juece yu shijian de huigu* (Reflections on Certain Major Decisions and Events), vol. 2 (Beijing: Zhonggong zhongyang dangxiao chubanshe, 1993), pp. 1216–17.

[36] The only direct involvement concerned extending the Cultural Revolution to the industry and communications front and to agriculture in December 1966, a case where he was clearly carrying out Mao's instructions; see above, p. 69.

Zhou Enlai-led moderate coalition winning the policy debate at this juncture both because of the continuing prevalence of high-speed economic policies, and given Zhou's leading role in implementing Mao's ambitious programme. Following Lin's death, although Zhou used the occasion – the occasion, in our view, being Mao's disorientation following the unanticipated flight and demise of his successor and the improving international outlook, rather than the removal of Lin's political influence[37] – to argue for more balanced policies, massive capital construction continued in 1972, and it was only in early 1973 that *slight* decreases were approved in spending on national defence and the defence industry. We can only conclude that the gradual and delayed changes in the expansionary economic policies over the period from the fall of 1970 to early 1973 were at best only indirectly linked to the fate of Lin Biao.[38]

In contrast to domestic policy, official accounts of Lin Biao's foreign policy views provide little of the sweeping assertions found in accounts of his alleged 'ultra-leftist' sabotage of the economy. Instead, such sources and statements by Chinese leaders only present a handful of specific incidents implying or claiming Lin's opposition to the major development in China's international posture, the opening to the United States. The most direct claim in this regard came from Mao himself who told Richard Nixon that a 'reactionary group [was] opposed to our contact with you. . . . The result was that they got on an airplane and fled abroad.'[39] Such slight pickings have been one basis for the widespread acceptance in Western scholarship of the view that Lin did indeed oppose Sino-American rapprochement in favour of an isolationist approach which confronted both the Soviet Union and the United States and relied on war preparations to

[37] On Mao's disorientation following Lin's death, see Teiwes, 'Mao and his lietenants', pp. 34–5. In this period Mao's health also deteriorated and Zhou assumed a particularly vital role in sorting out the problems created by the demise of the successor.

[38] Fang Weizhong, *Jingji dashiji*, pp. 469, 471, 486, 489, 496; and Ma Qibin, *Sishinian*, p. 355.

[39] See Pollack in *CHOC*, vol. 15, p. 414. Pollack, pp. 414–15, reviews the limited evidence for this interpretation.

keep these enemies at bay. In this interpretation the purported political logic of the situation is equally if not more important to sustaining the analysis. A key argument is that Lin's power declined at precisely the time of the warming in Sino-American relations. Moreover, since confrontation meant increased defence expenditures, Lin's institutional constituency assertedly required him to oppose rapprochement. Finally, Lin's personal position would be weakened by a diplomatic approach which would theoretically play to the strong suit of his presumed major competitor for the succession, Zhou Enlai.[40]

The foregoing analysis has already indicated several major problems with this interpretation. First, the defence build-up, which continued despite the moves toward rapprochement, can be traced to Mao in the first instance and not to Lin Biao. Secondly, Zhou Enlai's political *modus operandi* included a determination to avoid any friction with Maojiawan, and from the evidence available Lin bore no ill-will towards Zhou. There are, moreover, further considerations which cast doubt on the view of Lin Biao opposing the new foreign policy initiative. One is Zhang Yunsheng's account of Lin's limited interest in foreign policy issues as exemplified by his falling asleep while being briefed on the Cambodian situation in May 1970. Also, a substantial number of Party historians, including some of the most authoritative, and people working on Lin Biao all claim to have no knowledge of *any* position held by Lin Biao on foreign affairs, concluding, *inter alia*, that he played no role in Sino-American

---

[40] E.g., *ibid.*, pp. 413–19; MacFarquhar in *CHOC*, vol. 15, pp. 320–3; and Robert S. Ross, 'From Lin Biao to Deng Xiaoping: élite instability and China's U.S. policy', *CQ*, no. 118 (1989), pp. 267–6. For a more elaborate argument including an alleged 'pro-Soviet tilt' sponsored by Lin Biao in 1970, see John W. Garver, *China's Decision for Rapprochement with the United States, 1968–1971* (Boulder: Westview Press, 1982), especially ch. 4. This interpretation too is largely based on unverifiable assumptions about bureaucratic and factional interests, as well as by a Pekinological analysis of contemporary sources. The danger of Pekinological analysis is demonstrated by arguments (e.g., Garver, p. 138) that Huang Yongsheng's August 1971 speech condemning US imperialism represented continuing opposition to rapprochement by the Lin Biao group when in fact, as pointed out by Barnouin and Yu, *Ten Years of Turbulence*, p. 227, Huang's denunciation followed the official wording of the time.

relations. Where Lin was involved in foreign policy issues it was apparently from a military perspective alone, as in the briefings he received on the Zhenbao Island incident or his activities surrounding 'Order Number One'. Finally, when, in the tightly controlled sphere of foreign policy – which usually involved only Mao, Zhou and a small group of advisers – Mao took the unusual step in early 1969 of asking four old marshals – Chen Yi, Nie Rongzhen, Xu Xiangqian and Ye Jianying – to form a study group on the international situation, a group which concluded that 'contention between the superpowers' was the main trend and recommended a softening of policy toward the United States, there is no evidence of any participation by Lin in these discussions. Of particular significance given their generally hostile memoirs, the marshals give no indication that they were aware of any conflict with Lin on this major security question, an issue where according to the conventional analysis Lin held precisely the opposite view.[41]

The above is not to claim that Lin Biao had no private views on the new foreign policy orientation, but even these appear to have been rarely expressed. The only *concrete* example of Lin having articulated reservations about the policy toward the United States – as opposed to the generalised and highly suspicious *ex post facto* claim by Mao[42] – is a reported remark he made to Ye Qun in May or early June 1971 that Zhou's moves toward the United States would produce setbacks and disadvantages. The main subject of this conversation, however, was whether Lin should attend a central work conference in June dealing with foreign policy, with Lin initially deciding that he should put in a brief appearance, although in the event he did not participate.

---

[41] Zhang Yunsheng, *Maojiawan*, p. 218; Pollack in *CHOC*, vol. 15, p. 411; Xu Xiangqian, *Lishi de huigu* (Reflections on History) (3 vols, Beijing: Jiefangjun chubanshe, 1987), vol. 3, p. 848; *Chen Yi zhuan*, pp. 614–15; *Zhonggong dangshi tongxun* (CCP History Bulletin), no. 2 (1989), p. 7; above, pp. 10, 112–14; and oral sources.
[42] In addition to Mao's 1972 claim above, a purported text of a December 1971 report by Zhou published in Taiwan claimed that Lin opposed the new policy as a betrayal of Vietnam; *Issues and Studies*, January 1977, p. 117. Unfortunately, we are unable to determine whether this is a genuine CCP document.

But in terms of advancing specific views in policy councils, there is no evidence that Lin ever interfered in this policy area that was traditionally dominated by Mao and Zhou. This was nowhere more apparent than at the June work conference – attended by all large military region commanders but not by the Minister of Defence – which unanimously endorsed the approach advocated by Zhou and the four marshals, and thus the major departure in contemporary Chinese foreign policy. Moreover, when the issue did arise at a Politburo meeting following Henry Kissinger's visit in July and Li Zuopeng allegedly supported Albanian complaints about the visit, Lin and the other members of his 'clique' said nothing in support. Whatever his private thoughts concerning the new foreign policy line, Lin Biao certainly was not leading political opposition to it.[43]

Thus, in foreign policy, even more than domestic affairs, Lin Biao appears to have played a marginal, indeed virtually non-existent role. The prime movers in both areas were above all Mao who set the basic policy and Zhou Enlai who played the crucial role in implementation. On the domestic scene concrete evidence of Lin's involvement only exists where defence industry issues were central, and where Mao had provided clear authorization for action. Even this much involvement, oddly, does not appear to have occurred in national security policy apart from that strictly concerned with military preparations. But as the case of defence industry and overall economic policy shows, Lin's limited personal involvement did not detract from a major institutional role for the PLA. This basic consideration must be kept in mind as we examine the question of whether there was an attempt to perpetuate military control of the policy in this period when war preparations dominated the national economy.

---

[43] Chen Dunde, *Mao Zedong, Nikesun zai 1972* (Mao Zedong and Nixon in 1972) (Beijing: Kunlun chubanshe, 1992), pp. 144–5, 261; *Zhonggong dangshi tongxun*, No. 2 (1989), p. 7; and oral source. While we are suspicious of the claim that Li Zuopeng would have questioned a decision clearly endorsed by Mao, even in this account Lin remained passive. It is uncertain, moreover, whether Lin actually attended the Politburo meeting at issue.

The Politics of Military Dominance, 1969–1971

The question of Bonapartism – the alleged effort of Lin Biao to maintain army dominance over civilian affairs and Mao's struggle to reassert Party rule after the Ninth Congress – stands at the centre of the present accepted Western interpretation of the Lin Biao affair.[44] In this view, with the aim of overthrowing Liu Shaoqi accomplished, Mao became concerned at the power exercised by the PLA and by extension Lin, and attempted to reassert traditional Party control of the gun through measures to rectify the army, rehabilitate civilian cadres and rebuild Party committees – whereas Lin marshalled his forces in an effort to undermine this process and ensure military dominance of the new Party structure. Thus the alleged power struggle between Mao and Lin is seen as reflecting an institutional conflict between the Party and the army. While this analysis draws on official sources, it is at some variance with the mainstream CCP interpretation which focuses on a concrete military *coup* rather than a longer-term struggle to create a military *dictatorship*,[45] and when discussing post-Ninth Congress civil-military conflict, Party histories depict a struggle between the two cliques of Jiang Qing's radical intellectuals wielding the pen against Lin Biao's group of generals rather than a larger institutional confrontation.[46] How can these different emphases be resolved, and what do they tell us about both Lin Biao's role and the larger pattern of élite politics in the period from the Ninth Congress to Lin's death?

There is no doubt that the PLA emerged as the single most powerful institution in China at the Ninth Congress, that Mao initiated an effort to revive the Party organisation at that time but that the structure in place at the time of Lin Biao's death

---

[44] See MacFarquhar in *CHOC*, vol. 15, pp. 312–13.

[45] Chinese references to a military dictatorship did appear, however, particularly in the intial period following Lin's death as officials struggled to explain the affair to incredulous foreigners. The most high level example was Mao's assertion that Lin began his attempt to install a military dictatorship by infiltrating his partisans into key organs of state power before breaking ranks on a number of domestic and foreign issues; *The New York Times*, 28 July 1972, p. 2.

[46] E.g., Zong Huaiwen, *Years of Trial*, pp. 150–4.

was still heavily dominated by the military, and that concern had been shown over mistakes committed by army officers in political and administrative roles throughout the 1969–71 period. The PLA gained unprecedented representation on the leading bodies selected at the Ninth Congress with 52 per cent of Politburo and 38 per cent of Central Committee seats. This tendency was even more striking in the provinces where, at the time of the Congress, 62 per cent of chairmen of the new organs of power, the revolutionary committees, were military officers.[47] This, of course, was the inevitable outcome of the Cultural Revolution, which left the army as the only integrated national institution still standing. Yet the situation was essentially unchanged by the process of rehabilitating cadres, consolidating the revolutionary committees and rebuilding the Party after the Congress, a process guided by PLA propaganda teams in low-level units and by military-dominated Party core groups and existing revolutionary committee leaders at the provincial level. The unsurprising result was that army dominance of provincial revolutionary committees remained essentially unchanged during membership adjustments in 1969–70, while PLA leadership of the new provincial Party committees set up in 1970–1 was even more pronounced with 57 per cent of all secretaries and 69 per cent of first secretaries being serving military officers.[48]

If military dominance, particularly at subnational levels, was one inevitable outcome of the Cultural Revolution, another was tension between the military men thrown into unfamiliar civilian roles and other elements of the new élite structure. At the First Plenum following the Congress, Mao declared: 'The problem of the localities lies in the army, and the army's problem lies in its

[47] Kau, Lin Piao, p. xxxii; and Teiwes, Provincial Leadership, p. 31. PLA cadres also made up 38 per cent of the total number of chairmen and vice chairmen. This, however, understates their strength since large numbers of mass representatives who were appointed vice chairmen normally did not exercise significant power. Excluding such representatives, PLA representation stood at 60 per cent. Also, according to Li Ke and Hao Shengzhang, 'Wenhua dageming' de Jiefangjun, p. 244, military cadres made up an astonishing 98 and 97 per cent of the heads of revolutionary committees at the county level and above in Hubei and Yunnan respectively.

[48] Teiwes, Provincial Leadership, pp. 75–6, 79–80, 95–6, 145–6; and Domes, China after the Cultural Revolution, pp. 47–54.

work.' He went on to complain of unnecessarily harsh action taken against perceived opponents and to appeal for unity.[49] The need for the army to avoid high-handed dictatorial behaviour – behaviour which undoubtedly was unavoidable in a context of restoring order, war fears, production drives and the application of army-style mass mobilization methods to civilian society under such rhetoric as '700 million people . . . [in] a single military camp' – became a repeated official theme. In the fall of 1969 low-key press criticism was aimed at defects in the work style of the military-dominated political apparatus, while in early 1970 official publications stressed the CCP's leading role over all other organizations including the PLA. But concern with civilian leadership of the military was hardly the main trend in 1970, as ironically revealed by the case of the 'two resolutions' sometimes cited in scholarly studies as indicating an effort to restore Party control. In the summer of 1970 a campaign was launched to study Mao's famous 1929 Gutian resolution which asserted that the army must obey the Party, together with the 1960 MAC resolution on political work sponsored by Lin Biao. In the ensuing campaign the emphasis was clearly on those political concepts such as the 'living study' of Mao's thought and 'Politics in command' advocated by Lin since 1960 (see Appendix, pp. 188ff, for details) ratlier than on the organizational supremacy of Party committees. While the need to rectify PLA shortcomings was a major theme, in both the summer *and* the months after the Lushan plenum, it was a rectification to be accomplished by Lin Biao-style innovations rather than pre-Cultural Revolution organizational mechanisms. It was only following Lin's death that an even greater emphasis on the need for PLA discipline and learning from the people was linked to explicit demands that the military withdraw from direct involvement in administration.[50]

---

[49] *ZGDSJXCKZL*, vol. 26, pp. 336–7.

[50] Bridgham, 'Fall of Lin Piao', pp. 430ff; Domes, *China after the Cultural Revolution*, ch. 4; Kau, *Lin Piao*, pp. xxxiii, xlv–xlvi, 137–41, 152–9; Garver, *China's Decision for Rapprochement*, p. 121; and *China News Analysis*, no. 814 (1970), pp. 1–7, no. 817 (1970), pp. 3–7, no. 818 (1970), pp. 3–5, no. 830 (1971), pp. 4–6.

While the general concern with the work style of PLA leaders in political roles is clear, its significance for élite politics requires further examination, which naturally starts with Mao. Mao more than anyone else was responsible for the dominant role of the PLA, not only by virtue of destroying the civilian Party apparatus during the Cultural Revolution, but by specific decisions starting in January 1967 granting the military key powers in managing the movement. But for our purposes what is particularly relevant is that Mao sanctioned and abetted the new power structure confirmed at the Ninth Congress. The Chairman both appointed Huang Yongsheng to the crucial personnel group drawing up the Politburo list and endorsed an outcome that awarded more than half the seats to military figures. Perhaps most telling, at the very time when he began to articulate concern about the army's work style, was Mao's dismissive response to Soviet accusations that the Congress had ratified a 'military-bureaucratic system' as not worth refuting.[51]

While Mao appeared unconcerned about the prominence of the army in the power structure in the spring of 1969, it is not clear when his perception of the situation changed. In one view held by some excellent Party historians, by the summer of 1970 as objective conditions altered and tasks of military control increasingly gave way to those of construction, Mao would have been uneasy about the stranglehold of PLA leaders on top political positions throughout the country and felt the need to restore balance before they became too entrenched.[52] In reaching such a conclusion, however, no hard evidence was cited,[53] and in any case the issue did not necessarily relate to Lin Biao. Our alternative interpretation is that only after the Lushan plenum, when Lin fell into disfavour for largely extraneous reasons, did Mao begin to shift his focus from military *work style* to military *power* and link questions of the army's performance to Lin Biao. The connection

---

[51] Wang Nianyi, *Dadongluan*, p. 395.

[52] *Ibid.*; and oral source.

[53] Another oral source, moreover, noted the appointment of PLA cadres to leading ministerial positions in June 1970, a step arguably indicating Mao's relative unconcern with the power of the military at this late date.

was clearly made during his southern tour of August–September 1971, the main purpose of which was to inform local leaders of his estrangement from Lin, when Mao complained that the PLA was preoccupied with civilian affairs to the neglect of military training, and had become a cultural army; he also criticised the practice of military Party committees discussing matters already decided by local Party committees, and demanded that the military learn from the people of the whole country. Even more to the point, on that occasion Mao declared that it was only *following* Lushan that 'I started to take charge of the military by myself'; in other words, notwithstanding his general oversight previously, it was only then that his loss of confidence in Lin Biao led to doubts concerning political control of the army.[54]

But even with Mao drawing connections between excessive military power and Lin Biao from late 1970 to the summer of 1971, this situation sits oddly with the fact that this was precisely the period when heavily PLA-staffed provincial Party committees were being formed. If a struggle for institutional dominance was reaching its climax and, as was clearly the case, Lin was on the defensive, then the make-up of the new committees is difficult to explain. More broadly, if such a struggle were the *leitmotiv* of élite politics throughout 1969–71, then we would expect evidence of a struggle to control the process and, given the large number of military appointees, a key role for Lin and/or his close followers on the bodies responsible for Party building. But while a dominant military role is clear at the provincial and lower levels, this simply was not the case *at the national level*. Overall authority at the top for Party building was vested in the civilian radicals. Mao initially assigned responsibility for the task to Zhang Chunqiao and Yao Wenyuan in September 1967, with fellow-radical Xie Fuzhi also involved. In the period before late 1970, moreover, the main game was the revamping of state organs, the formation of revolutionary committees in the localities, and the rehabilitation of cadres, and here Zhou Enlai – not

---

[54] Kau, *Lin Piao*, pp. 63–4; and mimeo of leadership speeches in 1968–71 available at the Sinological Institute, University of Heidelberg, p. 70.

Lin Biao – played a major role, while top-level PLA input during the staffing of army-dominated revolutionary committees in late 1967 and early 1968 seems to have come from Yang Chengwu.[55] When Party building moved high on the agenda and a seminar on the subject was convened in April 1970, Kang Sheng played a particularly important role and was appointed to a Party rectification leadership group which also included Zhang Chunqiao and Xie Fuzhi. That such an unlikely collection of leaders presided over the appointment of the new Party committees which featured heavy military control, without any sign of conflict with Lin Biao or even his involvement in the process, strongly suggests that the PLA's grip on organizational power at lower levels was not in itself the vital issue of leadership politics.[56]

The politics of military dominance is best understood as arising out of necessity – the need to restore order and provide a backbone for political authority amidst the wreckage of the Cultural Revolution. This basic impulse was further bolstered by the threat of war which peaked in 1969 and remained an important feature of the situation over the next few years. In this process Mao was the driving force first in drawing the army into its political role, and then in sanctioning its new prominence at the Ninth Congress without any apparent hesitation despite emerging concerns over the heavy-handed methods of military cadres.

---

[55] See Thomas W. Robinson, 'Chou En-lai and the Cultural Revolution in China', in idem, *The Cultural Revolution in China* (Berkeley: University of California Press, 1971), pp. 230–8, 272–6; Harding in *CHOC*, vol. 15, p. 192; and above, pp. 91, 95–6. Lin was accused of wanting a large-scale purge of the old apparatus and thus, by implication, of opposing a broad rehabilitation of cadres, but these charges largely came in the form of unspecific and suspicious claims made by Chinese officials to the foreign press in the immediate period after Lin's death; see Bridgham, 'Fall of Lin Piao', p. 429.

[56] Wang Nianyi, *Dadongluan*, pp. 339–41; and *Dangshi yanyiu* (Research on Party History), no. 2 (1985), p. 59. Oral sources, however, point to the significant role of one PLA figure in Party building at the national level – Guo Yufeng, who became the leading figure in the CCP organization department during the Cultural Revolution. Guo, however, had close historical ties to the armies of Nie Rongzhen rather than Lin Biao, and according to oral sources was strictly subordinate to Kang Sheng, not Lin Biao, during the Party rebuilding process.

Perhaps by mid-1970, but more likely after Lushan, he started to worry about entrenched army power preventing the re-establishment of traditional civilian control and the effect which PLA involvement in political affairs was having on military pre-paredness. However, in this he would have had considerable sup-port in the army itself. Indeed, to the extent that evidence exists, this would also seem to have been the attitude of Lin Biao. When carrying out an inspection of Zhangjiakou in the fall of 1969, Lin met with perplexed generals who sought his advice on how to strike a balance between politics and military training. To Lin the answer seemed obvious: 'At present doing a good job of war pre-parations is the greatest politics.'[57] Far from a man on horseback, Lin stood aloof from the process of staffing the emerging Party structure and only seemed able to raise a modicum of interest in national affairs when purely military matters were concerned. The militarization of the new Party committees was carried out by provincial PLA leaders who were simply the only authori-tative local officials available for the job, leaders presumably answerable on this question to a leadership group in Beijing made up of civilian radicals, not Lin Biao and the heads of the central military. More broadly, evidence of a major Party-army struggle for political dominance simply does not exist. Mao's dissatisfac-tion with the local military may still have been a background factor in his estrangement from Lin in the summer of 1970, but it was surely not the central factor in the critical developments at Lushan. Finally, to state the obvious, if there had been intense institutional contention for power, one would expect some sign of significant military support for Lin Biao in September 1971 rather than merely the activities allegedly carried out by a small band of conspirators led by his son.

[57] Zhang Yunsheng, *Maojiawan*, pp. 313–14.

The State Chairmanship and the Lushan Plenum, March–September 1970

The August–September 1970 Lushan plenum is correctly portrayed in both official and Western accounts as the turning-point in Lin Biao's post-1966 career, a meeting where his relationship with Mao decisively worsened over the issues of the state chairmanship and Mao's genius. The interpretations of both Party historians and foreign scholars, however, also attach a political meaning to the events which can be traced directly to Mao's own analysis and which must be seriously questioned. This interpretation claims that an insecure Lin sought to bolster his position as successor by obtaining a new post which would place him above Zhou Enlai in the government structure, and therefore he campaigned for the state chairmanship. Lin was allegedly uncertain of his prospects given that Mao had spoken of Zhang Chunqiao as a possible successor to Lin when enquiring about his colleague's health, and due to a general realisation that Jiang Qing's forces (or those of Zhou Enlai, especially in earlier Western analyses) were growing. Lin's position as number-two required that he first offer the post to Mao on the calculation that the Chairman would decline and it would fall to him. But when Mao not only declined but declared that the position of state chairman should be abolished, Lin persisted with his proposal and the Chairman became uneasy with the perceived disloyalty of his colleague and set in train moves that would lead to Lin's downfall.[58]

In broad terms, though not in several crucial details, the outline of events is clear.[59] The state chairmanship issue arose in the spring of 1970 in a context where Mao, with the new 'construction' phase of the Cultural Revolution unfolding, placed the writing of a new state constitution high on the agenda of the

[58] See Gao Gao and Yan Jiaqi, '*Wenhua dageming*', pp. 346–50; Yu Nan, 'Jiujie erzhong quanhuishang de yichang fengbo' (A disturbance at the Second Plenum of the Ninth Central Committee), *Dang de wenxian*, no. 3 (1992), pp. 83–6; MacFarquhar in *CHOC*, vol. 15, pp. 313–20; and Domes, *China after the Cultural Revolution*, ch. 5. Mao's analysis was given during his August-September 1971 southern trip; see Kau, *Lin Piao*, pp. 59–62.
[59] See MacFarquhar in *CHOC*, vol. 15, pp. 313–20, for a concise overview.

Fourth National People's Congress (NPC) scheduled for later in the year. In early March 1970, Mao presented his opinions on the new state structure which included abolishing the post of state chairman. Mao's views were accepted by the Politburo the next day, but Lin soon raised the issue again in April, leading to another of what the Chairman would claim were six occasions when he declined to serve, although in fact he demurred only five times before Lushan.[60] In July and August the matter was involved in heated clashes in the Politburo between Lin's supporters and several of the civilian radicals. When the Lushan plenum convened, Lin again raised it, somewhat indirectly, at the start of the meeting but now the emphasis of Lin's group had shifted to the issue of Mao's genius. With Chen Boda playing a particularly prominent role, they pressed the latter question in a way that altered the meeting's agenda, and the onslaught was extended for a total of two and a half days in regional group meetings, and in the process the state chairmanship again emerged. At this point Mao intervened, rebuked Lin's associates, and began a major campaign directed against Chen Boda. Mao's attitude toward Lin was more ambiguous, however, and no specific actions were taken against the Defence Minister. According to some Western analyses, Mao's hesitation was perhaps due to uncertainty as to whether he could prevail against Lin's military support.[61]

This account of events is broadly sound but, as a military Party historian commented, the actual story of the state chairmanship matter is quite different from the standard Party history interpretation. The most fundamental issue is whether Lin Biao was actually seeking the post, and much evidence suggests that he was not. Wang Nianyi's careful account simply comments

[60] See Wang Nianyi, *Dadongluan*, pp. 393–4, 396; and Wang Dongxing, 'Yi Jiujie erzhong quanhui' (Recollecting the Second Plenum of the Ninth Central Committee), *Dangdai Zhongguoshi yanjiu* (Research on Contemporary Chinese History), no. 3 (1994), pp. 16–17. For Mao's claim of six occasions, see Kau, *Lin Piao*, pp. 61–2. Confusion is caused by the erroneous listing of an occasion on the eve of the plenum (see below, p. 142), and by the fact that the sixth occasion on 25 August 1970 came at the moment when Mao ended the discussion for good, and thus cannot be regarded as an instance of the Chairman's wishes being ignored despite his claims to this effect.
[61] See MacFarquhar in *CHOC*, vol. 15, pp. 319–20.

that there is no way of knowing whether Lin was interested in the position or aware of Ye Qun's efforts to promote the issue, while one member of Lin's household staff flatly claims that the whole state chairmanship matter was Ye's idea.[62] Several Party historians went further in interviews, stating that in their opinion Lin had no desire for the chairmanship. This was based on the heavy public duties of the job, which were ill-suited to Lin's poor health and reclusive tendencies, in particular its requirement of meeting foreign visitors, a task Lin reportedly hated.[63] There is also Lin's own explicit assertion in April 1970 when proposing that Mao become state chairman that the job of PRC vice chairman – the only one to which he could openly aspire – was not important and that in any case he would not undertake the position.[64] The final consideration is that much of the case concerning Lin's alleged craving for the job comes from comments attributed to Ye Qun by the tainted testimony of Wu Faxian, such as 'If there is no State Chairman, what will become of Lin Biao?' But even if Ye did make this and similar statements, they by no means provide irrefutable proof of Lin's objectives.[65]

---

[62] Wang Nianyi, *Dadongluan*, pp. 394, 396; and Jiao Ye, *Ye Qun zhi mi*, p. 340.

[63] According to Zhang Yunsheng, *Maojiawan*, p. 329, Lin so disliked meeting foreigners that he only received them twice during the four years of Zhang's service. This, however, is an exaggeration as there is photographic evidence from major contemporary PRC newspapers of at least nineteen occasions between May 1967 and September 1970 when Lin received foreigners.

[64] Ye Yonglie, *Chen Boda*, p. 478; and Yu Nan in *Dang de wenxian*, no. 3 (1992), p. 83.

[65] Although a generally reliable oral source claims Ye Qun's remarks were specific examples of what Wu Faxian made up in his efforts to please his interrogators, Mao already claimed in summer 1971 that 'disclosed materials' (perhaps provided by Wu or Wang Dongxing – see below – in the post-plenum investigations) revealed she had made such remarks; see mimeo of leadership speeches in 1968–71 available at the Sinological Institute, University of Heidelberg, p. 71. Another source suggesting Ye did express such sentiments is the account of Mao's doctor, Li Zhisui, *The Private Life of Chairman Mao: The Memoirs of Mao's Personal Physician* (London: Chatto and Windus, 1994), p. 529, which claims Wang Dongxing told him of a similar Ye approach before the Lushan plenum. In any case, even assuming the statements were Ye's, they may have simply reflected her own wish for 'first lady' status quite independent of Lin's wishes.

If Lin did not want to be state chairman, why did he persist in pushing the issue in the face of Mao's repeated statements on the subject? The answer advanced by oral sources sceptical of the official view is that Lin was simply performing the duty of a number-two to promote Mao[66] as well as following his own basic inclination to please the Chairman. Similarly, Chen Boda's involvement in the effort can be seen as the attempt by someone who perceived himself as having lost Mao's confidence to demonstrate 110 per cent loyalty. In this interpretation many people – including, as we shall see, not only Lin Biao's group but also Politburo members, other high-ranking leaders of various stripes and people very close to Mao – may at some point have believed that notwithstanding his statements the Chairman really wanted the position, or at least the honour implied in repeated offers of it. Although we do not think it likely, at least one historian believes that Lin was set up by Mao, who misled him into believing that he (Mao) wanted the post. A more credible view was expressed by another careful historian who concluded that no one could know whether Mao was serious when he disclaimed interest in the position: people therefore had to figure out for themselves how to act accordingly. Or, as yet another senior historian put it, since it was Mao's habit not to speak of his real intentions, Lin Biao (and others) would have taken the view that they could not go wrong by insisting on the Chairman accepting another honour.[67] In this regard, it is useful to recall the behaviour of Zhou Enlai at the time of the Ninth Congress. Zhou not only apparently agreed to Jiang Qing's inclusion in the Politburo despite Mao's explicit comments to the contrary, he

---

[66] Cf. Wang Nianyi, *Dadongluan*, p. 396.

[67] Another possibility separates the issue of whether there should be such a post from the question of who should hold it. In this interpretation Lin would have argued for the state chairmanship both because of Chinese tradition and international practice without trying to force Mao to take on duties he wished to avoid or seeking the ceremonial post for himself. In such circumstances a relatively non-political figure such as Dong Biwu could assume the position, as indeed Mao suggested during the discussions in April 1970 (see below), and as Dong in fact did in an acting capacity following Lin's death.

also used two of the adverbs proscribed by Mao shortly before to acclaim the Chairman's brilliance. This consideration, along with the likelihood that much of the drama was pushed forward by Ye Qun and Lin's involvement was probably limited at best, and that the real clash was between Ye Qun and people from Jiang Qing's group, becomes clearer as we examine the specific events more closely.

In the initial stage of the state chairman issue from March to May 1970 there was only one suggestion of significant conflict despite the different views expressed by Mao and Lin. At the very outset things moved smoothly after Mao's chief security officer and Central Committee General Office head, Wang Dongxing, brought the Chairman's proposals for convening the Fourth NPC and revising the state constitution from Wuhan to Beijing on 8 March, proposals which stipulated that there would be no state chairman. Mao's proposal was immediately accepted, and on the 16th the Politburo provided him with some principles for the NPC session and constitution, which he approved. However, at a four-day central work conference convened the next day, which fleshed out the agreed principles, some dissension emerged. While Lin Biao was probably not at this meeting, it was reportedly marked by sharp debate and a great disparity of views, with the result that Mao again stated his opinion that there should be no state chairman.[68] A few weeks later on 11 April, in what was apparently the only occasion that he personally advanced the specific proposal that the post of state chairman be re-established, Lin telephoned from his residence in Suzhou to Mao's in Changsha, and argued that it was necessary for Mao to serve in this capacity

---

[68] According to Jiang Huaxuan *et al.* (eds), *Zhongguo Gongchandang huiyi gaiyao* (Outline of CCP meetings) (Shenyang: Shenyang chubanshe, 1991), p. 554, Lin chaired this conference, but other accounts of the period including that of Wang Dongxing in *Dangdai Zhongguoshi yanjiu*, no. 3 (1994), p. 16, make no mention of his presence. In addition, Lin was known to be in Suzhou during March and April; see Zhang Yunsheng, *Maojiawan*, p. 375. The account of the discussions here comes from Wang Dongxing, p. 16, and is in some tension with the official claim that 'the great majority' of participants supported Mao's opinions.

to satisfy 'the psychology of the people'. This was also the occasion on which Lin declared that having or not having a vice chairman was not important, and that he himself was not suitable for such duties. Lin's proposal was transmitted at the same time to the Politburo which immediately met and provided majority – or perhaps unanimous[69] – support. As for Mao, Lin's suggestion reportedly drew a laugh from the Chairman and the comment that since he could not do it, why didn't they invite the Party elder Dong Biwu to do the job? However, on the 12th he issued a more formal response declaring the suggestion inappropriate. This fairly inconspicuous rejection seemingly did not stop further discussion of the idea, a development undoubtedly furthered by the fact that sometime after this, Wang Dongxing's office circulated two proposed constitutional drafts, one with and one without a state chairman. In any case, at a Politburo meeting in late April Mao restated his unwillingness to be state chairman again and reiterated his view that the post should be abolished, but in mid-May Lin allegedly asked Wu Faxian and Li Zuopeng, who sat on the constitution drafting group, to insert an article establishing a state chairman. In none of this, however, were there any indications of tension between Mao and Lin.[70]

The situation had changed by the summer. Much remains unclear about these developments, but matters apparently became heated in July–August with Ye Qun playing a prominent role in a conflict with several leading personalities from Diaoyutai. As Wang Nianyi has observed, the 'contradiction of the Lin Biao and Jiang Qing *cliques*' (our emphasis) was an important background cause of these developments, but his account is vague concerning precisely who from the respective 'cliques' was involved or why sharp differences should have broken out at this

---

[69] While written sources uniformly say a majority, a scholar specialising on the matter reports that this meeting chaired by Zhou Enlai unanimously supported Lin's proposal.
[70] Wang Nianyi, *Dadongluan*, pp. 392–4; Yu Nan in *Dang de wenxian*, no. 3 (1992), p. 83; Wang Dongxing in *Dangdai Zhongguoshi yanjiu*, no. 3 (1994), p. 16; Zhang Yunsheng, *Maojiawan*, p. 384; and MacFarquhar in *CHOC*, vol. 15, pp. 313–14.

moment, and he further observed that, given the contradictions between Lin and Ye Qun, it was impossible to know whether Lin was aware of or behind her activities.[71] In any case differences had certainly intensified when 'one day in July', according to Zhang Yunsheng's recollections, Ye Qun returned to Maojiawan from a Politburo meeting in a satisfied mood, telling her secretaries: 'The debate regarding the convening of the Fourth NPC was very exciting! I was on the side of the majority [and] the minority was isolated.' The secretaries could only deduce from the grapevine that the majority included the four generals and Chen Boda, while the minority included Kang Sheng, Zhang Chunqiao and Yao Wenyuan 'backed up by Jiang Qing'; the issue was Mao serving as state chairman.[72] This rendering implies that Jiang Qing may not have been present – which, if true, would be another factor clouding perceptions of Mao's actual wishes. It is also worth speculating on the position of Zhou Enlai, who surely would have chaired such a meeting. Despite the absence of explicit information concerning his role (or perhaps because of this omission), it is a reasonable conclusion that he would have supported the majority. In any case in mid-July, following a report from Zhou that some people on the group to revise the constitution were advocating a state chairman, Mao for the fifth time articulated his view that there should be no such post.[73]

Matters deteriorated further the following month with Ye Qun reportedly telling Wu Faxian on 11 August that Lin Biao still favoured having a state chairman; one could ask whether this was another of Wu's fabrications or if Ye was honestly representing Lin's view. In any case, the state chairmanship issue did not play a role in the clashes over the new state constitution during the following days as Lin's associates focused on issues where Mao's attitude was less explicit. On the 13th, at a meeting

---

[71] Wang Nianyi, *Dadongluan*, pp. 395–6.

[72] Zhang Yunsheng, *Maojiawan*, pp. 384–5.

[73] Wang Nianyi, *Dadongluan*, p. 394; and Wang Dongxing in *Dangdai Zhongguoshi yanjiu*, no. 3 (1994), p. 16.

of the small group to draft the constitution, Wu proposed that the document include a statement that 'Mao Zedong Thought is the guiding principle for all work of the entire country'. This was hardly a startling proposal, but more controversially – in view of the Ninth Congress discussions – he also advocated the incorporation of the three adverbs: 'with genius, creatively and comprehensively'. A quarrel with Zhang Chunqiao and Kang Sheng ensued, and Chen Boda entered the fray on Wu's side. The menace in the confrontation is suggested by Wu's reported remark that 'some people' used Mao's modesty to oppose Mao's Thought. Why the quarrel developed is unclear, and explanations focusing on Zhang's and Kang's awareness of Mao's Ninth Congress position are unconvincing given that Mao's role in the omission of the three adverbs from the Party constitution was widely known. Whatever the cause, the dispute led Ye Qun to rally support by phone, asking Chen Boda and Huang Yongsheng to prepare quotations concerning genius, while Huang phoned Li Zuopeng to have him come and add his backing. At the Politburo meeting the next day Zhang and Kang strangely remained silent and Wu's proposal was passed without a struggle. Nevertheless, even without the direct raising of the state chairmanship matter, a tense atmosphere had been created for the meeting of the Central Committee in Lushan a little over a week later.[74]

There is now a fair amount of detail available on what transpired at Lushan, but with some critical gaps and several contentious assertions.[75] The story begins with a Politburo Standing Committee meeting on the afternoon of the 22nd before the opening of the plenum the next day. Accounts of this meeting diverge sharply. According to the careful Central Party School historian, Yu Nan, Mao, perhaps motivated by some knowledge

[74] Yu Nan in *Dang de wenxian*, no. 3 (1992), pp. 83–4; and Xiao Sike, *Caoji shenpan*, vol. 1, p. 196.
[75] Yu Nan in *Dang de wenxian*, no. 3 (1992), presents the most detailed account by a serious scholar of the meeting, but an account basically endorsing the official interpretation of the Lin Biao affair. Wang Dongxing in *Dangdai Zhongguoshi yanjiu*, no. 3 (1994), offers another detailed account by a key participant which also follows the official view but differs from Yu Nan's on matters of detail. Challenges on key points and general interpretation come from oral sources.

of the 'contradiction between the two cliques', called for a plenum
of unity and victory, not a divisive and failed gathering. Lin Biao
and Chen Boda, however, assertedly again raised the state chairman issue producing Mao's angry retort: 'Whoever wants to be
state chairman can do it but I won't.' Mao then allegedly proceeded to criticize Lin severely on this issue.[76] This version of
events is considered completely unreliable by one of the most
meticulous chroniclers of the period, who asked how could Lin,
who made such a fetish of following Mao, have proceeded as
he did the next afternoon if he had been dressed down in that
way by the Chairman? More concretely, the recollections
of a key participant, Wang Dongxing, place the above remarks
by Mao on the afternoon of 25 August, when he decisively ter-
minated consideration of the issue. In Wang's account the Standing Committee session on the 22nd was quite different, essentially
involving a fairly unexcited discussion of the plenum's agenda.
When Mao did express irritation on this occasion it had nothing
to do with Lin Biao. Instead, he reacted to the emphasis placed
by Zhou Enlai and Kang Sheng on relying on his Thought, arguing that in industry it was necessary to rely on experts and scientists, even foreign experts, as well as on the working class.[77]

When the plenum formally opened on the 23rd, according to
the official version no speech by Lin Biao had been planned.
However, when Mao asked at an informal Standing Committee
gathering just before the opening session who would speak first,
Lin allegedly volunteered suddenly and at the meeting proceeded
to speak for over an hour. In this speech he did not directly raise
the state chairman (*guojia zhuxi*) issue, but alluded to it indirectly
by saying that it was extremely important for the new constitution to emphasise Mao's status as the great leader, supreme
commander and head of state (*guojia yuanshou*), a proposal arguably in accord with Mao's unspoken wishes as it avoided the

[76] Yu Nan in *Dang de wenxian*, no. 3 (1992), p. 84. Yu Nan incorrectly places this
meeting on the evening of the 22nd; in fact, after the Standing Committee meeting
at 2 p.m., an expanded Politburo meeting was convened by Zhou Enlai at 8 p.m.
Wang Dongxing in *Dangdai Zhongguoshi yanjiu*, no. 3 (1994), pp. 10–12.
[77] Wang Dongxing in *Dangdai Zhongguoshi yanjiu*, no. 3 (1994), p. 11.

onerous duties of the specific post of state chairman. Lin also praised Mao's writings and theories, stated that he still insisted Mao was a genius, and indirectly attacked those who did not agree. All of this, as Wang Dongxing noted more than two decades later, was not new and did not address the current situation, but it produced an enthusiastic response from the audience. According to the recollections of some of those who were present, the Chairman was smiling when Lin began but his demeanour changed to a lack of expression and then to some annoyance as Lin continued. Wang Dongxing confirms this, recalling both Mao's impatience and the expressions of anxiety on the faces of Zhou Enlai and Kang Sheng (that is, the two leaders who had received a mild rebuke for *their* excessive praise of Mao the previous day). Thus the orthodox view is that Lin spoke without prior approval of his remarks, and by the time he was finished Mao was displeased.[78]

Ye Qun, however, claimed at the time that Lin's talk had Mao's agreement in advance; Chen Boda said many years later that immediately after Lin's speech Lin told him that Mao had been aware of what he was going to say, and several Party historians believe that Lin had shown Mao an outline beforehand.[79] This view seems credible given not only Lin's personal style but general leadership practice – even though such precautions could never be a guarantee against Mao objecting after the fact.[80] And if Mao had been upset it must not have been widely apparent, for the events of the next two days are difficult to fathom if his discontent had been obvious. The first step in those events came at a Politburo meeting the same evening, when Wu Faxian proposed to alter the conference agenda, which listed the national economic plan and war preparations in addition to the

[78] Wang Dongxing in *Dangdai Zhongguoshi yanjiu*, no. 3 (1994), pp. 12-13; and Yu Nan in *Dang de wenxian*, no. 3 (1992), p. 84. Where there are differences of detail we have relied on Wang's version.

[79] Wang Nianyi, *Dadongluan*, p. 397; Ye Yonglie, *Chen Boda*, p. 486; and oral sources.

[80] The outstanding precedent was Liu Shaoqi's oral remarks at the 1962 7,000 cadres conference, remarks Mao had encouraged Liu to make, then approved in outline form, but found offensive in the event. See Teiwes, 'Mao and his lieutenants', pp. 61-2.

state constitution, and to make listening to a tape-recording of Lin's speech and discussing it the main item, a proposition apparently accepted without opposition. According to Wang Dongxing, everyone echoed Wu's proposal, while Zhou was 'forced' to act according to everybody's opinion. And most crucially, when on the following morning someone suggested printing Lin's speech and Zhou sent Wang to seek Mao's view, the Chairman simply said: 'I have no opinion, so print it.'[81]

The situation, as so often in the Lin Biao story, is further complicated by the role of Ye Qun, who continued to organize forces on the 23rd. After the fact Lin Liguo confided to Zhang Yunsheng that Ye had stoked the fire at Lushan while Lin Biao had not known ahead of time that she would create so much trouble. Her alleged advice to the other members of the 'clique' at this point had a shrewd side to it, however. Ye advised that since it was clear that the state chairmanship proposal would not be accepted,[82] they should shift their emphasis to the three adverbs and the genius question, and to the slogan of Mao's Thought as the guiding principle for the nation. She further instructed that they should avoid naming anyone, that Kang Sheng should not be criticized, and that not even half a word of criticism should be directed at Jiang Qing or there would be trouble. The need was to focus their fire – apparently on Zhang Chunqiao, for if the attack were too broad it would not be approved. It was with this advice suggesting *fairly limited* factional aims that the generals went to the regional group meetings which began on the afternoon and evening of the 24th.[83]

---

[81] Yu Nan in *Dang de wenxian*, no. 3 (1992), p. 84; and Wang Dongxing in *Dangdai Zhongguoshi yanjiu*, no. 3 (1994), p. 13.

[82] Whether this indeed was Ye's perception can be questioned, particularly if the source of the claim was Wu Faxian. In any case, the speed with which the state chairman issue resurfaced at the plenum suggests it was far from a closed issue in the minds of the participants.

[83] Zhang Yunsheng, *Maojiawan*, pp. 397–8; Ye Yonglie, *Chen Boda*, p. 488; and Tan Zhongji, *Shinianhou*, p. 88. Wu Faxian participated in the Southwest meetings, Ye Qun and Li Zuopeng in the Central-South group, and Qiu Huizuo in the Northwest sessions, while Huang Yongsheng did not arrive in Lushan until a week later. These regional group identifications which differ from other accounts are from Wang Dongxing in *Dangdai Zhongguoshi yanjiu*, no. 3 (1994), p. 15.

While Lin Biao's speech was apparently supported in all the regional groups including the East China group (where, significantly, Zhang Chunqiao's Shanghai deputy, Wang Hongwen, joined in the praise),[84] it was in the North China group that the most dramatic developments took place. At the meetings of this group Chen Boda, bolstered by materials he had prepared on the genius question, launched into an excited speech. It was difficult to understand because of his Fujian dialect, but he got across the main point that not only was Mao a genius but there were people who dared to oppose the three adverbs and Mao's Thought as the guiding ideology for the nation. What was particularly significant was the unanimity of the response in support of Chen and the range of people involved. Most crucial was the wholehearted support by Wang Dongxing, 'a comrade who had worked at Mao Zedong's side for a long period' as his chief security officer but who seemingly had developed ties to Maojiawan. This naturally had a profound effect on the participants, undoubtedly leading them to believe that the attack had Mao's blessing. The combined views of Chen and Wang greatly agitated those in attendance, who wanted to know who the people opposing Mao were so that they could be 'chopped into pieces', and Chen hinted that Zhang Chunqiao was such a person. When word spread that it was Zhang who denied Mao's genius, he reportedly was nervous and pale when attacked in the East China group. Back in the North China group one of the old marshals, Chen Yi, who had been tipped off early in the plenum by none other than Wang Dongxing that someone (apparently Zhang Chunqiao) would be criticized at the meeting,[85] pledged support for

---

[84] *RMRB*, 18 May 1978, in *FBIS*, 24 May 1978, p. E11.

[85] Oral source close to Chen Yi. Chen had sought out Wang to enquire whether he should make a self-criticism, but Wang replied 'It's not your turn' and indicated that criticism would be directed elsewhere. This incident suggests links between Wang and Lin Biao's group, perhaps based on the disdain of military men for literary types like Zhang, and significantly that at least in Wang's perception such an attack would not have been uncongenial to Mao. Li Zhisui, *Private Life*, pp. 511, 522, argues that Wang's hatred of Jiang Qing was a major factor in his alignment with Lin's group. Li, p. 519, also emphasises that there was no conflict in Wang's mind between loyalty to Mao and cooperation with Lin Biao.

Mao as state chairman if he changed his mind about taking up the position. Chen Yi also cited historical facts to demonstrate Mao's genius, and suggested that there must be a conspiracy if anyone denied such evidence. During the meeting Chen Boda also interjected that some counterrevolutionaries were overjoyed when hearing that Mao would not be state chairman, a statement which produced indignation among those present. In the passions which followed someone suggested that Mao serve as state chairman and Lin as vice chairman, and the group issued a strongly-worded bulletin demanding such an outcome and warning against swindlers within the Party. About the same time, various Central Committee members and alternates drafted a letter to Mao and Lin expressing support for Mao becoming state chairman, and both documents apparently reached Mao on the morning of 25 August. Whatever the initial intention of Ye Qun, Chen Boda *et al.* – or for that matter Lin Biao – the result of the North China meeting was to place the state chairmanship issue back at the top of the agenda.[86]

Several points concerning the resurfacing of the state chairman question require emphasis. First, the weight of evidence suggests that this was not part of a deliberate effort to obtain the post for Lin Biao. There is nothing to indicate that anyone in Lin's group promoted this objective,[87] and Wang Nianyi flatly states that no one at the plenum proposed that Lin become chairman. The only conflicting evidence is Yu Nan's claim that in some groups 'individuals' said that if Mao was unwilling to be chairman Lin should serve, but even this version does not lay the matter at Lin's door. Another aspect of the issue that emerges clearly from the events is that once the issue was posed in terms of feelings toward the Chairman, virtually all participants at the plenum felt

---

[86] Wang Nianyi, *Dadongluan*, pp. 398–9; Yu Nan in *Dang de wenxian*, no. 3 (1992), pp. 84–5; *Chen Yi zhuan*, pp. 617–18; Wang Dongxing in *Dangdai Zhongguoshi yanjiu*, no. 3 (1994), pp. 14–17; Tan Zhongji, *Shinianhou*, p. 89; and Barnouin and Yu, *Ten Years of Turbulence*, p. 219. According to Yu Nan, p. 84, Ye Qun had instructed the generals to push for the state chairmanship on the morning of the 24th.

[87] In speeches to regional group meetings, however, both Li Zuopeng and Qiu Huizuo sought to link alleged opposition to Mao to opposition to Lin Biao; Wang Dongxing in *Dangdai Zhongguoshi yanjiu*, no. 3 (1994), p. 15.

obliged to express fervent support for his assuming the post. Interestingly, the most extreme advocate at the North China meeting was the scientist Qian Xuesen, with the writer Guo Moruo not far behind. But of greatest importance for our analysis is the attitude of Wang Dongxing, who specifically supported re-establishing the state chairmanship and said that this was not merely his personal opinion but that the Central Committee's General Office and the 8341 guard unit responsible for the central leadership's security fervently hoped Mao would become chairman and Lin vice chairman. That someone so close to Mao, someone who had served him for decades and was acutely aware of the imperative of understanding his wishes, could have taken such a position can only reinforce our view that the Chairman's repeated statements were taken as less than definitive even by those in his immediate circle. Wang's subsequent explanations that he had been overcome by outrage when he heard Chen Boda claim that some people were overjoyed that Mao would not be state chairman, and had totally forgotten Mao's injunctions on the matter in the passion of the moment, only indicate further that he believed Mao to be at the very least receptive to the glorification inherent in raising the state chairmanship.[88]

In the context of the revived state chairinan issue and the attacks on those allegedly denigrating Mao, Jiang Qing went to see the Chairman on the morning of the 25th with Zhang Chunqiao and Yao Wenyuan in tow. As Mao later observed, the whole situation had become extremely tense ('The whole mountain was turned upside down'), and this meeting marked the turn of the tide. It is not known precisely who was in attendance or the full range of matters raised, but apparently Jiang Qing complained of the attacks which had been launched, observing that the situation was terrible and claiming that 'they want to drag people out'. Mao responded by backing Jiang. He convened

---

[88] Wang Nianyi, *Dadongluan*, p. 399; Yu Nan in *Dang de wenxian*, no. 3 (1992), p. 85; Wang Dongxing in *Dangdai Zhongguoshi yanjiu*, no. 3 (1994), pp. 16–17; Li Zhisui, *Private Life*, pp. 519, 529–30; and oral source. For a general insight into the Mao-Wang relationship see Li Zhisui, pp. 9, 49, 126, 184–6 and *passim*.

an expanded Politburo Standing Committee meeting the afternoon of the 25th where he criticised Chen Boda *et al.* for having violated the policy and spirit of the Ninth Congress, suspended the group discussions of Lin's speech, and withdrew from circulation the bulletin of the North China group. On the 26th and 27th, Zhou Enlai and Kang Sheng held talks with Wu Faxian, Li Zuopeng and Qiu Huizuo, pointing out the error of their ways, while Mao himself talked with various people – including Lin Biao.[89] Why Mao acted as he did remains a matter of speculation. Among the possibilities canvassed by Chinese scholars in interviews are his underlying uneasiness at the dominant position of the military; anger with those who violated his call for unity at the outset of the meeting and disrupted an agenda dealing with the critical issues of the national economy and war preparations; the fact that the activities of Ye Qun and associates were the type of organized manoeuvres behind people's backs banned by Party principles; alarm and annoyance that pressure might be put on him to take up a role he had made clear he wanted to avoid; and his closeness to Jiang Qing. In any case, by siding with his wife's group against that associated with his designated heir the Chairman had transformed the leadership equation.

However, none of the explanations offered in Chinese scholarly works or by historians in interviews focuses on what we believe to be the key to Mao's reaction and the larger meaning of Lushan. While the affair probably began as a factional sally launched by Ye Qun against Zhang Chunqiao, at the plenum it quickly became a microcosm of all the passions which had divided the élite since the onset of the Cultural Revolution. A key to understanding this development is the role of Chen Yi, one of the main actors in the 'February adverse current' more than three years earlier. For his passionate advocacy of the line of attack taken by Chen Boda at the North China group meeting

---

[89] Yu Nan in *Dang de wenxian*, no. 3 (1992), p. 85; Wang Dongxing in *Dangdai Zhongguoshi yanjiu*, no. 3 (1994), pp. 17–18; and Wang Nianyi, *Dadongluan*, pp. 402–3. The fourth general, Huang Yongsheng, arrived in Lushan on 31 August after allegedly burning material he had prepared in support of Lin, and visited Mao who advised Huang to study well.

should be seen as more than simply affirming Mao's genius as a tactic for political survival in the Cultural Revolution context. We argue that Chen Yi's fervent support, which was mirrored in large sections of the Central Committee and spread rapidly through them, was precisely due to the fact that Chen Boda's target was the CRG radical Zhang Chunqiao. The larger target was the *Cultural Revolution* itself, a target which could not be attacked directly but which the many veteran leaders, bitter over the developments of the previous several years, could get at through one of the main proponents of the movement. And this would explain the decisiveness of Mao's response in bringing the meeting to a halt before it could get further out of hand and backing Zhang and Jiang Qing, for what he was really defending was *his* Cultural Revolution. Just as during the 'February adverse current' he had regarded an attack on the CRG as virtually an attack on him, he now equated opposition to Zhang Chunqiao with opposition to himself.[90] Significantly, once the Chairman made his position clear, Kang Sheng derisively commented on 'the collaboration of the February adverse current and the August red current' and the 'combined force of the two Chens'. The state chairmanship and related questions aired at the plenum could not have aroused the passions unleashed by the old guard revolutionaries or triggered so sharp a reaction by Mao, but the visionary and destructive Cultural Revolution could.[91]

With Mao having acted, open criticism at the plenum became focused on the hapless Chen Boda. Mao's open letter to the meeting, 'My opinion', was issued on 31 August, and took Chen to task on both theoretical and *ad hominem* grounds, attacking his ideas on genius and claiming that he had sided with Peng Dehuai at the earlier 1959 Lushan meeting. This letter was the first shot in a criticism campaign targeting the 'sham Marxist' which saw Chen immediately stripped of all power and lasted well into 1971.

---

[90] A year later on his southern tour, Mao made precisely this observation; see mimeo of leadership speeches in 1968–71 available at the Sinological Institute, University of Heidelberg, p. 71. Cf. above, p. 76.
[91] *Chen Yi zhuan*, pp. 616–18.

From the next day the regional groups began the study of Mao's letter, and when the plenum adjourned on 6 September the Chairman advised the assembled officials to read more Marxist-Leninist books and emphasized Party unity. In all this not only was Lin Biao's individual problem not mentioned, but Mao's 'Opinion' included the claim that Lin completely agreed with him on the Chen Boda question. Indeed, on 2 September Lin presided over a meeting where participants were required to explain and confess their mistaken statements during the plenum.[92]

Thus for public consumption within the Party, action against Chen was presented as a move where the Chairman and Lin Biao had identical views on Chen's errors. A year later Mao declared that he had protected Lin at Lushan, while at the time Lin Liguo said that the Chairman had come to his father's rescue. According to Mao's version given in the summer of 1971, Lin in their private exchange had excused his actions by saying that he wanted to build the Chairman up, although Mao now dismissively commented that he really wanted to build himself up. A journalistic account of these events purports to provide more detail, portraying Mao as advising Lin to keep some distance from Chen and make clear that they were different. The Chairman further observed that he understood that Lin agreed with Chen concerning genius, but that Lin was a little different from Chen who was an anti-Communist agent. Lin reportedly accepted Mao's criticism and admitted 'lighting a match' with regard to both the genius and the state chairmanship issues, but Mao responded that his case was not that serious.[93] Clearly a great deal of ambiguity remained concerning Lin Biao's political health after this exchange.

[92] Wang Nianyi, *Dadongluan*, pp. 402–5; Yu Nan in *Dang de wenxian*, no. 3 (1992), p. 85; Wang Dongxing in *Dangdai Zhongguoshi yanjiu*, no. 3 (1994), p. 19; and *ZGDSJXCKZL*, vol. 26, p. 476. We believe the version of Mao's 'Opinion' from a Taiwan source in Kau, *Lin Piao*, pp. 67–8, is distorted as it contains assertions we have not found in any of the many PRC versions of the letter.

[93] Wang Nianyi, *Dadongluan*, pp. 403–4; Kau, *Lin Piao*, pp. 61–2; Zhang Yunsheng, *Maojiawan*, p. 398; and Nan Zhi, *Ye Qun yeshi* (Informal History of Ye Qun) (Liaoning: Shenyang chubanshe, 1988), pp. 106–7.

This ambiguity was strikingly revealed in an event which took place shortly before the plenum adjourned. On the evening of 5 September, Ye Qun called on Jiang Qing to smooth over the tensions of the past two weeks. Jiang accepted Ye's apologies for the events of the plenum but herself toned down their importance by portraying them as the result of a squabble among 'intellectuals' (xiucai). The differences between Chen Boda on the one hand and Zhang Chunqiao and Yao Wenyuan on the other were a case of 'literary people [wenren] scorning each other'. Jiang also held Ye's hand and declared her intent to follow Vice Chairman Lin even more closely.[94] This exchange indicated that even the 'victor' of Lushan could not be sure of Lin's standing or of Mao's intent, and under the circumstances she had to respect Lin's current superior status. It also suggests that the conflict at Lushan did indeed originate with the petty squabbles of scholars who detested each other and vied for a place in Mao's sun, an activity which also excited the jealousies of Ye Qun. This struggle for power was arguably of a less elevated sort than that implied by the filling of an office like the chairmanship of the state,[95] but in the heat of the plenum the conflict was quickly transformed into a deeply felt albeit oblique attack on the Cultural Revolution from sources wider than the 'Lin Biao clique'. Ironically, the views presented by Chen Yi and other revolutionary veterans probably mirrored Lin's own very closely, but in all likelihood Lin had been drawn into the most fundamental issue of contemporary Chinese politics by the uncontrolled actions of his wife seeking limited factional gains rather than by any large political strategy of his own making.

[94] Shao Yihai, Lin Biao wangchao heimu (The Inside Story of the Lin Biao Dynasty's Sinister Plot) (Chengdu: Sichuan wenyi chubanshe, 1988), p. 95. Gao Gao and Yan Jiaqi, 'Wenhua dageming', p. 365, place Lin Biao at this meeting, but this is surely an error because someone of Lin's higher status would not come personally even if apologies were required.
[95] Even in this interpretation the question may not have been entirely irrelevant in that Mao had canvassed the idea of Zhang Chunqiao becoming the successor to Lin Biao; see above, pp. 110, 134.

The Downward Spiral, September 1970–September 1971

The official view of the final year of Lin Biao's life claims that with his 'peaceful struggle' to seize power at Lushan unsuccessful, he then moved quickly to a strategy of seizing power by force. The *locus classicus* of this strategy is the comment reportedly made by Lin at Lushan – again according to Wu Faxian – that 'using civilian means doesn't work, using armed force works' (*gaowen de buxing, gaowu de xing*), a comment seriously distorted in official accounts.[96] In this view, after desperate efforts to cover up the conspiracy at Lushan, by early 1971 concrete plans for a coup began under Lin Biao's direct orders, and once Mao indicated his determination to settle matters with Lin in the summer of 1971 his heir authorised the assassination of the Chairman before taking the fatal plane ride on 13 September when that project was thwarted.[97] Western analyses have questioned the authenticity and authorship of so amateurish a plot,[98] but on the whole they have accepted the basic idea of a brutal struggle between Mao and Lin heading inexorably toward a violent showdown, albeit with an emphasis on the reactive and defensive nature of many of Lin's specific actions in response to Mao's increasing pressure.[99] Our aim in this brief section is not to examine all of the major events of the period in any detail, nor to address directly the vexing issues concerning what Lin knew or did not know about any coup or assassination schemes,[100]

---

[96] Rather than issuing a call to arms, we believe Lin was commenting on how his uneducated PLA supporters, although good at war, had been outmanoeuvred at the plenum by their more literate opponents. See Ye Yonglie, *Chen Boda*, p. 495; Tan Zhongji, *Shinianhou*, p. 91; and Xiao Sike, *Caoji shenpan*, vol. 1, pp. 195–6.

[97] E.g., Gao Gao and Yan Jiaqi, '*Wenhua dageming*', pp. 351–95.

[98] See Domes, *China after the Cultural Revolution*, pp. 131–2; and van Ginneken, *Rise and Fall*, pp. 270–4.

[99] See MacFarquhar in *CHOC*, vol. 15, pp. 323–34.

[100] While we accept that Lin's prior knowledge of these matters cannot be disproved, we are impressed with the paucity of direct evidence linking Lin to the alleged coup and assassination plans and share the doubts of various oral sources concerning his involvement. It is our best estimate that Lin would have become aware of Lin Liguo's plans, to the extent any existed, only in the days or hours before fleeing. His main responsibility, we believe, was that his inattention to his household allowed any such matters to develop.

but instead to challenge the accepted view in two crucial ways while refining the correct insight that Lin's position was largely determined by Mao's actions. The first feature of our alternative view is to emphasise the ambiguity of Lin's situation for most of the year in question, and the second is that in crucial ways his posture appears more passive than reactive.

A brief outline of events is necessary, however. At the close of the Lushan plenum Lin and his followers were required to engage in self-criticism and, in the official version, reportedly agreed on a strategy of false confessions in order to restore Wu Faxian's position and protect Lin Biao and Huang Yongsheng. In any case, the resultant written self-criticisms, when they reached Mao in October, failed to satisfy him and at the turn of the year a North China conference and a MAC seminar lasting from January to April again did not produce self-criticisms which satisfied the Chairman. Meanwhile, the public campaign against the anonymous 'sham Marxist' Chen Boda gradually built up from November 1970 to April 1971 and beyond. In November 1970, moreover, a central organization and propaganda group was established under the Politburo with Kang Sheng as head, but other residents of Diaoyutai, notably Jiang Qing and Zhang Chunqiao, were the key figures in this new organ. Thus for the first time since the Ninth Congress the other 'clique' now had an operational body at its command. In the following six months organizational changes also took place in the military, first with Politburo alternate Ji Dengkui and General Zhang Caiqian and then, more significantly, Politburo member Li Xiannian added to the MAC Office by April 1971, thus diluting the power of Lin's group. Earlier, the December–January North China conference convened by Zhou Enlai to criticise Chen Boda removed the hapless leaders of the Beijing Military Region, Li Xuefeng and Zheng Weishan, who had been tarred by their involvement in the North China group meeting at Lushan. Then at the end of April during a meeting to discuss the anti-Chen Boda rectification campaign, Zhou Enlai accused the four generals of mistakes in political line and of factionalism. Finally, in August–September Mao toured the south alerting local leaders to his dissatisfaction with Lin Biao and his followers, and indicated his intention to deal with them on his return to Beijing.[101]

The events of the year following Lushan are strangely at odds with what one would expect of an all-out struggle between contending forces. All the main actors, perhaps including the Chairman himself, seemed uncertain of what was in store for Lin Biao. Part of this was simply due to the reform motif. Mao had called for self-criticism and then sat in judgment on what was offered – no one could be sure of what might satisfy him.[102] The uncertainty was increased by the fact that knowledge that Lin was in trouble at all was tightly retained within the highest CCP circles. Not only was there no hint of any problem in the public media, but even fairly high-ranking figures within the Party and army were unaware of any tension between Mao and Lin. A case in point appeared during the criticism of Chen Boda after Lushan when the 38th Army, a unit historically connected to Lin Biao, submitted a report of an incident during the active phase of the Cultural Revolution when the army clashed with the Beijing Military Region which was backed by Chen at the time. In attacking the 'sham Marxist', the leaders of this army were oblivious to the fact that Chen was part of Lin's group at the Lushan plenum.[103]

There were signals to suggest that matters might not be excessively serious. For one thing, notwithstanding the measures to dilute their authority, the four generals remained in their key PLA posts. While some Western scholars interpret this as reflecting the limits of Mao's power, this was not the view of the Lin Biao camp as reflected in Lin Liguo's observation that the Chairman 'need only utter one sentence to remove anyone he chooses'. More broadly, as we have seen, the appointments to

---

[101] See the summary of events in MacFarquhar in *CHOC*, vol. 15, pp. 323–5, 328–9; and Ma Qibin, *Sishinian*, pp. 333ff.

[102] While Wang Dongxing had been severely criticised at Lushan along with Ye Qun and company, he was spared after his self-criticism for reasons which remain unclear. See Wen Feng, *Shentanxia*, pp. 279–80.

[103] Zhang Yunsheng, *Maojiawan*, p. 182; Barnouin and Yu, *Ten Years of Turbulence*, p. 223; and oral source.

the new provincial revolutionary committees were heavily dominated by the army, and while there appears to have been a
disproportionate appointment of Second and Third Field Army
veterans to leading central and regional military posts after
Lushan, Fourth Field Army men were not neglected in new
ministerial assignments. In any case, such ambiguous signs left
actors from various camps in the highest circles uncertain. Even
while allegedly preparing for a coup in March 1971, some conspirators in the group organized by Lin Liguo canvassed the
possibility that Lin Biao might assume power peacefully in five
or six years, and concluded that it was unlikely he would be
toppled in the next three years. Moreover, at this time Zhou
Enlai demonstrated uncertainty concerning Mao's intentions as
he adopted a conciliatory posture towards Qiu Huizuo[104] during the latter's self-criticisms in February–March. And Jiang
Qing, as we have seen, published a photograph of Lin in July
1971, an act which Zhang Chunqiao declared appropriate given
Lin's status, and which had insiders from Maojiawan later
wondering why she went out of her way to promote Lin right
before the '13 September incident'. Finally, there is evidence of
ambivalence in Mao's own mind. While it cannot be known
whether, as one authoritative oral source believes, Mao was not
even thinking of getting rid of Lin after Lushan, according to
the testimony of Jiang Qing as late as 12 September the Chairman was still expressing great forbearance toward his heir.[105]

  If the uncertainty surrounding Lin's position argues against a
no-holds-barred struggle, so does his basic political passivity during the year after the Lushan plenum. Here we set aside any
possible awareness of or directing role in the alleged coup and
assassination plots on Lin's part and focus on *political* activities,
activities which should have been intense if a major conflict were

---

[104] Even after Lin's demise Zhou demonstrated a similar posture towards Qiu on the
eve of his arrest in late September 1971; Xiao Sike, *Caoji shenpan*, vol. 1, p. 288.
[105] Kau, *Lin Piao* p. 92; Xiao Sike, *Caoji shenpan*, vol. 1, p. 287; Domes, *China after
the Cultural Revolution*, pp. 99, 101–2; Zhang Yunsheng, *Maojiawan*, pp. 385–9; Gao
Gao and Yan Jiaqi, '*Wenhua dageming*', p. 379; *RMRB*, 18 May 1978, in *FBIS*, 24
May 1978, p. E6; and oral source.

unfolding. In fact, there is hardly any evidence of political activity by Lin in this period; indeed he reportedly 'refused to report
for work' on the pretext of ill-health.[106] While making a
retreat by taking sick leave in politically difficult situations was
nothing new for top CCP leaders,[107] it was not something
which fitted well either the role of successor or the expected
response of someone fighting for his political life. Beyond the
purely political, the absence of any role by the four generals in
any coup plans, whatever the actual roles of Lin Biao, Ye Qun
and Lin Liguo, also points to less than concerted action organised
on a broad front by a leader struggling for survival. Finally,
while somewhat contentious, the available evidence indicates, in
the last days of early September 1971, a remarkably uninvolved
Lin who seemingly had to be roused from sleep and told that
it was time to flee.[108] As one careful scholar of the Lin Biao
affair put it in an interview, at this crucial juncture Lin was
basically in a passive position and being 'led by the nose'.

Two incidents in the post-Lushan period, moreover, suggest
an individual resigned to his fate, or at least someone aware that
there was little he could do to affect it.[109] First, when Edgar
Snow visited China in late 1970, Mao initially asked Lin to
receive Snow but he declined. Rather than 'follow Mao' on this
minor request and try to use the meeting to advance his cause,
Lin explained his action to Ye Qun with the curiously personal
observation that since Snow was an old friend from Yan'an days
he would probably raise questions that he (Lin) could not afford
to answer, and indicated that he was unwilling to provide false
answers.[110] An event even more rich in pathos occurred on

[106] Kau, Lin Piao, p. 72.

[107] On the use of sick leave in élite politics, see Teiwes, Politics and Purges, p. lxv.

[108] Lin Doudou claimed that her father was virtually kidnapped by Ye Qun and Lin
Liguo, a view challenged by Zhou Enlai. While probably overstated, her account fits
well with the general picture of frantic last minute activity at Lin's summer residence
in Beidaihe but very little sign of Lin himself. See the report of an interview with
Lin Doudou in Jingbao yuekan, June 1988, p. 20.

[109] There is evidence, however, of efforts to keep tabs on the situation in spring and
summer 1971, but in all likelihood these originated with Ye Qun. See Zhou Ming,
Lishi zai zheli chensi, vol. 2, p. 109.

[110] Guan Weixun, Ye Qun, p. 210.

May Day in 1971. On that evening as the leaders gathered at Tiananmen for the celebrations, Lin Biao was late in appearing – to the consternation of Zhou Enlai who, throughout this period, acted as someone trying to mend fences between the two leading figures of the regime rather than as a potential beneficiary from Lin's distress. Zhou had earlier phoned Maojiawan to persuade Lin to come despite the claim of the Vice Chairman's office that he was not in good health. Notwithstanding Lin's previous practice of arriving at official functions before Mao, the Chairman now arrived to find his deputy missing. Zhou attempted to make excuses for Lin by citing his health, excuses which Mao brushed aside with the comment that Lin was 'always idealistic about his health'. When Lin finally appeared Mao ignored him, and Lin for his part did not look at or greet Mao but simply sat down for a short time before suddenly leaving without excusing himself. Thus the great sycophant, with his career slipping away, demonstrated a certain dignity by refusing to debase himself before the Chairman.[111]

If the meaning of the events of September 1970–September 1971 was unclear to the participants in élite politics and Lin Biao's essential response was to avoid political action, in retrospect what gives shape to the period is the steady build-up of pressure by Mao. While the ostensible rectification goals in one sense clouded what unfolded, in another sense Mao's demand for reform and his dissatisfaction with the repentance offered drove events forward. As early as mid-October 1970 Mao wrote on Wu Faxian's self-examination that there had been 'a plot by a few people to cheat more than 200 Central Committee members, a thing not witnessed in all the days of the Party'. Matters were also escalated by the criticism of Chen Boda as in the unwitting attacks of the 38th Army which caused Mao to reach the ludicrous conclusion that Chen had become the 'overlord' of the Beijing Military Region and the North China

---

[111] Quan Yanchi, *Zhou Enlai*, pp. 365, 370. Another incident soon after the May Day event gives a similar picture. On this occasion Romanian leader Ceauşescu visited China and Mao wanted Lin to receive him, but Lin refused. It was only after Ye Qun's tearful pleas that Lin must think of his family that he reluctantly consented to go; Nan Zhi, *Ye Qun yeshi*, p. 137.

area, and to call for the December–January North China conference to investigate the matter. The Chairman's preoccupation
with the self-criticisms of the 'clique' was strikingly revealed in
June 1971 at the time of Henry Kissinger's visit to Beijing to
arrange for President Nixon's subsequent trip to China. On this
occasion Mao called in Xiong Xianghui, a PLA General Staff
Department official who had been working closely with Zhou
Enlai on the visit. While Xiong expected to be consulted on such
a major departure in Chinese foreign policy, he instead found
Mao wanting to know whether Huang Yongsheng had made
his Lushan errors and self-criticism known within the department. The Chairman showed great concern with Xiong's reply
that Huang and Wu Faxian had claimed that there were no links
between Huang and Chen Boda at Lushan, and observed that their
self-criticisms were fake, the problem was not solved, and they
had 'a backstage boss' – thus implicating Lin for the first time.[112]
However unreasonable Mao's attitude given the secrecy surrounding the case to which he himself had crucially contributed and
which was common practice in cases of top-level conflict,[113] the
exchange with Xiong was seemingly another factor contributing
to the Chairman's determination to bring matters to a head.

   The personnel changes in the military in the early months of
1971, which weakened the position of Lin's group, must also
have added to the sense of building pressure notwithstanding the
speculation that Lin could survive for at least another three years.
By the spring of 1971, moreover, there was an escalation of the
rhetoric against the four generals. Although Zhou Enlai had referred to Huang Yongsheng and Li Zuopeng in comradely terms in
December at the North China conference, at the April meeting
to criticise Chen Boda he accused all the generals *and Ye Qun* of
errors of line in politics and factionalism in organisation.[114] This,

---

[112] Ma Qibin, *Sishinian*, p. 333; Gao Gao and Yan Jiaqi, '*Wenhua dageming*', p. 356;
Kau, *Lin Piao*, p. 63; Barnouin and Yu, *Ten Years of Turbulence*, pp. 223, 226; and
oral source. The claims by Huang and Wu may indeed have been true since Huang
only arrived at Lushan after Chen was under attack; see above, nn. 83, 89.
[113] Cf. developments during the Gao Gang affair; Teiwes, *Politics and Purges*,
pp. lxiii–lxiv.
[114] Wang Nianyi, *Dadongluan*, pp. 411, 415.

as Mao later claimed, may have seemed to those involved as the high-water mark of an affair which was now resolved, but the process of escalating pressure, of tightening the screw turn by turn and pushing Lin into a corner, reached new heights with Mao's southern trip in August–September. The apparent aim of this tour was to let regional leaders know that Lin Biao was no longer trusted, and despite his injunctions that the talks be kept secret, he must have suspected that their contents would get back to Lin's group. In this sense a careful student of the case regards Mao's trip not only as reflecting paranoia on his part but as a deliberate trap, as an attempt to force Lin into some unacceptable act that would justify his disgrace. Mao's comments certainly appear designed to cause alarm for the whole Lin family, with Ye Qun and Lin Liguo as well as Lin Biao receiving the Chairman's barbs. He described the events at Lushan as a 'struggle of two headquarters' and the 'tenth line struggle' in the history of the CCP – thus placing Lin in the same category as Gao Gang, Peng Dehuai and Liu Shaoqi, two of whom had died as a result of events flowing from Mao's disapproval, the third (Peng) remaining incarcerated. Lin was mentioned by name and said to lust after the state chairmanship and to be impatient to seize power, while the bulletin of the North China group supporting Lin's speech at Lushan was dubbed a 'counterrevolutionary' document. And ominously, despite claiming he still wanted to protect Lin and that people should not jump to conclusions, Mao clearly stated that he would pursue matters on returning to Beijing and would seek Lin and company out, going to them if they were unwilling to come to him, and observing that while some could probably be saved others, 'especially the leader', could not.[115]

Mao's remarks must also be seen in the context of another ominous development: by mid-August it was clear that a Central Committee plenum and the long-delayed Fourth NPC session would be convened around the time of the 1 October National Day activities. This must have reinforced the sense of crisis in Lin's inner circle, and perhaps led its members to ponder parallels

[115] Kau, *Lin Piao*, pp. 57–63; *ZGDSJXCKZL*, vol. 26, p. 555; and oral sources.

with the Eleventh Plenum in 1966 when, following expressions of Mao's discontent, Liu Shaoqi was dropped as the successor before suffering an even worse fate. Yet in key circles outside Lin's household there was little sign of any recognition of impending crisis with Li Zuopeng visiting the Summer Palace on 12 September, the same day that Jiang Qing also relaxed there and bragged about gifts she had received from Lin.[116] Lin himself had spent a relaxed summer at Beidaihe, and even in the week before his flight he concerned himself with the marriage plans of his children. But with the pressure building in the days before the 13th, two different responses were advocated by his offspring. His daughter Lin Doudou argued that Lin should simply retire and assume a position without power like that of Zhu De; from what we know of Lin Biao's career such a position would undoubtedly have been congenial to him. Lin Liguo, however, declared such thinking to be completely naive and observed that Lin Biao's poor health could not have withstood even a few days in prison. While it is a moot point whether such dark fears were fully justified, under the tension of the day the option to flee was the one taken.[117]

---

[116] *Zhongguo dabeiju de renwu* (Personalities in China's Great Tragedy) (Beijing: Zhongguo Renmin Daxue chubanshe, 1989), pp. 213–14; Zhou Ming, *Lishi zai zheli chensi*, vol. 2, pp. 226–7; Jin Chunming, '*Wenhua dageming*' *lunxi* (Discussion and Analysis of the 'Cultural Revolution') (Shanghai: Shanghai renmin chubanshe, 1985), p. 179; and Guan Weixun, *Ye Qun*, p. 231. Apart from Li Zuopeng's visit to the Summer Palace and the official admission that there was no evidence of their role in any coup plans, other indications that the four generals had no idea, or were perceived to have no idea, of what was coming were Qiu Huizuo's participation in a routine departmental meeting on the 12th and the presence of Huang Yongsheng at a meeting with Zhou Enlai dealing with the Fourth NPC the same evening, their shock when confronted with evidence of military coup plans, and the fact that they were treated very leniently in the initial period following Lin's demise with Mao, who referred to them as old comrades who should be allowed mistakes, giving the generals ten days to write confessions in comparatively pleasant circumstances. Xiao Sike, *Caoji shenpan*, vol. 1, p. 64; Guan Weixun, *Ye Qun*, p. 234–5; and Wang Dongxing, 'Mao Zhuxi zai fensui Lin Biao fangeming zhengbian yinmoude rizili' (Chairman Mao during the days of smashing the Lin Biao counterrevolutionary coup plot), *Dangdai Zhongguoshi yanjiu*, no. 1 (1994), pp. 34–5.

[117] Guan Weixun, *Ye Qun*, pp. 229–32, 242; *Jingbao yuekan* (see above, n. 108), June 1988, p. 18; MacFarquhar in *CHOC*, vol. 15, p. 331; and oral sources.

5

WESTERN ASSUMPTIONS AND CHINESE REALITIES

With so much taking place behind closed doors at Maojiawan the possibility of greater personal involvement by Lin Biao than is suggested by our account cannot be ruled out in specific events such as the manoeuvres surrounding the state chairman issue or the persecutions of various military leaders. Nevertheless, any such involvement would seem to have been spasmodic at best, and perhaps Lin's greatest sin – and political weakness – was his inability to control his own household. In terms of the broad issues and events confronting him as the regime's number-two leader from 1966 to 1971, Lin's responses can be categorised as follows. Where broad issues of domestic and foreign policy were concerned, e.g. economic strategy or diplomatic initiatives, he was basically passive to the point of being virtually invisible; the attitude was truly one of 'Do whatever the Chairman says'. With regard to dealing with perceived political enemies or people in whom he had lost confidence, Lin apparently used the opportunities presented to push such people aside, though probably on a smaller scale than was generally supposed, and the harsher edges of that process were arguably the doings of Ye Qun, Jiang Qing or Mao himself. As for pushing the Cultural Revolution forward – certainly the prime duty of the successor in 1966–8 – Lin played a significant public role but one which was fundamentally reactive, again responding to Mao's cues. Finally, with regard to curbing the excesses of the movement and particularly protecting the institutional integrity of the army, Lin took guarded initiatives on several key occasions, such as the eight-point directive and the disruptions following the Wuhan incident, to nudge the Chairman in a moderate direction.

The Lin Biao case, however, must be seen in the broader

context of the evolution of élite politics during the Maoist era. It is perhaps best conceptualised as yet another case of politics at Mao's court, but a case where such politics was now taken to unprecedented extremes. Throughout the post-1949 period Politburo leaders recognised the absolute priority of the need to retain Mao's trust, but initially this was still compatible with openly pursuing policy and institutional interests. The purge of Gao Gang in the early 1950s was in some ways similar to the Lin Biao case given the focus on power, Mao's fluctuating attitudes toward his top colleagues, and the hesitancy of these individuals to approach the Chairman on such sensitive issues, but various actors nevertheless tried to protect bureaucratic turf and advance policy preferences.[1] In 1955 Mao demonstrated his ability to override a policy consensus and greatly speed up the process of agricultural cooperativization, but it was an intervention which substantially reflected rational assessments of real policy problems and did not inhibit his Politburo colleagues from taking vigorous policy initiatives – with Mao's assent – when it became necessary in 1956 to cope with dislocations arising from cooperativization and related decisions.[2] By the time the Great Leap Forward was launched in 1957–8, Mao was dragging the entire leadership with him in a tense atmosphere where, according to Party historians, it was impossible to articulate alternative views, but in a context where genuine questions of developmental strategy were at issue, broad-based enthusiasm for the new programme existed within the élite initially, and the whole process was considered 'democratic' given such support.[3] By the early 1960s, after Mao's arbitrary dismissal of Lin's predecessor as Dftence Minister, Peng Dehuai, leaders approached Mao with heightened nervousness, but there was still the expectation that a normal policy process

---

[1] See Teiwes, *Politics at Mao's Court*, especially pp. 58–61.

[2] See the Editors' Introduction in Frederick C. Teiwes and Warren Sun (eds), *The Politics of Agricultural Cooperativization in China: Mao, Deng Zihui, and the 'High Tide' of 1955* (Armonk, NY: M.E. Sharpe, 1993); and Teiwes with Sun, 'Politics of an "un-Maoist" interlude'.

[3] See Teiwes with Sun, 'Politics of an "un-Maoist" interlude', concluding section.

could proceed subject to clearing every major decision with the Chairman.[4]

The Cultural Revolution, however, marked a significant change in the way politics was played at Mao's court. Now there was an extreme concern with slogans and the Mao cult, a game that was *de rigueur* for all actors, not just Lin Biao and the civilian radicals. We need only recall Zhou Enlai's speech at the Ninth Congress to realize just how pervasive this fact of élite life was. Similarly, the opportunities for policy initiatives shrunk. Even Zhou Enlai, who unlike Lin Biao often did exchange ideas with Mao, basically could only operate within the narrow parameters set by the Chairman. In the case of economic policy Zhou presided over the new 'rash advance' of 1970-1, only starting to push for moderation when Mao was prepared to listen in the shocked aftermath of Lin's death and in view of the easing international situation. The submersion of policy concerns by the imperatives of the cult was probably nowhere demonstrated more clearly than at the critical Lushan plenum where an agenda including the national economic plan and war preparations was pushed aside so that the assembled officials could listen to a tape-recording of a paean of praise for the Chairman's genius – a step apparently taken without objection. Finally, the court politics of the Cultural Revolution era was inundated by petty disputes, the 'squabbles of literary people', old resentments of several decades standing, and the overweening ambitions of the wives of the two leading figures. While large ideological themes hung over the scene and the side-effects of these trivial concerns had profound implications for national wellbeing, in essence much of the political activity of the period had all the hallmarks of palace intrigues unrelated to real issues that are so reminiscent of Chinese imperial courts in decline. These features have been present in existing analyses of the Lin Biao affair, but they have been obscured by various distortions and misperceptions.

While the distortions of official histories can easily be explained in terms of the political sensitivity of the case, why has Western

---

[4] See Teiwes, *Politics and Purges*, pp. xxxvii–xxxviii, lvi–lxii, 504.

scholarship got the story so wrong? Part of the problem, not for the first time, has been the dependence of outside analysts on Chinese sources for information, a dependence which creates great vulnerability to the official interpretations behind such information, no matter how much they are adapted to foreign frameworks. Indeed, a problem which is perhaps even more basic is the reliance on such frameworks to sift the available information. Simply put, Westerners think of politics in certain ways which make it difficult to accept Chinese realities. The most basic stumbling-block, whether reflected in adaptations of the official 'two-line struggle' model for the pre-1966 period or in depicting a bitter struggle between Mao and Lin in 1970–1, is the difficulty of acknowledging the absolute authority of a single leader, Mao Zedong. Even within the authoritarian Chinese political tradition Mao's power was exceptional, a power comparable only to that exercized by the most awesome emperors.[5] Coming from cultures where even the most dominant leaders – such as Franklin Roosevelt, Winston Churchill or Charles de Gaulle – face major opposition and sometimes bitter defeat, there is an understandable reluctance to accept such statements as Lin Liguo's observation that a sentence from Mao could overthrow anyone. Yet the evidence of the events examined here, and numerous general observations by Chinese Party historians,[6] demonstrate repeatedly that once Mao spoke the Party obeyed.

Another Western assumption is that politics is about policy, that a great country has a large policy agenda which naturally preoccupies the politicians. This does not mean that the petty hatreds which mark political life everywhere are ignored in Western interpretations, but merely that they are believed to be secondary to the larger issues that must dominate the day. That during the Cultural Revolution fundamental policy issues could

[5] Cf. Peng Dehuai's 1959 comparison of Mao to 'the first emperor of any dynasty in the past [who] was always ruthless and brilliant'; see Teiwes, *Politics and Purges*, p. 323.
[6] In discussions with dozens of Party historians over the past decade a repeated theme concerning a variety of post-1949 events has been the 'impossibility' or 'unreality' of opposition to Mao.

be pushed aside at Lushan, that the management of 'number-one' and Jiang Qing would dominate concern at Maojiawan with the real affairs of state only spasmodically breaking through, is antithetical to the way politics should be played and hard to accept. Thus analysts have looked for policy conflict on the basis of thin evidence when in fact, whatever private views were held and bitter differences suppressed, the only viable option was to implement the line laid down by Mao.[7]

Similarly, Western analysts come from systems where large institutions constrain and often dominate political leaders, and the interests of such institutions are naturally seen as driving political conflict.[8] In examining the 1966–71 period when there were dramatic fluctuations in the fortunes of China's leading institutions, outside observers naturally imagined that a major conflict of interest existed between those most affected – the Party and army – and was central to élite politics. And clearly there were tensions, and on the part of Lin Biao (and many others) a deep commitment to his beloved PLA, but in a context where a leader-initiated movement gripped both institutions, such tensions never developed into direct conflict organized around those structures. In our view, PLA leaders, including Lin Biao, would have welcomed the order to withdraw to the barracks throughout this period, but circumstances kept them involved longer than they wished.

Western scholars also think that political power flows to people with certain skills and capabilities, with a capacity to 'deliver

---

[7] To a certain extent the view expressed here is similar to Lucian W. Pye's emphasis in *The Dynamics of Chinese Politics* (Cambridge, MA: Oelgeschlager, Gunn and Hain, 1981) on the irrelevance of policy issues and the manipulation of symbols to test loyalties as key features of Chinese politics. We differ from Pye in that he treats such phenomena as dominant in all periods of CCP élite politics while we see them especially relevant to the Cultural Revolution, and because his analysis fails to focus on the overarching role of Mao in shaping such behaviour.

[8] This view as applied to China in the 1950s is argued in David Bachman, *Bureaucracy, Economy, and Leadership in China: The Institutional Origins of the Great Leap Forward* (Cambridge University Press, 1991). See also Frederick C. Teiwes, 'Leaders, insitutions, and the origins of the Great Leap Forward'; and Bachman's 'Response to Teiwes' in *Pacific Affairs*, Summer 1993. For the Cultural Revolution period, see especially Garver, *China's Decision for Rapprochement*, pp. 108ff.

the goods'.[9] Such capabilities are naturally relevant in the Chinese case as well, but they have been far less weighty in élite politics than Party status based on contributions to the revolution. Western analyses have noted Lin's ill-health and doubts about his leadership abilities, and this has by and large led to conclusions about Lin's alleged political weakness, e.g. *vis-à-vis* Zhou Enlai, when in fact those real disabilities paled in comparison to Lin's extraordinary prestige as a great general and his new status as the successor. Indeed, the evidence shows the multi-talented and tireless Zhou scrupulously maintaining a subservient posture toward Lin at least up to the Lushan plenum in the summer of 1970.

Finally, Westerners believe that politics is about seeking power and about wanting it badly, although this is at least as prevalent in popular Chinese thinking.[10] Given that politics is an exacting game, someone who has clawed his or her way to the top must be determined and tough. Given this mindset, it is difficult to come to terms with a number-two leader who was content to stay on the sidelines for a decade and was apparently thrust into the successor role against his desires and expectations. It is easier to imagine such an elevated personality plotting for even more power, but in Lin Biao's case the evidence shows someone basically answering Mao's call in a system where Party discipline left no realistic alternative, and subsequently rarely doing much apart from endorsing the Chairman's views and continuing the flow of praise to which the great leader had become accustomed.

Lin Biao was indeed tragically entrapped by his political system and political culture. He had no choice but to become the

[9] See Teiwes, *Leadership*, ch. III, for an analysis which, while not ignoring historical contributions, places too much weight on 'delivering the goods'. See idem, *Politics and Purges*, pp. lxiii–lxiv, for a discussion giving revolutionary status its proper due.

[10] Indeed, the proverbial 'man in the street' in China undoubtedly places even greater emphasis on contention among the country's rulers than Western political scientists with their concern with the processes and constraints of decision-making and policy implementation. Nevertheless, foreign academic writing on Communist systems in particular generally assumes a hard-edged struggle for power.

successor and face limited choices once elevated. Even a mini-malist approach of following Mao in all things could not save Lin when the all-powerful leader suddenly and, as it must have seemed, inexplicably lashed out against proclamations of his genius. Yet Lin certainly contributed to his own downfall through the fatal flaw of his weakness which allowed the petty concerns of his entourage to drag him into an unnecessary con-flict. The larger problem, however, was Mao and the culture of subservience to authority, a culture which was magnified by the fact that Mao was the founder of the regime and that the political élite consisted of leaders who could not separate their historic achievements from loyalty to the leader. In this sense, whatever his faults or indeed crimes, Lin Biao was a victim who could not escape Mao's increasingly unpredictable demands.

Lin Biao's essential tragedy was that he found himself at the centre of a totalistic political system at its most extreme, where pervasive politics allowed no honourable exit, no legitimate pur-suit of personal or institutional interests. All that could be legiti-mately sought was to contribute to Mao's glory, and Lin was in the unenviable position of being chosen to play the leading role in promoting that glory. This transformed a man who dur-ing the revolutionary period demonstrated great energy and skill in winning stunning victories on the battlefield, and who even in the Cultural Revolution occasionally displayed bursts of interest in military affairs.[11] Whether because of ill-health, personal pre-ference or some combination of the two, Lin tried after 1949 to position himself on the fringe of leadership politics. Yet as he was increasingly drawn toward the centre of power from 1959 on, he helped to make the fearsome 'tiger' of CCP politics into an even more formidable (in popular Chinese parlance) 'tiger with wings' (ru hu tian yi) by taking the leading role in building up the Mao cult, even as his own private views departed more starkly from those of the Chairman. During the Cultural

---

[11] During the crisis surounding 'Order Number One' in 1969, Lin's secretaries noted his involvement in defence matters and commented about him 'getting back on the horse'; Wen Feng, *Shentanxia*, p. 237. Cf. above, p. 112.

Revolution itself the public sycophant avoided the cult within the confines of Maojiawan.[12] The real Lin Biao could not simply offer his country the military talents which had made him such a respected figure, or even retreat into a well-earned retirement. Once thrust into a central role at Mao's court he was forced to 'ride the tiger' of the Chairman's designs.

[12] When Guan Weixun came to work at Maojiawan he was struck by the absence of Mao rituals that so marked Chinese life at the time. Ye Qun, however, was something of a Mao devotee who filled her room with Mao badges and other articles of worship, but Lin's room was devoid of such things. Guan, *Ye Qun*, pp. 28, 42–5.

LIN BIAO'S PRE-CULTURAL REVOLUTION CAREER, 1949–1965: A CRITICAL CHRONOLOGY[1]

[Lin Biao was born on 5 December 1907 in Huanggang county, Hubei. In 1925 he became a cadet at the Guomindang's Whampoa Military Academy where Chiang Kai-shek was commandant and Zhou Enlai political commissar during the first period of Nationalist-Communist collaboration. Already a CCP member, he participated in the breakaway military units which formed the Red Army following the 1927 Nanchang Uprising, and soon became a battalion commander in the Fourth Red Army led by Mao Zedong in the Jinggang Mountains on the Hunan-Jiangxi border, thus beginning a long association with Mao. Lin's military achievements were acknowledged with a series of promotions which in 1932 saw him at the age of twenty-six succeed Zhu De as commander of the First Army Corps, and with the establishment of the Chinese Soviet Republic in 1931 he was also named to its highest political body, the Central Executive Committee.

Following further military successes in repulsing the Guomindang's fourth encirclement campaign, when the fifth encirclement campaign forced the Communists out of Jiangxi Lin played a leading role on the epic Long March, again as commander of the First Army Corps. Accounts of the Long March indicate that he had even by this time developed an extraordinarily high military reputation. With the CCP then established in north Shaanxi, Lin was soon named head of the Red Army Academy (later Kangda, the Anti-Japanese Military and Political Academy), but he was again in a command role with the outbreak of the Anti-Japanese War. As leader of the 115th Division,

---

[1] In this chronology, we provide detailed information and critical analysis concerning Lin's known activities before 1966, as well as relevant information concerning military affairs and a number of major developments on the road to the Cultural Revolution. We have not provided sources for more straightforward events such as appointments, appearances on ceremonial occasions etc., which can be located in standard sources, nor for specific instances where Lin was acting in a general way consistent with accepted perceptions of him, e.g. emphasizing politics within the PLA. We have cited sources where Lin's behaviour was at variance with conventional assumptions, where he interacted with other leaders (particularly in conflict situations), and where the sources themselves are difficult or impossible to access.

with Nie Rongzhen as political commissar, Lin won a famous victory over the Japanese at Pingxingguan in northern Shanxi in September 1937. In spring 1938 he was seriously wounded and subsequently resumed the presidency of Kangda. From late 1938 to February 1942 he was in the Soviet Union for medical treatment, and on his return became involved, along with Zhou Enlai, in negotiations with Chiang Kai-shek in Chongqing. For the remainder of the Anti-Japanese War he was involved in military education and training, but did not hold command positions. Nevertheless, his reputation was such that he secured the sixth highest total of votes for the Central Committee at the Seventh Party Congress in 1945. He was not, however, named to the Politburo as his Central Committee votes entitled him, apparently because in the pursuit of Party unity Mao preferred a wider range of members to someone so closely identified with himself.

Lin's active military career resumed in August 1945 when he led Communist forces into the key Northeast region in the effort to gain a foothold before the return of the Guomindang. After an initial organizational phase, Lin's troops began to occupy major Northeast cities following the withdrawal of Soviet forces. With the outbreak of full scale civil war by mid-1946, and in the context of a conflict with Peng Zhen who held the leading position of regional Party secretary (until replaced by Lin at this juncture) and who preferred a more confrontational stance against the Nationalists, Lin evolved a policy of 'Abandoning the towns for the countryside', and his forces concentrated as much on land reform as fighting the Nationalists. By early 1947, however, Lin began his counterattack, and in winter 1947–8 launched an offensive against the increasingly overcommitted Guomindang armies. Further victories followed in 1948, and by the end of the year the entire Northeast was in Communist hands. In the last weeks of the year Lin's armies moved south of the Great Wall and quickly, in combination with Nie Rongzhen's forces, captured Tianjin and Beijing. In March 1949 Lin was appointed commander of the Fourth Field Army, and in April his forces crossed the Yangtze and soon took Wuhan in May and Guangzhou in October. Lin's military achievements in sweeping all before him from the far north to far south of China in less than a year were seen as truly awesome, leaving him arguably the most admired of all CCP military leaders.][2]

---

[2] The above summary draws heavily on Lin's biography in Klein and Clark, *Biographic Dictionary*, 1, 559–64.

1949

1 October
Mao declared the founding of the PRC at a Beijing rally. Lin Biao was one of a number of top leaders who did not participate, presumably because of ongoing military campaigns against the Nationalists. Lin also did not participate in the earlier September meetings which decided the key organizational and personnel issues involved in setting up the new regime. He was in any case named a member of the three key bodies established, the Central People's Government Council, the People's Revolutionary Military Committee (later on 19 October), and the Standing Committee of the Chinese People's Political Consultative Committee.

2 December
Appointed Chairman of the Military and Administrative Committee of Central-South China, one of the five new large administrative regions in the immediate post-1949 period, with Deng Zihui and Ye Jianying as his deputies. Lin Biao had also served since May as first Party secretary and commander of the now renamed Central-South Bureau and Military Region, clearly making him one of the half dozen top regional leaders in this period.

1950

11 April
Presented the 'Report on the work of the Central-South [region]' to the sixth meeting of the centeal People's Government Council.

17–30 April
The Fourth Field Army under Lin Biao's command liberated Hainan Island, the last stronghold of the Guomindang on the mainland.

6–9 June
Unable to participate in the Third Plenum of the Seventh Central Committee because of poor health. Kang Sheng and Zheng Weisan also missed the meeting while on sick leave.

6 October
Figured very prominently in arguing against China's involvement in the Korean War at a MAC standing members' meeting. Lin Biao said: 'Fight, fight. We have been fighting over several decades in the past. . . . People now want peace. It is utterly against the people's will

to engage in more fighting. [Our] nation has just been liberated, the domestic economy is a great mess, the army's equipment is still to be updated. . . . How can we afford more warfare? Besides, we could be pretty confident fighting the Guomindang, yet to fight the modern American [army] equipped with atom bombs [is quite another matter]. Are we [really] capable? In my view the Party Centre should consider the matter carefully and adopt a safe approach.' Lin expressed this view despite the fact that Mao had already disclosed his inclination to intervene in Korea, while the Politburo majority opposed involvement.[3]

About 8 October and thereafter
Arrived in Moscow for medical treatment. On the 10th joined by Zhou Enlai for a secret meeting with Stalin concerning the Korean situation. Both Lin and Zhou argued against sending Chinese troops to Korea, while Stalin was particularly unimpressed with Lin's view that the North Koreans should conduct their own protracted guerrilla warfare. Lin reportedly declined Stalin's toast despite the latter's sarcastic remark that the drink contained no poison, and he embarrassed his Russian hosts and Chinese colleagues by refusing even a token sip, apparently for medical reasons. Zhou Enlai subsequently changed his position on Chinese participation in the Korean War as soon as he received Mao's final decision to confront the Americans.[4]

Mao initially considered appointing Lin Biao rather than Peng Dehuai as commander of Chinese forces in Korea. Lin declined Mao's offer, citing health reasons, but apparently largely due to his belief that it was primarily Stalin's war and hardly in China's national interest. He also believed privately that instead of pursuing the war China should take the opportunity to improve her international standing, including relations with the United States.[5]

When the Korean truce was signed in 1953, Lin reportedly remarked to Liu Yalou: 'The Americans claim they won the war, and we Chinese claim we have defeated the Americans. I'll say this, neither side won, it was Stalin who emerged as the real victor.'[6]

[3] Lei Yingfu *et al.*, *Tongshuabu canmo de zhuihuai* (Recollections of the Headquarters Staff) (Jiangsu: Jiangsu wenyi chubanshe, 1994), pp. 169–70.
[4] Shi Zhe, *Zai lishi juren shenbian – Shi Zhe huiyilu* (At the Side of a Historical Giant – The Memoirs of Shi Zhe) (Beijing: Zhongyang wenxian chubanshe, 1991, pp. 497–500.
[5] Oral source close to Lin Biao.
[6] Idem.

1951

5 November
Promoted to Vice Chairman of the People's Revolutionary Military Committee along with Northeast regional leader Gao Gang.

November
Spoke to the PLA propaganda and cultural work conference, saying: 'The purpose of political education . . . is to promote proletarian class consciousness within our army. . . . To achieve this we must adopt Marxism-Leninism and Mao Zedong Thought to upgrade our theoretical competence.'

1952

January
Recommended Xiao Xiangrong for appointment as director of the MAC General Office (*Junwei bangongting*),[7] a position Xiao retained until November 1965. (Cf. entries for 19 November 1965 and 21 November 1965 and thereafter.)

About August
Again went to the Soviet Union for medical treatment for about two months. During his stay he missed his daughter, Lin Doudou, so much that Su Yu arranged for her to be included in a delegation to Moscow led by Zhou Enlai, thus enabling her to visit her father.[8]

16 November
The SPC established with Gao Gang as Chairman and Deng Zihui Vice Chairman. Lin Biao was appointed one of 15 commission members along with Chen Yun, Deng Xiaoping, Bo Yibo and others.

1953

Spring
Lin Biao's illness worsened and the Party Centre arranged for a female nurse to look after him. This caused great uneasiness on the part of

---

[7] Huang Yao, *Sanci danan busi de Luo Ruiqing Dajiang* (General Luo Ruiqing Survives Three Calamities) (Beijing: Zhonggong dangshi chubanshe, 1994), p. 275.
[8] Oral source close to Lin Biao in the early 1950s.

the shy Lin who demanded that all medical and other staff in his household be male. This practice, in sharp contrast to that adopted by Mao, was maintained for the remainder of Lin's life.[9]

May
Ye Jianying appointed acting Party secretary and acting military commander of the Central-South region, thus indicating that Lin was now officially on sick leave.

August–September
Moved from the Summer Palace to the headquarters of the MAC at Yuquanshan. There he was visted several times by Gao Gang who was lobbying for support in an effort to displace Liu Shaoqi and Zhou Enlai as part of the so-called Gao Gang-Rao Shushi affair. Yet in the same period Zhou also visited Lin, and it is reported that on the last two of Gao's visits Lin declined to receive him by pretending to have gone to bed.[10]

Mid-October
Paid an hour long morning visit to Mao at Zhongnanhai; afterwards Mao showed respect by seeing Lin off at the door. In the afternoon Lin left for Hangzhou where he was soon visited by Gao Gang's wife but by not Gao himself despite claims in some Party histories. Liu Shaoqi, Zhou Enlai and Chen Yun also came to extend their regards to Lin during his stay in Hangzhou.[11]

About 20 December
Mao called in Luo Ruiqing and Tan Zheng and asked them, 'If I retreat to the second front, who should be in charge of the first front? . . . Isn't Gao Gang in favour of Lin Biao? [But let me tell you that Gao] not only wants to overthrow Liu Shaoqi [which means] to overthrow me, he would also overthrow Lin Biao eventually.'[12]

24 December
Mao chaired a Politiburo meeting and exposed, although not by name, Gao Gang's 'plot'. The same evening Gao invited Luo Ruiqing to

---

[9] Idem. On Mao's relations with women on his staff, see Li Zhisui, *Private Life, passim.*

[10] Oral source close to Lin Biao in the early 1950s.

[11] Idem. For official claims see, e.g., Tan Zhongji, *Shinianhou*, p. 61.

[12] Huang Yao, *Luo Ruiqing*, p. 140.

his residence and said that he favoured Lin Biao as Chairman of a new Council of Ministers.

During this period Mao reportedly remarked that '[Gao] proposed that Lin Biao take over the Premiership, [but] in fact he wants the Premiership himself. Lin Biao is in poor health, how would he be able to become the Premier?'[13]

End of December
Mao left Beijing for Hangzhou after the 24 December Politburo meeting, and Lin Biao received him at the Hangzhou railway station. Mao visited Lin the next day, and soon afterwards paid a second call. According to one account, Mao actually celebrated his 60th birthday on 26 December at Lin's temporary residence. Jiang Qing also dropped by at Lin's residence several times, ostensibly to convey Mao's regards.[14]

1954

March and thereafter
Moved to Guangzhou while continuing on sick leave. While staying at Tan Zheng's local residence Lin Biao was frequently visited by Tao Zhu, one of the very few privileged to visit Lin without notice.

Soon afterwards Lin was on the move again, taking his family on sightseeing tours of Guilin and Nanchang before settling briefly in Qingdao for the summer. People serving him closely at the time never observed Lin engaging in discussions on political or military matters in conversations with colleagues during this long sick leave.

Lin returned to his Beijing residence at Maojiawan in the fall.[15]

15-28 September
The First NPC convened in Beijing. Lin attended the Congress only briefly. Apparently in view of his poor health, two small group sessions were held on the 25th and 26th at Lin's residence attended by Peng Dehuai, Deng Xiaoping, He Long, Chen Yi and others. The group unanimously elected Lin Biao group leader, but Lin insisted that

---

[13] Quan Yanchi, 'Peng Dehuai luonan yu Lin Biao deshi zhenxiang' (The Truth about Peng Dehuai's downfall and Lin Biao's ascendancy), *Yanhuang chunqiu* (The Spring and Autumn of the Chinese People), no. 4 (1993), p. 31.
[14] Oral source close to Lin Biao in the early 1950s.
[15] Idem.

Deng be leader.[16] On the 27th Lin appeared at the Congress to cast his ballot for Mao as PRC chairman. By the end of the Congress Lin was elected the second-ranking Vice Premier after Chen Yun, but above Peng Dehuai, the newly appointed Minister of Defence, and Deng Xiaoping.

28 September
Appointed a member of the Party's reconstituted MAC. Peng Dehuai was placed in charge of daily work, with Mao reconfirmed as Chairman and no Vice Chairmen designated.

29 September
Appointed one of fifteen Vice Chairmen of the newly established PRC National Defence Council.

1955

Spring
Moved to Guangzhou again while still on sick leave. In this period Lin reportedly read Peng Zhen's self-criticism during the Party's review of the 1946 Siping campaign in the Northeast concerning which he had clashed with Peng at the time. Clearly unimpressed, Lin commented: 'Is this self-criticism? Can the Party Centre possibly approve this?'[17]

4 April
The Fifth Plenum of the Seventh Central Committee added Lin Biao and Deng Xiaoping to the Politburo. Although notified in advance, Lin did not inform his family of the promotion. When his wife, Ye Qun, became aware of what had happened and went to congratulate Lin, he reportedly remained expressionless.[18]

27 September
Named one of the ten marshals of the PRC, ranked third after Zhu De and Peng Dehuai despite being the youngest of the marshals. Lin Biao was on sick leave at Qingdao and, along with Liu Bocheng, was one of the two marshals to miss the formal ceremony at which Mao awarded the new military ranks. When official reporters were sent to

[16] Idem.
[17] Idem.
[18] Idem.

Qingdao, Lin reportedly showed little enthusiasm for putting on his marshal's uniform and posing for photographs.[19]

Latter half of the year
Sometime in this period Lin Biao received Party documents concerning the development of agricultural cooperativization, and expressed ardent support for Mao's call for a high tide in the movement.[20] This is the only indication of any reaction on Lin's part to the cooperativization issue as he is completely missing from detailed Party history accounts of this key issue.

1956

About this year
In the 'mid-1950s' Mao urged Lin Biao to be 'prepared to shoulder responsibility in the Party's highest leadership core'.[21]

Spring
Lin Doudou asked Ye Qun the ostensibly puzzling question, 'Who ranks higher, Peng Dehuai or father?' Ye replied, 'Your father, of course.' Lin reportedly reprimanded them for both the question and the reply.[22]

15–28 September
The Eighth Party Congress held from 15 to 27 September. Lin Biao returned to Beijing to attend the Congress and was elected a standing member of the Congress Presidium. On the 27th he was re-elected a full member of the Central Committee, receiving the ninth highest total of votes. Apparently due to poor health, Lin only attended the Congress briefly on the opening and election sessions (the 15th and 27th respectively). He was the only top leader who failed to deliver a speech to the Congress.

On the 28th, at the First Plenum of the Eighth Central Committee, Lin was re-elected to the Politburo in the seventh-ranking position just outside the Standing Committee. In this he was now ranked above six previously senior leaders including Peng Zhen and Peng Dehuai.

---

[19] Oral source familiar with the literature on Lin Biao.
[20] Oral source close to Lin Biao in the early 1950s.
[21] Huang Yao, *Luo Ruiqing*, p. 200.
[22] Oral source close to Lin Biao in the early 1950s.

Several official Party histories claim that Mao received one vote less than the total cast for Party Chairman, and that he himself had cast that vote for Lin Biao.[23]

1957

During this year
Peng Dehuai visited Lin Biao and discussed an unknown topic, perhaps the rectification campaign carried out in the PLA during 1957. As recalled by Lin at the 1959 Lushan conference: '[Peng] came to talk to me [and acted] as if he were reading lecture notes, well prepared and talking like a machine-gun. As soon as he finished he was gone. He was so alert, it was hardly like talking to a comrade.'[24]

January
At the meeting of provincial and municipal secretaries Mao remarked, 'A deterioration of political work among military cadres has appeared. How can this be allowed to happen!'[25]

In contrast to attempts in official histories to portray Lin Biao as the person mainly at fault in the attack on military dogmatism in 1958, this indicates that Mao had raised the problem at a much earlier stage.

20 September–9 October
The Third Plenum of the Eighth Central Committee held in Beijing. Mao criticised the cautious economic policies of 'opposing rash advance' for the first time, and set in motion the process leading to the Great Leap Forward. Lin Biao was presumably among the six full members absent from this crucial meeting which saw Mao, Deng Xiaoping, Chen Yun and Zhou Enlai give keynote speeches. In addition, Zhu De, Peng Zhen, Li Fuchun, Li Xiannian, Bo Yibo and Deng Zihui made important speeches.

---

[23] See Gai Jun, *Bolan zhuanghuo de qishinian*, p. 447; and Quan Yanchi, 'Peng Dehuai yu Lin Biao', p. 30. The claims concerning Mao's vote have been contested by several Party historians, however; see above, p. 20, n. 28.
[24] Li Rui, *Lushan shilu*, p. 250.
[25] *Mao Zedong sixiang wansui* (Long Live Mao Zedong Thought) (Beijing: 1967), p. 110.

1958

January–August
Lin Biao was absent from crucial meetings providing political pressure and policy guidelines for the Great Leap, except for the Second Session of the Eighth Congress in May. He definitely missed the January Nanning conference, where Mao raised the question of 'opposing rash advance' to the level of political line and severely criticized Zhou Enlai and Chen Yun, and the March Chengdu conference, and by all available evidence did not attend the August Beidaihe meeting.

21 February
Xiao Ke, who previously served in Lin Biao's Fourth Field Army and had been unhappy with Peng Dehuai's and Tan Zheng's early 1957 criticism of dogmatism which probably echoed Mao's similar criticism, wrote to Peng expressing doubt over Peng's emphasis on 'revolutionizing the army'. This letter was later used by Peng to attack Xiao at the enlarged May–July MAC conference.[26] This is one indication that Peng Dehuai – not Lin Biao – was the key military critic of excessive PLA modernization during this period.

8–26 March
Mao chaired the Chengdu conference where he criticized dogmatism on both the economic and military fronts and cited the need for a personality cult. Although Lin Biao did not attend the conference, he would have been well aware of Mao's emphases given his closeness to Tao Zhu who, along with Ke Qingshi and Wang Renzhong, was particularly prominent in promoting Mao's cult at Chengdu.

Claims in several Party histories that Lin Biao attended the Chengdu conference are clearly inaccurate as we now have a full list of participants,[27] as is the implication that Lin's activities at Chengdu made him the chief culprit in bringing about the May–July MAC conference where Liu Bocheng and Xiao Ke were severely criticized for dogmatism.

---

[26] Cong Jin, *Quzhe fazhan*, pp. 283–4, 289.
[27] Participant lists for this conference and also the January Nanning conference (cf. entry for January–August 1958) are given in 'Unpublished Chinese documents on opposing rash advance and the Great Leap Forward nos 2 and 3', and deposit copies are available at the Menzies Library, Australian National University, and the Fairbank Center Library, Harvard University.

April
After being visited by Peng Dehuai who discussed the Xiao Ke problem, Lin proposed to Mao that criticism of dogmatism be placed on the agenda of the forthcoming MAC conference.[28] Notably, Peng had attended the Chengdu conference, the only military leader apart from Luo Ronghuan to have done so, and subsequently played the leading role in the attack on dogmatism at the MAC gathering.

5–23 May
Attended the Second Session of the Eighth Party Congress in Beijing. On 8 May when Mao praised Qinshihuang during a speech, Lin interrupted to comment that Qinshihuang burned books and buried [460] scholars, to which Mao replied, 'That was nothing compared to our burying of 46,000 scholars.'[29]

25 May
The Fifth Plenum of the Eighth Central Committee promoted Lin Biao to Party Vice Chairman and member of the Politburo Standing Committee.

27 May–22 July
Enlarged MAC conference held. Lin Biao spoke at opening session on the 27th, declaring his support for Peng Dehuai and emphasizing 'the army's unity under Peng's leadership'. On 30 May Peng referred to the Zhukov affair in the Soviet Union as a justification of the need 'to criticize seriously dogmatism'. On 1 June Peng continued to criticize Xiao Ke over his February letter. In speeches on 21, 23 and 29 June Mao emphasized 'getting rid of slavish thought and burying dogmatism [once and for all]'.[30] As a result of these pressures, Marshal Liu Bocheng suffered greatly, Xiao Ke was permanently posted to non-military duties, and Su Yu, who had been particularly close to Lin in the past (cf. entry for about August 1952), was replaced by Huang Kecheng as PLA Chief of Staff.

May
In a speech to a senior military cadres meeting (probably a part of the MAC conference), Lin Biao spoke of walking on two legs, 'one left,

---

[28] Cong Jin, *Quzhe fazhan*, pp. 286–7.
[29] *Mao Zedong sixiang wansui* (Long Live Mao Zedong Thought), vol. covering 1958–9 (no pub. data), p. 58.
[30] Cong Jin, *Quzhe fazhan*, p. 290.

one right – both indispensible'. Lin declared the same applied to the relationship of military training and political work, but apparently to redress the 'pure military viewpoint' he placed primary emphasis on political work: 'The army serves politics, . . . politics is the most fundamental thing; whoever lags behind in politics will lag behind in all other work.'

Interestingly, Lin made no specific reference to 'dogmatism' in this speech. He came closest to the themes of the conference in saying that 'Some people say only foreign things are scientific, this is incorrect'; and '[We] should not whet our appetite only on foreign things while dismissing native things as if they were country bumpkins.'[31]

9 June
Attended Politburo Standing Committee meeting considering the question of Zhou Enlai's proposed resignation following Mao's extensive criticism of Zhou since the Nanning conference for his moderate economic policies in 1956–7. Apart from Standing Committee members, others present were Peng Zhen, Peng Dehuai, He Long, Luo Ronghuan, Chen Yi, Li Xiannian, Chen Boda, Ye Jianying and Huang Kecheng. It is unclear as to who said what at this meeting, but the conclusion was that '[Zhou] should carry on [his] present work, there is no need for change.'[32]

31 July–3 August
Khrushchev visited China. Lin Biao attended banquet to greet Khrushchev at Mao's request.

1959

2 January
Inspected the Red Second Company, an army unit in Guangzhou. Lin had been the first commander of its predecessor in 1927.

---

[31] *Gaoju Mao Zedong sixiang weida hongqi* (Raise High the Great Red Banner of Mao Zedong Thought) (Beijing: April 1967), pp. 130–1.
[32] Li Ping, *Kaiguo Zongli Zhou Enlai* (Founding Premier Zhou Enlai) (Beijing: Zhonggong zhongyang dangxiao chubanshe, 1994), pp. 362–3. See also Shi Zhongquan, *Zhou Enlai de zhuoyue fengxian* (Zhou Enlai's Brilliant Commitment) (Beijing: Zhonggong zhongyang dangxiao chubanshe, 1993), p. 412.

23 July
Arrived at the Lushan conference after being summoned by Mao to lend support for his handling of the Peng Dehuai issue, i.e. Peng's criticism of aspects of the Great Leap Forward in his private letter of 14 July to Mao which was soon distorted into anti-Party activities. Mao greeted Lin with the question, 'How has your health been lately?'[33]

While the most detailed account of the conference by Li Rui makes conflicting claims variously dating Lin's arrival on the 17th and the 29th, these dates are much less credible than the 23rd. The 29th is unlikely since Lin declared on 4 August that he came 'halfway through the conference' which had begun on 2 July, thus ruling out so recent an arrival as the 29th. While this leaves the 17th a possibility, on 16 July in response to Peng Dehuai's letter the Politburo Standing Committee decided to ask Peng Zhen, Huang Kecheng and An Ziwen – but not Lin Biao – to join the conference. Apparently it was only subsequently, as Mao's attitude toward Peng Dehuai hardened, that he decided to call for Lin Biao.[34]

31 July
Lin Biao made his first public appearance at the conference at a Politburo Standing Committee meeting. Before this he reportedly stayed in seclusion, not attending social gatherings where the other marshals participated and declining to receive guests.[35]

Since Standing Committee members Chen Yun and Deng Xiaoping were away on sick leave, the meeting chaired by Mao involved the remaining members (Liu Shaoqi, Zhou Enlai and Zhu De as well as Mao and Lin) and two others, He Long and Peng Zhen. The remaining participants were the targets of criticism. Lin's role was low key, consisting of only a few interjections during Mao's day-long speech. One of these interjections amounted to a mild self-criticism in acknowledging partial responsibility for the heavy losses suffered during the Pingxingguan campaign in 1937.[36]

[33] Quan Yanchi, 'Peng Dehuai yu Lin Biao', p. 31.
[34] See Li Rui, *Luishan shilu*, pp. 246, 285. For Lin's remarks on 4 August, see *ibid.*, p. 278. For the summons of other leaders on 16 July, see Cong Jin, *Quzhe fazhan*, p. 205.
[35] Quan Yanchi, 'Peng Dehuai yu Lin Biao', p. 30.
[36] Li Rui, *Lushan shilu*, p. 223.

1 August
The Standing Committee meeting continued. Zhu De spoke first and offered a mild criticism of Peng Dehuai, much to Mao's displeasure. Mao then reviewed the 31 years of his relationship with Peng which he described as '30 per cent cooperative and 70 per cent uncooperative'. When Mao touched on the Huili meeting in 1935 during the Long March where Peng asked him to relinquish day-to-day control of military operations, Lin Biao interrupted to say it was *his* idea which had nothing to do with Peng, a truly remarkable intervention given the atmosphere of the time. In one account Peng was greatly moved by Lin's action which he felt cleared up decades of misunderstanding between Mao and himself, and apparently after Lin's demise in 1971 Peng refused to join other marshals in 'exposing' Lin's 'crimes'.[37]

Two points in Mao's speech merit comment. First, after describing Peng as 'unsociable and eccentric', he went on to declare that Lin was 'even worse' in these respects. Second, during his long discourse on his own relations with Peng, Mao gave particular attention to the struggle against Xiao Ke and Su Yu at the 1958 enlarged MAC conference as an example of 'very good cooperation' – thus providing yet futher proof that Peng and Mao, not Lin Biao, were the main 'culprits' on that occasion.

Lin was probably the last Standing Committee member to speak at length. While toeing Mao's line in attacking Peng, his speech was in striking contrast to those of others in two regards. First, apart from general character assassination (e.g. labelling Peng as individualistic, arrogant, ambitious and cunning), Lin made no specific allegations such as illicit relations with foreigners – a claim pursued by Xiao Hua and Zhou Enlai in particular. Second, Lin did not criticize other alleged members of Peng's 'anti-Party clique'. In fact, his only reference to Peng's followers was that 'Old Huang [Kecheng] is an honest man.' With regard to Peng himself, Lin seemingly also manifested considerable moderation, as evidenced in his comment immediately following Mao's talk. When Mao declared: 'I think there are two possibilities, you [Peng] may come around or you may not'; Lin said: '[This is] not meant to knock [you] out, to place no more trust in you. The job [of Defence Minister] still needs you to carry it out.'

Finally, Lin observed with regard to himself: 'The Chairman says that there is apathy [as with old men] among our marshals. . . . I have

[37] *Ibid.*, p. 232; and oral source close to Lin Biao.

such a shortcoming. I have such apathy, with no ambition or confidence [in my ability] to create a great situation. . . . Chairman Mao is the only great hero, both you [Peng] and I are miles away [from being a great hero].'[38]

4 August
Together with Liu Shaoqi, Zhou Enlai and Zhu De, Lin Biao briefed participants at the Eighth Plenum of the Eighth Central Committee on the results of the 31 July–1 August Standing Committee meeting. Lin accused Peng of opposing the 'three red flags' (the general line, the Great Leap Forward and the people's communes), as well as opposing Chairman Mao. He maintained that Peng's criticism of the SPC during the conference was actually a criticism of Mao because everyone knew that 'It is Chairman Mao who leads economic construction [at present]'. Zhou Enlai followed a similar logic in claiming that Peng's criticism of Tan Zhenlin concerning agriculture was actually directed at Mao since agriculture was under the Chairman's direct leadership. But despite his harsh criticism, Lin acknowledged Peng's merits by saying: '[Peng] is morally decent and simple in life style, this is his strength.'[39]

11 August
In a long speech to the plenum, Mao decided to convene an enlarged MAC conference to expose further Peng Dehuai, a motion immediately seconded by Zhou Enlai.

16 August
At the concluding session of the plenum Lin Biao remarked that the Lushan conference had avoided a U-shaped disruption of economic development and a Party split. In commenting on these remarks by Lin during his concluding speech, Mao addressed Peng Dehuai as follows: 'For the sake of reassuring you of our confidence I let Lin Biao retire early. . . . You proposed to resign [as Defence Minister] last year, but we decided to allow you to carry on. We supported you in struggling against Xiao Ke [during the enlarged MAC conference].'[40]

This seems to suggest that Peng contemplated resignation in 1958 in the context of his conflict with Xiao and other military leaders

[38] Li Rui, *Lushan shilu*, pp. 249–52, 255.
[39] *Ibid.*, p. 282.
[40] *Ibid.*, p. 349.

including Liu Bocheng and Lin Biao's friend Su Yu. In supporting Peng on that occasion, Lin arguably sought to sustain Peng as Minister of Defence, thus avoiding the role himself.

17 August
A brief Party Centre work conference chaired by Mao appointed Lin Biao Minister of Defence and to the unprecedented position of First Vice Chairman of the MAC, although formal announcement was made one month later. While it has been widely reported that Luo Ronghuan strongly opposed Lin's appointment and advocated He Long for Defence Minister, our source claims that both Luo Ronghuan and Luo Ruiqing expressed disagreement with the arrangement *in accordance with Lin Biao's private request*, indicating that Lin had no interest in the job.[41]

Liu Shaoqi gave the keynote address to the work conference in which he focused on Mao's 'best and most correct leadership', claiming that 'whoever opposes Comrade Mao Zedong's personal cult is completely wrong, it is in fact an act of sabotage against the Party, the cause of the proletariat and the cause of the people'. Thus a new Party consensus on promoting Mao's cult was established as a result of the dismissal of Peng Dehuai. Mao also spoke at the meeting, again citing Lin Biao's remarks about preventing U-shaped development and a Party split.[42]

18 August–12 September
Enlarged MAC conference held in Beijing. On 31 August Lin Biao spoke to a small group session; the full content of his speech is unclear. Nor can we be sure of the exact role Lin played in the second stage of the conference when Mao, Liu Shaoqi, Li Fuchun and Zhou Enlai all spoke with Zhou in particular condemning Peng Dehuai's past. However, two abstracts of Lin's speeches undoubtedly pertain to the conference. First, in an undated 'Speech concerning Peng Dehuai and Zhu X',[43] Lin called for a resolute struggle against Peng to defend the general line and consolidate the Party Centre under Mao's leadership. He added harshly critical remarks directed at Zhu De: 'You, Zhu De, [also] harbour personal ambition, your self-criticism is not good

---

[41] Oral source close to Lin Biao.
[42] Li Rui, *Lushan shilu*, p. 360. For Mao's speech, see the second edition of Li Rui's *Lushan shilu* (Taibei: Xinrui chubanshe, 1994), p. 371.
[43] *Gaoju Mao Zedong sixiang weida hongqi*, pp. 87–8.

enough. . . . Chen Yi's criticism of [Zhu] is hardly excessive. [Zhu] is not impressed with Chairman Mao, he himself wants to be the Chairman. During the Gao Gang affair he also favoured rotating the leadership. . . . Yet is he good enough? . . . At no time have you [Zhu De] been the commander-in-chief. During the Nanchang Uprising [you] lost your way like an anarchist; it was Chen Yi who directed [the Red Army] to the Jinggang Mountains. Before the Zunyi conference Li De [Otto Braun] was the commander, . . . whereas Chairman Mao was the real commander of the liberation war.' Secondly, in a September 1959 'Speech at the senior military cadres conference',[44] Lin advocated the 'theory of shortcuts' whereby 'Learning Mao's works is a shortcut to learning Marxism-Leninism' because Mao had 'advanced Marxism-Leninism in a comprehensive and creative way. . . . Students of geometry do not have to read Euclid, neither do we have to read the original works of Marx and Lenin.' These remarks are often quoted out of context in Party histories; in the same speech Lin gave great weight to Marx and Lenin, e.g. 'Not learning Marxism-Leninism is tantamount to a doctor without knowledge of medicine [and] could only lead to a failed revolution'. In any case, it must be remembered that Lin was addressing generally poorly educated military officers.

On 9 September Liu Shaoqi again focused on the question of Mao's cult: 'Well before the Seventh Congress I promoted Chairman Mao. . . . I shall continue to do so at the present time. And this is not all, I shall also promote the "personal cults" of Comrade Lin Biao and Comrade [Deng] Xiaoping. You may not approve of this, but I'll continue to do so.'[45] Also, at this conference Kang Sheng advocated that Mao Zedong Thought was 'the highest and ultimate criterion'.

26 September
The MAC reorganized with Lin Biao, He Long and Nie Rongzhen as Vice Chairmen. Zhu De was demoted from second to fifth in the Standing Committee, while He and Nie were promoted from sixth and eleventh to third and fourth respectively. Two long standing Lin Biao associates, Luo Ruiqing and Tan Zheng, were added. Lin was put in charge of MAC daily work, while Luo Ruiqing was made secretary-general. Mao as MAC Chairman instructed that 'Lin take charge of

---

[44] *Ibid.*, p. 132.
[45] Cong Jin, *Quzhe fazhan*, pp. 305-6.

the work of the MAC when he is at home, when he is not He [Long] shall be in charge.'[46]

30 September
Red Flag published Lin Biao's article, 'Raise high and march far with the Party's general line and the red flag of Mao Zedong Military Thought', to celebrate the tenth anniversary of the PRC. The article declared the necessity of ideological struggle between socialist and capitalist thinking, and cited Mao's words that 'Politics is the lifeline for our army' to argue that 'Politics in command' was still valid in modernizing the PLA.

1 October
Made National Day speech praising the Great Leap and people's communes and asserting the correctness of the general line.

October
Long time Lin Biao associate Qiu Huizuo appointed head of PLA Logistics Department, replacing Hong Xuezhi. Qiu later became one of the 'four generals' that Party histories claim were key elements of 'the Lin Biao clique'.

December
He Long appointed head of National Defence Industry Commission.

1960

About this year
Mao singled out Lin Biao and Deng Xiaoping as future successors, presumably after the older Liu Shaoqi.[47] In any case, this reflected Mao's long-standing favouritism toward both Lin and Deng.

Early (?) this year
Ye Qun became director of Lin Biao's office, apparently with Mao's blessing.[48]

---

[46] Quan Yanchi, 'Peng Dehuai yu Lin Biao', p. 33.
[47] Interview with Party historian specialising on Lin Biao.
[48] Jiang Bo and Li Qing, *Lin Biao 1959 yihou*, p. 135. Concerning Mao's blessing, see Guan Weixun, *Ye Qun*, p. 223.

188 APPENDIX

1–17 January
Enlarged Politburo meeting held in Shanghai. During the meeting Lin Biao presented a report to the Party Centre concerning national defence which stressed the primary importance of political work in military affairs, and for the first time avocated the 'three eight work style' – i.e. the three sentences of resolute and correct political direction, simple and austere work style, and flexible and mobile tactics and strategies, and the eight characters (in four pairs) referring to unity, intensity, seriousness and liveliness. This was clearly a reformulation of Mao's 1939 ideas as now applied to 'high speed socialist construction'. Lin also reportedly proposed setting up a 600-division-strong militia force.

11–19 January
National militia work conference held in Beijing under auspices of PLA General Staff and General Political Work Departments.

February
Spoke at senior military cadres meeting during enlarged MAC conference held in Guangzhou, 22 January–27 February. Lin elaborated on the idea of the 'three eight work style' and urged the army to recite Mao's most important works.

March–April
PLA political work conference held. GPD head Tan Zheng allegedly failed to heed and convey Lin Biao's instruction on the 'three eight work style' during the conference, which soon drew Lin's rebuke in May: 'Do you understand the [appropriate] relationship between an institution and its Party committee [i.e. Lin himself]?'[49]

April
Wrote inscription for the PLA Political Academy: 'Political and ideological work are the primary factor among all factors measuring the combat ability of our army.'

27 April
Made concluding speech at national conference of delegates from the militia condemning American imperialism and justifying strengthening the militia to complement regular forces in coping with nuclear and missile warfare. The conference was chaired by Luo Ronghuan and attended by Zhu De, He Long, Luo Ruiqing and others.

[49] Cong Jin, *Quzhe fazhan*, p. 310.

21–27 May
PLA representative conference of culture and education enthusiasts held. During the conference Luo Ruiqing and Xiao Hua (Tan Zheng's GPD deputy) enthusiatically emphasized the primacy of the 'three eight work style'.

May–July
Issued various instructions during inspection tours of certain navy, air force and army units in the Jinan Military Region. Lin Biao invariably reiterated the point that 'Man, not weapons, is the decisive factor in military victory', and that 'We must at all times rely on politics, [namely] on the political awareness and enthusiasm of the masses, to do our work well ...'

August
Spoke at a small group session of the eighth work conference of PLA military academies. Lin instructed that the curriculum of military academies should be compressed and simplified with a better focus, citing Lao Tzu's proverb that '*Less* is the key to wisdom, *more* can only lead to bewilderment.'

September
Replying to correspondents from the *PLA Daily*, Lin Biao stated: 'We must strive to grasp the *essence and spirit* of Mao Zedong Thought', and 'empty dogmatism and being bookish is no good for our combat capability.'

12 September
On the eve of an enlarged MAC conference, Lin Biao spoke to the MAC Standing Committee and articulated the 'four firsts' – the human factor, political work, ideological work and living thought. The term 'four firsts' was later coined by Wu Faxian, and the concept soon became famous as a result of Mao's praise. Lin's implicit criticism of the GPD under Tan Zheng set the tone for the conference.

14 September–20 October
Enlarged MAC conference held in Beijing. Apparently unhappy with Tan Zheng's reluctance to toe the line as reflected in his 20 September report on political and ideological work, on the 22nd Lin Biao decided to 'expose the issue thoroughly'. Tan's GPD was soon accused of 'coming very close to being an independent kingdom'. The conference concluded with two resolutions, one on PLA political and ideological

work, and the other on the 'mistakes of Comrade Tan Zheng'. While
the resolution on political and ideological work referred to Mao's 1929
Gutian resolution which stipulated military obedience to the Party, the
main emphasis of the new resolution was on Mao's Thought which,
Lin declared at the meeting, 'represents the peak [of Marxism-
Leninism] in the world today'.

In the struggle against Tan Zheng, a long time associate of Lin Biao,
two other old Lin Biao associates, Luo Ruiqing and Xiao Hua, played
prominent roles. Luo had a great input into the resolutions, first by
proposing to Lin that he emphasise the Gutian resolution, and then
by setting up a separate drafting group. Before submitting what was
initially a single resolution to Lin, Luo carefully vetted and revised the
draft, placing great emphasis on Lin's 'three eight work style'. Lin in
turn submitted the draft to Mao who, clearly delighted, asked his
secretary Tian Jiaying, Luo and Xiao Hua to polish the draft. Mao's
endorsement of Lin's approach was clearly indicated by his own addition, that all military units 'should carry out the resolution and make
annual reports of their progress'. Luo Ruiqing's heavy involvement
was further indicated by Lin's remark some years later: 'In 1960, Luo
and I cooperated very well with each other.'[50]

1 October
Published an essay, 'The victory of the Chinese people's revolutionary
warfare is none other than the victory of Mao Zedong Thought', to
mark the release of Volume IV of Mao's *Selected Works*.

October
*Collection of Marshal Lin Biao's Abridged Speeches on Political and
Ideological Work* edited and published by the GPD.

20 October
Made long speech to concluding session of the enlarged MAC conference. In this speech Lin made several interesting points, some well
known and some seemingly deliberately overlooked by Party histories.
While noting the primacy of matter over mind in dialectical materialism, Lin reminded his audience that this should not be misunderstood
as underestimating the critical force of the mind and coined the
notorious term, 'the spiritual atom bomb'. Also, in discussing the meaning of political and ideological work, Lin stated the most important

---

[50] Huang Yao, *Luo Ruiqing*, pp. 210–12.

aspect was to 'grab and consolidate political power' – a theme he again picked up on the eve of the Cultural Revolution – *and* to develop the productivity of the people – a point usually ignored by Party histories. Lin further stressed the principle of 'Politics takes command', but went on to say that this did not mean sacrificing military training: 'In fact, as far as allocating time is concerned, 60 to 70 to even 80 per cent should be spent on military training. . . . Otherwise it would be empty politics, and we would become a fake army.'

With regard to the ouster of Tan Zheng, Lin's speech was probably one of the most benign statements at the conference. Although critical of the GPD's 'deviation', Lin did not make specific allegations nor name anyone. Only a very careful reader of Lin's speech could sense that Tan was in trouble.[51]

October–December
Issued various instructions on a variety of topics from military journalism to military recreational activities.

3 November
Luo Ronghuan urged Xiao Hua to write a report to the Party Centre arguing that the PLA should play a more positive role in local affairs, particularly in those areas that had been seriously mismanaged during the Great Leap. This met the opposition of Lin Biao who, while acknowledging Luo's good intentions, said: 'This may lead the PLA to indulge in presumptuous intervention in local civilian affairs.' On 15 November Mao agreed with Lin in his comment on Xiao Hua's report: 'Do it according to Comrade Lin Biao's view.'[52]

31 December
Set the agenda for military work in 1961, namely, to create a new army in which every soldier was good at five things – political thought, military technique, work style, performance of duties, and physical fitness; while every company focused on four things – political work and unbookish ideas, good work style, military training, and good life style. Soon afterwards a campaign to create 'five good soldiers' and 'four good companies' was launched throughout the entire army.

---

[51] *Guoju Mao Zedong sixiang weida hongqi*, pp. 145–54.
[52] *Luo Ronghuan zhuan* (Biography of Luo Ronghuan) (Beijing: Dangdai Zhongguo chubanshe, 1991), p. 576.

1961

January

Issued 'Instruction on strengthening political and ideological work in the army' which expressed Lin's distinctive method of studying Mao's works. This method, 'to learn with questions in mind, to learn in an unbookish and practical manner, to combine theory and practice, to give priority according to the need to solve imminent problems, [and] to achieve immediate results', was subsequently reproduced in Lin's 1966 preface to the second edition of *Quotations from Chairman Mao Zedong*. Some Party histories wrongly claim this formulation was advanced by Zhang Chunqiao and reflected an alliance between the 'Lin Biao clique' and 'the Gang of Four'.

January–early February

In Guangzhou during January, Lin Biao instructed the Guangzhou Military Region to 'Tell cadres of various ranks that they should not lightly launch struggle sessions against soldiers. Even where criticism is warranted they should not impose political labels, nor should they openly criticize soldiers by name.'[53]

In the same month and early February, Lin gave further instructions while on inspection tours.

20 January

Tan Zheng deprived of MAC Standing Committee membership and demoted to GPD deputy head following internal rectification during enlarged GPD Party committee meeting held from 25 October 1960 to 25 January 1961. Marshal Luo Ronghuan resumed the GPD directorship, probably on Lin Biao's recommendation.

February

Spoke at meeting of commissioners checking PLA progress and called for debunking myths about theory. Arguing that theory was an ordinary rather than a mythical matter, Lin stated: 'Although it cannot be found in books, whatever has been tested and summarized through practice and experience can be called theory. Thus Chairman Mao is a great theorist.'

21 February

Peng Zhen, who is often depicted as being at the opposite end of the political spectrum from Lin Biao, spoke at a national coal industry

---

[53] *Guoju Mao Zedong sixiang weida hongqi*, p. 156.

telephone conference. Concerning what had to be done to deal with the severe downturn in coal production, Peng argued: 'The first measure is to let politics take command. . . . The core issue at present is to stick to the principle of politics taking command; [when we say] strengthen leadership [we mean] first of all to strengthen political and ideological work.'[54]

March
Issued instructions on PLA management and education work.

April
When inspecting the Beijing Military Region, Lin Biao commented that military training should be like practising traditional martial arts by doing it every day, and that grasping military technique is like playing table tennis. 'There is nothing profound about it, it is a question of practising repeatedly and vigorously.' Lin also instructed the *PLA Daily* to publish Mao's quotations regularly. Beginning 1 May, Mao's words were published topic by topic on the paper's masthead.

30 April
Chaired the 26th meeting of the MAC Standing Committee in Beijing, attended by He Long, Luo Ronghuan, Ye Jianying and Luo Ruiqing with Liu Yalou, Liang Biye and others as observers. Luo Ronghuan disagreed with Lin's method of 'learning [Mao's works] with quotations in mind', and proposed deleting the expression from the document under discussion. Standard Party histories claim that Lin Biao had to agree to the deletion, but he failed to conceal his anger and left the meeting unexpectedly.[55]

May
Spoke at PLA management and education work conference.

June
Reportedly complained to Luo Ruiqing about Luo Ronghuan, saying '[Luo Ronghuan] maintains that the *army* should bombard [i.e. criticize] the localities. Isn't this anti-*Party*?'[56] This was an apparent reference to Luo's 3 November 1960 proposal (see above) growing out of his unhappiness with local leaders' exaggerations of production. Lin's reluctance to intervene in civilian affairs in this instance stands

[54] Ma Qibin, *Sishinian*, p. 196.
[55] Huang Yao, *Luo Ruiqing*, p. 205.
[56] *Ibid.*, p. 203 (emphasis added).

in sharp contrast to claims that he wished to set up a military dictatorship in the 1969–71 period.

12 June
At Party Centre work conference Mao praised Lin Biao's good work in conducting field investigations. This was in the context of Mao's call at the start of the year for high ranking cadres to go to the countryside, declaring 1961 'the year of investigation and research'. Mao now said: 'Lately Comrade Lin Biao went down to combat units to carry out investigation work, once at Guangzhou, once at Yangcun. As a result, he has gained a lot of [firsthand] knowledge, discovered major problems in the building of our army, and come up with several good proposals.'[57]

12 June–15 July
Enlarged MAC conference held. It approved policy of 'Reducing national defence expenditure in order to support local economic construction'.

July
On inspection tour instructed that 'The value of foot soldiers is mainly limited to 200 metres, any greater distance must rely on fire power. Hence we must train [our troops] well with all close-range fighting techniques.'

August–September
Continued inspection tours and gave instructions to a military academy, the Nanjing Military Region and various combat units.

3 November
Gave speech at PLA political and ideological work conference. Lin Biao advocated combining subjective initiative with objective possibilities, noting that simply relying on subjective initiative would result in idealism while ignoring it would lead to mechanical materialism. He went on to argue that investigation and research were not sufficient in themselves, and knowledge obtained in this manner must be subjected to the test of practice – otherwise it could only be called 'half-done knowledge'. Finally, expressing a view similar to those denounced as 'revisionist' during the Cultural Revolution, Lin declared that it would be a big mistake to ignore military training, and its importance had become 'far, far greater than in the past'. Thus 'we must give

[57] *Mao Zedong sixiang wansui* (Beijing: 1967), p. 365.

prominence to military training, the main task for military academies is military training. . . . There is no politics in the abstract sense. . . . Doing military work well is doing political work in the absolute sense. . . . If a scientist merely does political work without doing professional work, can science be successful?'[58]

December
Made new inspection tour and gave instructions on various topics.

18 December
National Defence Industry Office set up with Luo Ruiqing as director. This apparently overlapped somewhat with the National Defence Industry Commission headed by He Long, which eventually was abolished in September 1963.

End of December
Began preparations for January 1962 7,000 cadres conference. Lin Biao initially asked Luo Ruiqing to organise a drafting group to prepare his speech, and Ye Qun proposed including a section on Mao's genius. Luo disagreed and indicated that he had consulted Mao's secretary Tian Jiaying on the matter. Lin reportedly became unhappy and decided to draft his own speech.[59]

1962

During this year
Sometime in 1962 Lin Biao advanced principles concerning high-tech aspects of the national defence industry: '[Producing] two [types of] bombs [i.e. atom bombs and hydrogen bombs] is [our] primary [objective], [producing long-range] missiles is [our] first [priority].'[60] Subsequently in 1964 China successfully detonated its first atom bomb, and in 1967 its first hydrogen bomb. In late 1967 the PLA also shot down a US plane with a missile.

---

[58] *Gaoju Mao Zedong sixiang weida hongqi kuobu qianjin* (Raise High and Advance Far the Great Red Banner of Mao Zedong Thought) (Beijing: 1968), pp. 209–13. This source is the most comprehensive collection to date of Lin Biao's speeches and writings from April 1933 to July 1968.
[59] Huang Yao, *Luo Ruiqing*, p. 206.
[60] *ZGDSRWZ*, v. 49, p. 130.

29 January
Made speech to 7,000 cadres conference at Beijing. Although Mao
would make a rare self-criticism at the conference, Lin Biao took the
lead and strongly defended Mao's infallible leadership and absolute
authority. Although widely cited in Party histories as both excessive
and unique in the context of the conference, other leaders also showed
great respect to Mao in their speeches and Deng Xiaoping, speaking
a few days after Lin, also expressed far reaching praise of the Chairman.
What actually set Lin's speech apart was its comparatively sanguine
picture of the situation facing the Party in the wake of the Great Leap,
arguing that things weren't nearly as bad as they seemed and all that
was needed was a little faith. The speech was received coolly by the
conference participants.[61]

In any case, Mao was extremely impressed with Lin's speech and
took the lead in the applause. He also made several private statements
indicating his appreciation, as in his 29 April 1962 question to Luo
Ruiqing, 'Can you write anything as good as Lin Biao's speech?'[62]

April
Spoke at February–April MAC staff and equipment conference. Lin
stated: 'We have said the political commissar should focus on political
work and the commander on military training. This is quite correct
[but] the military commander must also do a good job with political
work. Otherwise good military training won't be achieved.'

In the same month Lin Biao appointed Li Zuopeng, another of the
'four generals' (cf. entry for October 1959), navy vice commander in
charge of daily affairs to 'assist' Xiao Jingguang following the defection
of a navy officer to Taiwan the previous month.

June
Gave instruction concerning recreational activities in the army.

10 June and thereafter
The Party Centre issued an instruction on preparations for crushing
any Guomindang attempt to take advantage of the grim conditions
in post-Great Leap China and invade the southeastern coastal area. Lin
Biao subsequently became intensely involved in implementing the

---

[61] Printed text provided by Chinese sources of Lin Biao's speech to the 7,000 cadres
conference; and Cong Jin, *Quzhe fazhan*, pp. 406–7, 410–12.
[62] Huang Yao, *Luo Ruiqing*, p. 207.

instruction including the redeployment of strong forces in the Fujian area prior to taking sick leave in the fall.

Fall

After nearly three hectic years of carrying a heavy work load, particularly in view of his fragile health, Lin Biao once again became seriously ill. According to our sources, at this point in time Lin was considering retirement and proposed that He Long succeed him as Defence Minister and take charge of the MAC. These proposals were immediately rejected by the other old marshals. Party histories, in contrast, merely state that Ye Qun reported to the Party Centre requesting sick leave for Lin, saying that 'Commander Lin is in a state of exhaustion after directing the deployment of troops to Fujian. He needs a good rest.' Mao then instructed that He Long take charge of MAC daily work during Lin's sick leave.[63]

24–27 September

The Tenth Plenum of the Eighth Central Committee held in Beijing. Our sources claim that Lin Biao made a self-criticism during the plenum concerning the household contract system in the countryside, saying that Liu Shaoqi was being blamed on the question but he himself had also been wrong. Earlier, probably in early July, Chen Yun had sought Lin's views on household contracting, and Lin praised Chen's wisdom but expressed concern by asking whether Chen could find any justification for the proposal in the Marxist-Leninist classics. When Chen replied in the negative, Lin advised him to seek Mao's understanding.[64]

This account is questionable in that the available evidence indicates Lin Biao, as well as Chen Yun, did not attend the Tenth Plenum. Yet it is plausible that Lin did privately hold the views attributed to him given his long-standing relations with Deng Zihui and Tao Zhu. Deng was the central figure in the controversy and suffered greatly after the plenum with his Central Rural Work Department abolished by Mao. Tao Zhu was also in trouble at the August Party Centre work conference in Beidaihe preceeding the plenum for having advocated 'individual farming'. Thus the above account could be wrong in timing but credible in substance.

On the 24th at Huairentang, while talking about Peng Dehuai, Mao

---

[63] *Ibid.*, p. 209; and oral source close to Lin Biao.
[64] Oral source close to Lin Biao.

remarked favourably on Lin Biao, although not by name: 'Our military line during these [past] few years is clearly very different from that of the previous [disgraceful] years.'[65]

20 October
The Sino-Indian border war broke out. Lin Biao's role in the war is unclear, but it is likely his direct involvement, if any, was minimal given that he was on sick leave, and Liu Bocheng as leader of the MAC strategic small group and Luo Ruiqing were largely responsible for the exercise. However, in commenting during a briefing on the war in February 1963, Mao acknowledged Lin's indirect contribution to the war effort by drawing attention to the role of political work and the 'four firsts'.[66]

1963

2–27 February
PLA political work conference held in Beijing. Lin Biao, although presumably absent from the conference, issued an instruction insisting on the principles of the 'four firsts' and the 'three eight work style'.

March
Following the example of other leaders including Chen Yun and Deng Xiaoping, Lin Biao wrote calligraphy for the 'Learn from Lei Feng' campaign.

7 May
Reportedly conveyed to Luo Ruiqing through his secretary that 'I'm now in poor health. It is difficult for me to consider military problems. . . . Let those on the first front feel free to do their work. Do not worry unduly about my opinion. The [MAC] General Office meetings can decide on general issues; more important issues should be submitted to the [MAC] Standing Committee members. The most important issues must be reported to the Party Centre and the Chairman [in order to seek their wisdom].'[67]

[65] *Mao Zedong sixiang wansui* (Beijing: 1967), p. 413.
[66] Huang Yao, *Luo Ruiqing*, pp. 188–9. For Mao's response, see *Mao Zedong sixiang wansui* (Beijing: 1967), p. 419.
[67] Huang Yao, *Luo Ruiqing*, p. 209.

7-11 May
Mao made a favourable reference to Lin Biao at the Hangzhou conference which considered rural problems.[68]

20 May and thereafter
The Party Centre issued the 'first ten points' on the rural Socialist Education Movement. Lin Biao reportedly wrote Mao expressing his support for the campaign.[69] The exact timing of Lin's letter is unclear, but from late May the PLA began to send groups of cadres to localities participating in the Socialist Education Movement.

June
Moved to Jinan for a rest cure. Sometime in 1963 Lin Biao was also in Changchun for the same reason.[70]

12 December
Mao criticized the Ministry of Culture's performance in the arts saying very little had been achieved in socialist transformation in many departments. He complained that the 'dead' still dominated in many departments, and called for investigation and study in order to handle the problem in earnest.

14 December
Mao wrote to Lin Biao: 'I have received your letter some time ago. I am very delighted [to know] that you are getting better. Spring is not far away. You better take some walks outside [for exercise]. Your views on the two documents [the "first ten points" – see entry for 20 May 1963 – and the September 1963 "second ten points" concerning the Socialist Education Movement] are quite correct. Now both the domestic and international situations are heading for the better on the correct track. It is expected that even greater developments will occur.... P.S. Cao Cao once composed a poem entitled "Long live the wonder turtle" which was about how to stay in good health. It is a very good poem. I suggest you find a copy for your reading which will do your confidence good [for preserving your health].'[71]

---

[68] *Mao Zedong sixiang wansui* (Beijing: 1967), p. 456.
[69] *Mao Zhuxi de jiebanren – Lin Biao Futongshuai* (Chairman Mao's Successor – Deputy Commander Lin Biao) (n.p.: June 1969), p. 53.
[70] Huang Yao, *Luo Ruiqing*, p. 209.
[71] *Mao Zedong sixiang wansui* (Beijing: 1967), pp. 476-7.

16 December
Mao wrote to Lin Biao, He Long, Nie Rongzhen, Luo Ruiqing and Xiao Hua, calling for the industrial sector to learn from the PLA (an idea which seems to have originated with Minister of Metallurgy Wang Heshou), and asking the military leaders to send cadres for stationing in every industrial department.

In his letter Mao expressed special praise of Lin: 'After Comrade Lin Biao's formulation of the "four firsts" and the "three eight work style", PLA military work has made great progress in comparison to the past, both in concrete work and theory. Thus [the PLA] is a worthy model for various industry departments.' Mao also remarked that he would talk to other MAC Standing Committee members and heads of industrial departments concerning learning from the PLA, but 'Lin Biao need not be present in view of his illness.'[72]

1964

January and thereafter
Issued instruction to PLA political work conference held from 23 December 1963 to 14 January 1964: 'Now that the localities are engaged in learning from the army, our army should be all the more modest.'[73]

In the same month Lin Biao gave instructions on running the *PLA Daily*: 'Now we are facing a new situation. The Chairman is calling for the whole country to learn from the PLA. This means we must do even better with our army and that our newspaper must be run even better.'[74] Lin issued several further instructions on the same topic in the following months leading up to the PLA journalism work conference in April.

13 February and thereafter
Liu Yalou and Wu Faxian visited Lin Biao on Chinese New Year. The next day Yang Chengwu visited to extend his greetings, followed

---

[72] Ma Qibin, *Sishinian*, p. 238; and *Xuexi wenxuan* (Collected Study Documents) (Beijing: 1967), v. 3, pp. 345–46. See also *Mao Zhuxi de geming luxian shengli wansui – dangnei liangtiao luxian douzheng dashiji (1921.7–1969.4)* (Long Live the Victory of Chairman Mao's Revolutionary Line – A Chronology of the Two-Line Struggle within the Party, July 1921–April 1969) (Beijing: 1969), p. 318.
[73] *Guoju Mao Zedong sixiang weida hongqi*, p. 177.
[74] *Ibid.*

by Luo Ruiqing on the 15th. Lin praised the work of Liu and Wu highly and urged other PLA units to learn from the air force. Lin also gave instructions on how to overhaul military institutions. Part of his instructions were repeated later in the month in a report to the Party Centre on overhauling institutions, including the injunction to get rid of red tape by 'grasping the two ends', i.e., 'Anything from above must be conveyed below in good time; anything from below must be swiftly reflected to the superior levels'.[75]

1 May
Quotations from Chairman Mao Zedong published by the GPD.

9 May
Following a briefing on the third PLA art festival, Lin Biao made long remarks subsequently issued as 'Instruction on the PLA's literature and art work'. Lin stated that 'There must be two criteria for revolutionary literature and art work. We cannot afford only one criterion. That is to say, we need both a political standard and an aesthetic standard. The two must be chemically combined, not simply lumped together.'[76] The festival concluded the next day with Liu Shaoqi, Zhou Enlai, Zhu De, Deng Xiaoping, He Long, Lu Dingyi, Nie Rongzhen and Luo Ruiqing present at the closing ceremony.

15–16 June
Mao, Liu Shaoqi and other top leaders observed the PLA's military competition exercises, the programme enthusiatically promoted by Ye Jianying, He Long and Luo Ruiqing. Lin Biao stayed in Kunming, probably the only top leader absent from the exercises.

June–July
On two occasions in June and July (the first probably on 16 June when Mao discussed the implementation of military policy), Mao 'severely criticised' Luo Ruiqing for failing to carry out his instruction concerning strengthening the local militia in coastal areas.[77]

27 June
Mao commented on rectification plans for literary and art circles, launching a new and more vehement attack on responsible cultural officials

[75] For the visits of the generals, see Huang Yao, *Luo Ruiqing*, p. 221. For Lin Biao's instruction, see *Gaoju Mao Zedong sixiang weida hongqi*, p. 179.
[76] *Gaoju Mao Zedong sixiang weida hongqi*, p. 183.
[77] *Zhonggong wenhua dageming zhongyao wenjian huibian*, p. 25.

(cf. entry for 12 December 1963). He declared that for the past fifteen years the relevant organizations and most of the people in them 'have not carried out the policies of the Party. They have acted as high and mighty bureaucrats. . . . *In recent years*, they slid right down to the brink of revisionism.'

9 July
Zhou Enlai and Chen Yi visited Lin Biao in Kunming and extended their regards on their way to Burma.[78]

21 September
Appointment of Xiao Hua as GPD head formally announced. Xiao had been functioning as head since shortly after Luo Ronghuan's death in December 1963.

October
Luo Ruiqing visited Lin Biao to discuss staffing questions. On the eve of the Cultural Revolution, on Ye Qun's testimony, it was claimed that Luo made an extraordinary outburst: 'To hell with the sick! Nurse your illness, what's the worry! Make way for the deserving! No more intervention! Do not block my path!'[79] This account is highly dubious given the relative status of the two men and their past relations. It is possible, however, that Luo raised the issue of sick cadres generally, and this was misconstrued by Ye Qun and/or Lin Biao as aiming at Lin.

26 November
Mao made critical remarks concerning the Ministry of Culture: 'All the cultural institutions are not in our hands. . . . I think less than half are in our hands. The whole Ministry of Culture has collapsed. . . . [it would be better] to find a clear-headed military man to take charge [of cultural matters].'[80] (Cf. entries for 12 December 1963, 27 June 1964, and April–May 1965.)

15 December–January 1965
National work conference held in Beijing. During the conference Mao displayed unusual unhappiness with Liu Shaoqi and Deng Xiaoping. He claimed that Deng tried to prevent him from attending the meeting

[78] Huang Yao, *Luo Ruiqing*, p. 230.
[79] *Zhonggong wenhua dageming zhongyao huibian*, p. 30.
[80] Liao Gailong, *Xin Zhongguo*, pp. 242–3.

and Liu would not allow him to speak at the session, both petulant and distorted assertions. Mao also criticised both the Secretariat under Deng and the SPC under Li Fuchun as 'two independent kingdoms in Beijing'. There is no evidence that Lin Biao attended this important conference.[81]

29 December
Received Liu Zhijian, GPD deputy director, and Tang Pingcou, head of *PLA Daily*, who, following a recent investigation tour, together with Ye Qun reported unfavourably on the military competition exercises which had dominated PLA work in 1964. Lin Biao then spelled out his criticism of what he considered excessive military training and demanded that political work predominate in 1965.[82]

1965

4 January
Re-elected Vice Premier, now ranking first ahead of Chen Yun, at end of the Third NPC held in Beijing from 20 December 1964 to 4 January 1965.

9 January
Recieved Luo Ruiqing after enlarged meeting of MAC General Office on 1–3 January. Lin Biao expressed his views on military training in 1964 and priority work for 1965. Perhaps aware of Luo's disagreement with his criticism of the 1964 military competition, Lin softened the criticism while insisting on the priority of political work for 1965.[83]

13 January
Mao warned local leaders of the danger of revisionism.[84]

February
Moved to Shanghai and received Liu Yalou. On the 14th and 15th Liu allegedly complained that Luo Ruiqing had said Lin Biao should play a vital role on the *political* stage, leaving *military* affairs 'to other

---

[81] See Cong Jin, *Quzhe fazhan*, pp. 602–5. ·
[82] Huang Yao, *Luo Ruiqing*, p. 236. See also *Gaoju Mao Zedong sixiang weida hongqi kuobu qianjin*, pp. 230–2.
[83] Huang Yao, *Luo Ruiqing*, p. 245.
[84] Cong Jin, *Quzhe fazhan*, p. 604.

MAC Vice Chairmen' or to Luo himself. Thus Lin 'should no longer intervene in military work'.[85]

22 February
Mao praised Lin Biao's work highly during his reception of navy cadres and *PLA Daily* journalists: 'Who says that we Chinese are not creative and inventive? The "four firsts" is just such a creative and inventive [feat]. In the past we relied on the PLA, [and] we still need to rely on the PLA in the future.'[86]

End of February
Luo Ruiqing came to visit Lin Biao in Shanghai. Lin instructed Luo to see Liu Yalou first, and Liu reportedly conveyed that Lin still placed great trust in Luo and wished their misunderstanding could be quickly resolved so Luo would feel relaxed in his work. According to Luo's late 1970s recollection, the next day during his conversation with Luo, Lin made further efforts to reassure or 'win him over'.[87]

15 March
Ye Jianying published a *PLA Daily* article, 'Raise high the great red flag of Mao Zedong Thought to make military academies very proletarian and combative', which declared the main criterion of military academy work was how well political and ideological work was conducted.

March–July
On three occasions in March, June and July,[88] the *PLA Daily* published editorials citing Lin Biao's instructions on political work. These, however, appear to be the recycling of earlier statements rather than new initiatives by Lin. While he continued on sick leave, Lin's public appearances were reduced to a bare minimum for the remainder of the year.

---

[85] *Ibid.*, p. 633; and Huang Yao, *Luo Ruiqing*, pp. 247, 286–7. Liu Yalou was dead by the time this allegation was raised by Ye Qun, thus creating doubts as to whether the incident was distorted, if not fabricated.

[86] *Xuexi ziliao (1962–1967)* (Study Materials, 1962–1967) (n.p.: n.d.), p. 176. See also Ma Qibin, *Sishinian*, p. 254; and *Mao Zedong sixiang wansui* (Beijing: 1967), p. 200.

[87] Huang Yao, *Luo Ruiqing*, pp. 248–9.

[88] Namely, 18 March, 10 June and 14 July.

April

During his stay in Wuhan, Mao remarked to local leaders including Tan Qilong: 'I simply cannot agree with Lin Biao's view that the military should not criticize local leaders. Why not?'[89]

April–May

On 7 April the Party Centre issued a comment concerning the readjustment of the Ministry of Culture's leadership. This document relieved Vice Ministers Qi Yanming, Xia Yan and Chen Huangmei of their positions, with Minister and noted writer Shen Yanbing (Mao Dun) having already been replaced by Party propaganda chief Lu Dingyi at the start of the year.

In May, as part of carrying out Mao's criticism and rectification of the ministry, a leadership reorganization appointed PLA officer Xiao Wangdong (see entry for 26 November 1964) and Shanghai propaganda official Shi Ximin vice ministers and leaders of the ministry's Party group.

Mid–April

Moved to Suzhou. Lin Biao received Yang Chengwu and discussed the new military uniform to be adopted once the system of military ranks was abolished in May.[90]

22 April

Visited Mao, apparently in Wuchang, to discuss staffing issues in view of the increasing threat of war.[91]

23 April

Wrote to He Long, Nie Rongzhen and Luo Ruiqing on staffing. Lin Biao ordered the strengthening of leadership over MAC daily work by adding Yang Chengwu as a deputy secretary-general, while at the same time appointing Yang Deputy Chief of Staff.[92] This could be interpreted as an effort to weaken Luo's power in view of the difficult Lin-Luo relationship.

2 May

Received Luo Ruiqing and Yang Chengwu. Lin Biao apparently was unhappy with Luo who, together with He Long, bypassed Lin and

[89] Huang Yao, *Luo Ruiqing*, p. 264.
[90] *Ibid.*, p. 251.
[91] *Ibid.*, p. 252.
[92] *Ibid.*

reported directly to Mao on the proceedings of the PLA warfare conference then being held, and he reminded Luo of 'the organizational principle' that he should be kept informed.[93]

9 May
Presided over funeral service for Liu Yalou. Liu Shaoqi, Zhou Enlai, Zhu De, Deng Xiaoping *et al.* attended.

11 May
After the national industry and communications work conference held over the previous months, the Party Centre issued a directive stipulating that all industry and communications departments should learn from the PLA and give first priority to ideological and political work.

19 May
Received participants of PLA warfare conference together with all other top leaders except Mao. During the briefing most Politburo Standing Committee members as well as Luo Ruiqing were critical of a report presented by the warfare department, a report allegedly reflecting Lin Biao's view.

24 May
Wu Faxian, another of the 'four generals' (cf. entry for October 1959), appointed air force commander.

25 May
After reading the bulletin of the warfare conference which foreshadowed Luo Ruiqing's summary speech, Lin Biao immediately instructed that no individual was allowed to dictate the summary which must incorporate the views of the Party Chairman and Politburo Standing Committee as well as those of the majority of participants. Party histories regard this as a slap in Luo's face. The next day Ye Qun arranged a meeting between Lin and Luo to defuse the situation. Earlier Luo had made the mistake of again bypassing Lin concerning 'cadre assessment and rewards'.[94]

29 June
After consulting Mao's secretary Tian Jiaying, Luo Ruiqing deleted Lin Biao's characteristic expression that Mao's works were 'the highest

[93] *Ibid.*
[94] *Ibid.*, pp. 254, 256, 258.

and most living' of all Marxist classics from the proposed preface to the second edition of *Quotations from Chairman Mao Zedong*.[95]

7 July and thereafter

Moved to Dalian after a short stay at the capital of Inner Mongolia in June. Telephone records of 9 and 22 July from Luo Ruiqing's office reveal telling family diplomacy between Luo and Lin Biao. One recorded Ye Qun's thanks for Luo's concern for Lin's health, while the other noted Luo's recent visit to Lin's two children.[96]

1 August

He Long's article, 'The democratic tradition of the PLA', was published in *Guangming Daily* to celebrate Army Day. According to Ye Qun, it was Lin Biao's idea, rather than Luo Ruiqing's as asserted by Party histories, to have this published in He Long's name.[97]

4 August

Luo Ruiqing visited Lin Biao in Dalian, a cordial meeting according to Luo's later recollections. Luo reported to Lin on the progress of certain defence construction work Lin had previously ordered. Luo also reported on the drafting, on Lin's behalf, of the article 'Long live the victory of people's war'.[98]

26 August

Lin Biao's secretary, Guo Liankai, informed Luo Ruiqing that 'Vice Chairman Lin said "I have been pretty sick and am feeling much weaker now, [so I] need some time to recover. Please do not bother to brief me over the next two months".'[99]

2 September

The SPC issued outline of the Third Five-Year Plan, based on Mao's instructions given at Hangzhou emphasizing the guiding principle of preparing for war in the context of the conflict in Indochina, and giving priority to national defence construction including speeding up construction on the 'third front' in the interior.

---

[95] *Ibid.*, p. 261.

[96] *Ibid.*, p. 262.

[97] *He Long zhuan* (Biography of He Long) (Beijing: Dangdai Zhongguo chubanshe, 1993), p. 603.

[98] Huang Yao, *Luo Ruiqing*, p. 263.

[99] *Ibid.*, p. 265.

3 September
People's Daily published under Lin Biao's name the long article 'Long live the victory of people's war – commemorate the 20th anniversary of the victory of the Chinese people's resistance against Japan'. The drafting of the article began in May by a MAC writing group, with the first draft finished on 5 August and submitted to the Party Centre's theoretical writing group under Kang Sheng for revision. Kang apparently was unimpressed with the MAC draft and came up with a new draft. Although the MAC writing group reportedly was was not particularly happy with Kang's version, Luo Ruiqing insisted it was very good while urging the MAC group to keep on working. Eventually both versions were submitted to the Secretariat, with Deng Xiaoping and Peng Zhen preferring Kang's version which was to be supplemented with the good parts of the MAC draft. The final draft was completed on 25 August, and Luo submitted it to members of the Politburo Standing Committee. Zhou Enlai carefully vetted the draft, making suggestions for improvement and stylistic changes to certain passages. When reminded that these passages cited Lin Biao's actual words, Zhou immediately dropped the corrections, saying that 'Since this is his original wording, we should change it back.' Overall, Lin's role in producing this article was minimal while Luo's was central, notwithstanding various Western analyses depicting Luo as having views diametrically opposed to its line of argument.[100]

Early September
Stayed briefly in Beijing on his way to Shanghai. Lin Biao reportedly refused to see Luo Ruiqing in Beijing, and arrived in Shanghai on 13 September.[101]

Early October
Allegedly made critical remarks concerning Luo Ruiqing in private: 'He cooperated well with me in 1960, but since 1961 he started to keep his distance from me and kept me in the dark. By 1965 he was opposing me head to head.'[102]

10 October and thereafter
During the Party Centre work conference held in Beijing from 18 September to 12 October, Mao talked to, among others, regional

[100] *Ibid.*, pp. 263, 270–1.
[101] *Ibid.*, pp. 266, 273.
[102] *Ibid.*, p. 270.

leaders and clearly indicated his dissatisfaction with 'the Party Centre' and his distrust of leaders on the 'first front' by posing the question: 'What will you do if revisionism appears in the Party Centre? . . . Rebel! Do not be afraid of rebelling. . . . [Do not] put blind faith in the Party Centre. . . . Do not carry out [the Party Centre's orders] if they do not [follow] the correct line.'[103]

After the conference Tao Zhu visited Lin Biao in Shanghai. In contrast, Lin kept Luo Ruiqing at arms length, while the following month when Luo met Tao in Guangzhou he could detect Tao's reluctance to discuss serious matters with him.[104]

9 and 12 November
Commented on the Guangzhou Military Region's report on sixty articles concerning 'How to grasp the living thought of Mao Zedong'.

10 November
The Party Centre announced the sacking of Yang Shangkun as head of the Central Committee General Office, and his replacement by Mao's chief bodyguard, Wang Dongxing.

On the same day Yao Wenyuan's article 'Hai Rui dismissed from office', which had been secretly prepared with Mao's blessing and was one of the earliest shots of the Cultural Revolution, was published in Shanghai. Significantly, it took the *PLA Daily* two and a half weeks to reprint the article, and then only after Luo Ruiqing intervened to instruct Liu Zhijian to do so.[105]

18 November
Formulated the 'five principles of giving prominence to politics' on the eve of a PLA political work conference. These included the comparatively non-political stipulations that ranking cadres should conduct investigations at the grassroots, good combat personnel should be promoted to leading posts, and training in close range and night combat should be intensified. The work conference was unexpectedly delayed till 30 December, probably due to the Luo Ruiqing affair.[106]

On the same day Lin Biao relayed to Mao a report from the Lanzhou Military Region concerning the primacy of political work. Lin attached a note stressing the need for further prominence to political work.

---

[103] Ma Qibin, *Sishinian*, p. 260.
[104] Huang Yao, *Luo Ruiqing*, pp. 273, 277.
[105] See Cong Jin, *Quzhe fazhan*, p. 618.
[106] *Gaoju Mao Zedong sixiang weida hongqi*, p. 188.

Party histories, perhaps unduly, have interpreted this as Lin Biao testing the waters for the purge of Luo Ruiqing.[107]

19 November
Despite his longstanding ties with Lin Biao (cf. entry for January 1952), MAC General Office head Xiao Xiangrong came under attack during an enlarged meeting of the MAC General Office Party committee.

21 November and thereafter
Luo Ruiqing spoke up for Xiao Xiangrong at the enlarged meeting of the MAC General Office Party committee. In an apparent negative response, Lin Biao ordered the meeting adjourned for three days before declaring on 25 November the need to 'expose thoroughly [Comrade Xiao Xiangrong] without any misgivings. . . . Otherwise it will lead to serious consequences if we allow those who oppose giving prominence to politics to hold leadership posts.' Xiao was immediately replaced by Yang Chengwu who performed in an acting capacity.[108] When a new MAC Office (*Junwei banshizu*) was set up in September 1967, Yang became its head.

Also about this time in 'late November' Lin was visited by 'a Party Centre comrade' who discussed the Yang Shangkun case (cf. entry for 10 November 1965), an encounter which some believe encouraged Lin to move against Luo.[109]

23 November
Listened to Zhang Aiping's briefing and made comments on how the PLA should carry out the Socialist Education Movement.

26 November
Luo Ruiqing reported to Mao at Shanghai and proposed to visit Lin Biao the next day. Mao nodded and commented, 'Go and tell him to take good care of himself, [and keep] as fit as as he was during the 7,000 cadres conference so that he can [again] make a three-hour speech.' Zhou Enlai was present and clearly impressed with Mao's great expectations of Lin, and also instructed Luo to convey to Lin his (Zhou's) report to Mao.[110]

[107] Huang Yao, *Luo Ruiqing*, pp. 281–2.
[108] *Ibid.*, p. 277.
[109] Interview with Party historian specializing on Lin Biao.
[110] Huang Yao, *Luo Ruiqing*, p. 278.

27 November
Luo Ruiqing visited Lin Biao at Suzhou. Intriguingly, Ye Qun rushed back from the countryside where she had been carrying out the Socialist Education Movement to eavesdrop on the conversation from the next room. According to Luo's daughter, this meeting was cordial and Lin even enquired about Luo's health and offered a prescription for his toothache.[111]

On the same day navy leaders Li Zuopeng, Zhang Xiucuan *et al.* wrote to Lin Biao disclosing Luo's heated exchange with Zhang Xiucuan two days earlier concerning the enlarged conference of the navy's Party committee where Zhang accused Luo of a biased position in favour of other navy leaders, Xiao Jingguang and Su Zhenhua. Presumably after reading the letter from Li *et al.*, Lin instructed his secretary to phone Li requesting a report on the navy's ideological struggle over the previous two years with special reference to the performances of Luo Ruiqing and Xiao Jingguang.[112] Li thus had the report in hand at the December Shanghai conference (see entry for 8–15 December 1965), but he apparently remained silent at that meeting.

30 November
According to standard Party histories, Lin Biao sent Ye Qun, together with his letter and 11 items of materials exposing Luo Ruiqing, to see Mao at Hangzhou. The letter said in part: '[I] feel compelled to report to you an important development. Earlier several ranking leaders had already suggested I report [this] to you, but I failed to do so for fear of affecting your health. Now I am starting to see the relationship [of this] to [the] Yang Shangkun [affair] and feel that I must report to you.' The whole letter, however, contains no direct reference to Luo Ruiqing although the attached materials from various military institutions all implicated Luo. Ye Qun reportedly made a six to seven hour oral report to Mao with no one else, not even Wang Dongxing, present. After the report Mao assertedly instructed Wang Dongxing to escort Ye back to Suzhou as a security precaution.[113]

Other versions of this development claim that it was Mao who summoned Ye, with one variation that Ye had first conveyed Lin's view

---

[111] [Luo] Diandian, *Feifan*, p. 197.
[112] *Lishi de shenpan*, p. 109; Huang Yao, *Luo Ruiqing*, p. 278; and Jiang Bo and Li Qing, *Lin Biao 1959 yihou*, p. 173.
[113] Huang Yao, *Luo Ruiqing*, p. 282.

to Jiang Qing who then informed Mao, leading the Chairman to summon Ye.[114]

Also on 30 November, Yang Chengwu, after presiding over the MAC General Office meeting concerning Xiao Xiangrong, conveyed to He Long that 'Luo Ruiqing is Xiao Xiangrong's backstage boss [houtai]' – a view reportedly not shared by He Long.[115]

2 December

In a comment on a military report Mao denounced 'eclecticism, i.e. wavering between the concern for military work and ideological and political work and the reluctance to give prominence to the latter', a tendency he also classified as 'opportunism'. It soon became clear that this referred to Luo Ruiqing.[116]

8–15 December

Mao chaired an enlarged Politburo Standing Committee meeting in Shanghai dealing with the Luo Ruiqing issue. Standard Party histories assert that Lin Biao framed Luo at this meeting, but no details of Lin's reported allegations or actual activities have been revealed despite the post-Mao rehabilitation of Luo. Zhou Enlai and Deng Xiaoping relayed Mao's verdict on Luo during the gathering. The nature of this highly secret meeting remains puzzling as indicated by Tan Zhenlin's account. A Politburo member and participant in the meeting, Tan later asserted that during the conference there was no discussion at plenary sessions concerning Luo, although he conceded he could not be sure whether the matter had been discussed by the Politburo Standing Committee members.[117]

One may even doubt that Lin Biao attended the conference despite repeated claims in Party histories. Given the nature of the conference and Ye Qun's extraordinarily active role during the meeting, Party historians may simply have taken Lin Biao's presence for granted. Yet the very fact that Ye was active *on Lin's behalf* may suggest his absence. One interesting aspect is a report of the exchange of visits between Ye and Xue Ming, the wife of He Long with whom Ye had long-standing emnity going back to Yan'an, an account without any

---

[114] Hei Yannan, *Shinian haojie*, p. 20; and interview with senior military historian.
[115] *He Long zhuan*, p. 601.
[116] Ma Qibin, *Sishinian*, p. 262. See also Cong Jin, *Quzhe fazhan*, p. 635.
[117] [Luo] Diandian, *Feifan*, pp. 199–200. For the standard view, see Cong Jin, *Quzhe fazhan*, p. 630.

explicit mention of Lin's presence. Another possible clue is the account of some Party histories that Luo Ruiqing asked to *telephone* Lin from Shanghai to give a personal explanation concerning the accusations against him, only to meet Zhou Enlai's rebuke: 'How can you be so naive?'[118]

In the aftermath of the meeting Ye Jianying was placed in charge of a group investigating the Luo Ruiqing case, while He Long was deprived of his former responsibilities for overseeing MAC daily work.

Late December
Soon after the Shanghai conference, Mao raised the issue of a *coup d'etat* during a conversation with Xu Shiyou: 'What will you do if a *coup d'etat* takes place in Beijing? Revisionism is likely to appear within the Party, the government and the army, [and] not merely be limited to the cultural sphere. It is most likely to arise within the Party and the military, which are the most dangerous.'[119] Mao's articulation for the first time of his concern about a *coup d'etat* was probably the earliest indication of what prompted Lin Biao to deliver his notorious May 1966 speech on the same topic.

30 December and thereafter
PLA political work conference (which lasted to 18 January 1966) convened, presumably with the Luo Ruiqing case added to the agenda which centred on implementing Lin Biao's 18 November instruction concerning the 'five principles of giving prominence to politics'. During the conference GPD head Xiao Hua conveyed Lin's instruction that 'Every sentence of Chairman Mao's speeches is the truth, [his] one sentence is equal to [our] 10,000 sentences.'[120]

---

[118] For the exchange of visits, see *He Long zhuan*, p. 603. For Zhou's remarks, see Huang Yao, *Luo Ruiqing*, p. 290.
[119] Cong Jin, *Quzhe fazhan*, p. 635.
[120] *Gaoju Mao Zedong sixiang weida hongqi*, p. 1.

SELECT BIBLIOGRAPHY

CHINESE-LANGUAGE SOURCES

Books

Bo Yibo. *Ruogan zhongda juece yu shijian de huigu* (Reflections on Certain Major Decisions and Events), vol. 2. Beijing: Zhonggong zhongyang dangxiao chubanshe, 1993.

Cao Hua *et al.* (eds). *Dakangzheng* (The Great Resistance Struggle). Beijing: Tuanjie chubanshe, 1993.

Cao Weidong. *Hong bingli* (Red Medical Record). Taiyuan: Shanxi renmin chubanshe, 1993.

Chen Dunde. *Mao Zedong, Nikesun zai 1972* (Mao Zedong and Nixon in 1972). Beijing: Kunlun chubanshe, 1992.

Chen Yi zhuan (Biography of Chen Yi). Beijing: Dangdai Zhongguo chubanshe, 1991.

Chen Zaidao. *Huodong zhongde yimu – Wuhan qierling shijian qinliji* (A Scene in the Movement – Personal Historical Notes on the Wuhan 20 July Incident). Beijing: Jiefangjun chubanshe, 1989.

Cheng Hua. *Zhou Enlai he tade mishumen* (Zhou Enlai and his Secretaries). Beijing: Zhongguo guangbo dianshi chubanshe, 1992.

Cong Jin. *1949–1989 nian de Zhongguo: Quzhe fazhan de suiye* (China 1949–1989: The Years of Circuitous Development). Henan: Henan renmin chubanshe, 1989.

Dong Baochun. *Tan Zhenlin waizhuan* (Unofficial Biography of Tan Zhenlin). Beijing: Zuojia chubanshe, 1992.

———. *Yang-Yu-Fu shijian zhenxiang* (The True Account of the Yang-Yu-Fu Affair). Beijing: Jiefangjun chubanshe, 1987.

Gai Jun. *Zhongguo Gongchandang bolan zhuangkuo de qishinian* (The CCP's Seventy Years of Magnificent Surging Forward). Beijing: Zhongguo qingnian chubanshe, 1991.

Gao Gao and Yan Jiaqi. *'Wenhua dageming' shinianshi 1966–1976* (History of the 'Cultural Revolution' Decade 1966–1976). Tianjin: Tianjin renmin chubanshe, 1986.

Gu Baozi. *Hongqiang lide shunjian* (The Twinkling in the Red Wall). Beijing: Jiefangjun wenyi chubanshe, 1992).

Guan Weixun. *Wo suo zhidaode Ye Qun* (The Ye Qun I Knew). Beijing: Zhongguo wenxue chubanshe, 1993.

Han Zi (ed.). *Dadi cangsang – Zhongnanhai renwu chenfu neimu* (Great Changes

SELECT BIBLIOGRAPHY   215

in this Land – The Inside Story of the Rise and Fall of Personalities in Zhongnanhai). Beijing: Zhongguo dadi chubanshe, 1993.

He Li (ed.). *Lin Biao jiazu jishi* (Report on Lin Biao's Family). Beijing: Guangming ribao chubanshe, 1989.

He Long zhuan (Biography of the Long). Beijing: Dangdai Zhongguo chubanshe, 1993.

Hei Yannan. *Shinian haojie* (A Disastrous Decade). Hong Kong: Fengfu wenhua qiye gongsi, 1986.

Huang Yao. *Sanzi danan busi de Luo Ruiqing Dajiang* (General Luo Ruiqing Survives Three Calamities). Beijing: Zhonggong dangshi chubanshe, 1994.

Huang Zheng *et al. Zai lishi de dang'anli – wenge fengyunlu* (In the Historical Archives – A Record of the Cultural Revolution Storm). Shenyang: Liaoning Daxue chubanshe, 1988.

Huiyi Xiao Hua bianjizu (Remember Xiao Hua editorial group). *Huiyi Xiao Hua* (Remember Xiao Hua). Beijing: Junshi kexue chubanshe, 1988.

Jia Sinan (ed.) *Mao Zedong renji jiaowang shilu* (A True Record of Mao Zedong's Interaction with Others). Jiangsu: Jiangsu wenyi chubanshe, 1989.

Jiang Bo and Li Qing (eds). *Lin Biao 1959 yihou* (Lin Biao after 1959). Chengdu: Sichuan renmin chubanshe, 1993.

Jiao Ye. *Ye Qun zhi mi – yige mishu yanzhongde Ye Qun yu Lin Biao* (The Riddle of Ye Qun – Ye Qun and Lin Biao in the Eyes of a Secretary). Beijing: Zhongguo wenlian chubangongsi, 1993.

Jin Chunming. *Jianguohou sanshisannian* (The Thrity-three Years since the Founding of the PRC). Shanghai: Shanghai renmin chubanshe, 1987.

——. *'Wenge' shiqi guaishi guaiyu* (Strange Events and Strange Words of the 'Cultural Revolution' Period). Beijing: Qiushi chubanshe, 1989.

——. *'Wenhua dageming' lunxi* (Discussion and Analysis of the 'Cultural Revolution'). Shanghai: Shanghai renmin chubanshe, 1985.

Lei Yingfu *et al. Tongshuaibu canmon de zhuihuai* (Recollections of the Headquarters Staff). Jiangsu: Jiangsu wenyi chubanshe, 1994).

Li Ke and Hao Shengzhang. *'Wenhua dageming' zhongde Renmin Jiefangjun* (The PLA during the 'Cultural Revolution'). Beijing: Zhonggong dangshi ziliao chubanshe, 1989.

Li Ping. *Kaiguo Zongli Zhou Enlai* (Founding Premier Zhou Enlai). Beijing: Zhonggong zhongyang dangxiao chubanshe, 1994.

Li Ping *et al. 'Wenhua dageming' zhongde Zhou Enlai* (Zhou Enlai during the 'Cultural Revolution'). Beijing: Zhonggong zhongyang dangxiao chubanshe, 1991.

Li Rui. *Lushan huiyi shilu* (True Record of the Lushan Conference). Beijing: Chunqiu chubanshe, 1989. 2nd edn, Taibei: Xinrue chubanshe, 1994.

Li Zhishun (ed.). *Mao Zedong yu shida yuanshuai* (Mao Zedong and the Ten Marshals). Beijing: Zhonggong zhongyang dangxiao chubanshe, 1994.

Lin Qing. *Zhou Enlai zaixiang shengya* (Zhou Enlai's Career as a Feudal Prime

Minister). N.p.: Changcheng wenhua chubangongsi, 1991. Pirated from a Hong Kong publication.

Lin Qingshan. *Lin Biao zhuan* (Biography of Lin Biao), 2 vols. Beijing: Zhishi chubanshe, 1988.

Lin Yunhui (ed.). *Feng-yu jian cheng – Xin Zhongguo sishinian fazhan zhanlue de yanbian* (A Journey through the Storm – the Evolution of New China's 40 Years of Development Strategy). Shenzhen: Haitian chubanshe, 1993.

Lishi de shenpan (The Historic Trial). Beijing: Qunzhong chubanshe, 1981.

Liu Han *et al. Luo Ronghuan Yuanshuai* (Marshal Luo Ronghuan). Beijing: Jiefangjun chubanshe, 1987.

[Luo] Diandian. *Feifan de niandai* (Those Extraordinary Years). Shanghai: Shanghai wenyi chubanshe, 1987.

Luo Ronghuan zhuan (Biography of Luo Ronghuan). Beijing: Dangdai Zhongguo chubanshe 1991.

Nan Zhi. *Ye Qun yeshi* (Informal History of Ye Qun). Liaoning: Shenyang chubanshe, 1988.

Nie Rongzhen. *Nie Rongzhen huiyilu* (Memoirs of Nie Rongzhen). Beijing: Jiefangjun chubanshe, 1984.

Quan Yanchi. *Tao Zhu zai 'Wenhua dageming' zhong* (Tao Zhu during the 'Cultural Revolution'). N.p.: Zhonggong zhongyang dangxiao chubanshe, 1991.

––––––. *Zouxia shengtande Zhou Enlai* (Zhou Enlai Down to Earth). Taibei: Xinrui chubanshe, 1994.

Shao Yihai. *Lianhe jiandui de fumie* (The Destruction of the Joint Fleet). Henan: Chunqiu chubanshe, 1988.

––––––. *Lin Biao wangchao heimu* (The Inside Story of the Lin Biao Dynasty's Sinister Plot). Chengdu: Sichuan wenyi chubanshe, 1988.

Shi Zhe. *Zai lishi juren – Shi Zhe huiyilu* (At the Side of a Historical Giant – The Memoirs of Shi Zhe). Beijing: Zhongyang wenxian chubanshe, 1991.

Shi Zhongquan. *Zhou Enlai de zhuoyue fengxian* (Zhou Enlai's Brilliant Commitment). Beijing: Zhonggong zhongyang dangxiao chubanshe, 1993.

Tan Zhongji (ed.). *Shinianhou de pingshuo – 'Wenhua dageming' shilunji* (Critical Explanations after Ten Years – Collected Historical Essays on the 'Cultural Revolution'). Beijing: Zhonggong dangshi ziliao chubanshe, 1987.

Wang Nianyi. *1949–1989 nian de Zhongguo: Dadongluan de niandai* (China 1949–1989: The Years of Great Turmoil). Henan: Henan renmin chubanshe, 1988.

Wen Feng. *Shentanxia de Lin Biao* (Lin Biao Down to Earth). Beijing: Zhongguo huaqiao chubanshe, 1993.

'Wenhua dageming' fengyun renwu fangtanlu (Record of Conversations with 'Cultural Revolution' Men of the Hour). Beijing: Zhongyang minzu xueyuan chubanshe, 1994.

'Wenhua dageming' zhongde mingren zhi sheng (Famous People who Rose during the Cultural Revolution). Beijing: Zhongyang minzu xueyuan chubanshe, 1993.

Xiao Jingguang. *Xiao Jingguang huiyiluxuji* (Sequel to Memoirs of Xiao Jingguang). Beijing: Jiefangjun chubanshe, 1989.

Xiao Liang (ed.). *Shida yuanshuai zhi mi* (The Riddle of the Ten Marshals), 2 vols. Henan: Henan renmin chubanshe, 1993.

Xiao Sike. *Caoji shenpan: shenli Lin Biao fangeming jituan qinliji* (The Super Trial: A Participant's Account of the Trial of the Case of the Lin Biao Counterrevolutionary Clique), 2 vols. Jinan: Jinan chubanshe, 1992.

Xu Xiangqian. *Lishi de huigu* (Reflections on History), 3 vols. Beijing: Jiefangjun chubanshe, 1987.

Xu Xiangqian zhuan (Biography of Xu Xiangqian). Beijing: Dangdai Zhongguo chubanshe, 1991.

Ye Yonglie. *Chen Boda* (Chen Boda). Hong Kong: Wenhua jiaoyu chubanshe youxian gongsi, 1990.

———. *Ye Yonglie caifang shouji* (Reporter's Notes of Ye Yonglie). Shanghai: Shanghai shehui kexueyuan chubanshe, 1993.

———. *Zhang Chunqiao fuchenshi* (A History of Zhang Chunqiao Drifting with the Tide). Changchun: Shidai wenyi chubanshe, 1988.

———. *Zhonggong shenmi zhangquanzhe* (The CCP's Mysterious Powerholders). Taibei: Fengyun shidai chuban youxian gongsi, 1993.

Yu Qingtian *et al.* *Mao Zedong yu tongshi* (Mao Zedong and his Colleagues), 2 vols. Beijing: Zhongguo Renmin Daxue chubanshe, 1993.

Zhang Ning *et al.* *Lishi neimu* (History's Inside Story), 2 vols. Kansu: Kansu renmin chubanshe, 1988.

Zhang Yunsheng. *Maojiawan jishi: Lin Biao mishu huiyilu* (True Account of Maojiawan: Reminiscences of Lin Biao's Secretary). Chunqiu chubanshe, 1988.

——— *et al.* *Tongshuaibu de douzheng* (Struggle in the Supreme Command). Sichuan: Sichuan renmin chubanshe, 1993.

Zheng Xiaofeng *et al.* *Tao Zhu zhuan* (Biography of Tao Zhu). Beijing: Zhongguo qingnian chubanshe, 1992.

Zhong Kan. *Kang Sheng pingzhuan* (Critical Biography of Kang Sheng). Beijing: Hongqi chubanshe, 1982.

Zhongguo dabeiju de renwu (Personalities in China's Great Tragedy). Beijing: Zhongguo Renmin Daxue chubanshe, 1989.

Zhou Kang. *Qiushi lunji* (Collected Essays Seeking Truth). Fuzhou: Fujian renmin chubanshe, 1984.

Zhou Ming (ed.). *Lishi zai zheli chensi – 1966–1976 nian jishi* (Contemplating History – A True Record of 1966–1976), vols. 1–3. Beijing: Huaxia chubanshe, 1986.

Zi Gong (ed.). *Lin Biao shijian zhenxiang* (The Truth about the Lin Biao Affair). Beijing: Zhongguo guangbo dianshi chubanshe, 1988.

Zi Ping. *Hu Yaobang, Yang Chengwu, Li Desheng* (Hu Yaobang, Yang Chengwu, Li Desheng). Hong Kong: Kehua dushu chubangongsi, 1982.

Extensively Consulted Party History Journals

Dang de wenxian (The Party's Documents). Beijing: Zhongyang wenxian chubanshe, 1988–94.

Dangshi tongxun (Party History Bulletin). Beijing: Zhongyang dangshi yan-jiushi, 1983–7.

Dangshi wenhui (Collected Articles on Party History). Taiyuan: Zhonggong Shanxi shengwei dangshi yanjiushi, 1985–94.

Dangshi yanjiu (Research on Party History). Beijing: Zhonggong zhongyang dangxiao chubanshe, 1980–7.

Renwu (Personalities). Beijing: Renmin chubanshe, 1980–94.

Wenxian he yanjiu (Documents and Research). Beijing: Renmin chubanshe, 1982–7.

Zhonggong dangshi tongxun (CCP History Bulletin). Beijing: Zhonggong dangshi chubanshe, 1989–94.

Zhonggong dangshi yanjiu (Research on CCP History). Beijing: Zhonggong dangshi chubanshe, 1988–94.

Zhonggong dangshi ziliao (CCP History Materials). Beijing: Zhonggong dangshi ziliao chubanshe, 1982–94.

Articles

An Jianshe. 'Zhou Enlai yu "Wenhua dageming" qianqi de zhua geming cu shengchan' (Zhou Enlai and the early 'Cultural Revolution' period's grasp revolution and promote production [policy]). *Zhonggong dangshi ziliao* (CCP History Materials), vol. 49, February 1994.

———. 'Zhou Enali yu 1967 nian eryue kangzheng' (Zhou Enlai and the February resistance of 1967). *Zhonggong dangshi yanjiu* (Research on CCP History), no. 2, 1993.

Beijing tiyu xueyuan 'He Long' bianxiezu ('He Long' Writing Group of the Beijing Physical Education Academy). 'He Long' (He Long). In *Zhonggong dangshi renwu zhuan* (Biographies of Personalities in CCP History), edited by Hu Hua. Vol. 2, Xi'an: Shaanxi renmin chubanshe, 1981.

Bo Yibo. 'Wenhua lingyu de dapipan' (The big criticism in the cultural realm). *Zhonggong dangshi yanjiu* (Research on CCP History), no. 4, 1993.

[Chen] Donglin. '1970 nian Lin Biao weishenme yao jianchi she guojia zhuxi' (Why did Lin Biao persist in wanting to establish the state chairmanship in 1970). *Guoshi yanjiu tongxun* (Bulletin of Research on National History, Beijing), no. 3, 1993.

Chen Hong. '"Dashu teshu" de youlai' (The origin of 'greatly and specially establishing [Mao's cult]'). *Zhonggong dangshi ziliao* (CCP History Materials), June 1993.

Chen Zaidao. '"Qierling shijian" qianhou Mao Zedong dui wo de baohu' (Mao Zedong's protection of me before and after the '20 July incident').

Dang de wenxian (The Party's Documents), no. 3, 1993.

Cong Jin. 'Ping yijiuliuling nian Junwei kuoda huiyi' (An appraisal of the 1960 expanded Military Affairs Committee conference). *Dangshi tongxun* (Party History Bulletin), no. 3, 1987.

Fu Hao. 'Jiuyisan shijian bubai' (Supplement to the 13 September incident). *Dang de wenxian* (The Party's Documents), no. 1, 1988.

Gong Li. 'Dakai Zhong-Mei guanxi damen de jushou' (The giant hand [of Mao] in opening the great door of Sino-US relations). *Dangshi wenhui* (Collected Articles on Party History), no. 7, 1993.

———. 'Mao Zedong zai 60 niandaimo 70 niandaichu dui Mei zhengce de yanbian' (The evolution of Mao Zedong's policy toward the US at the end of the 1960s and the start of the 1970s). *Guoshi yanjiu cankao ziliao* (Reference Material for Research on National History, Beijing), no. 4, 1993.

———. 'Miandui Lin Biao jituan xianqi de Lushan elang' (Confronting the Lin Biao clique's surging evil wave at Lushan). *Dangshi wenhui* (Collected Articles on Party History), no. 5, 1993.

———. 'Yu jiding jiebanren de zuihou juezhan' (The final decisive battle with the established successor). *Dangshi wenhui* (Collected Articles on Party History), no. 9, 1993.

'He Long zhuan' bianxiezu ('He Long Biography' Writing Group). 'He Long mengnan jishi' (True record of He Long in the clutches of the enemy). *Guoshi yanjiu cankao ziliao* (Reference Material for Research on National History, Beijing), no. 2, 1993.

Hu Changshui. 'Zhongyang Junwei "batiao mingling" de chansheng' (The emergence of the Central Military Affairs Committee's 'eight point order'). *Zhonggong dangshi yanjiu* (Research on CCP History), no. 6, 1991.

Huang Kecheng. 'Huang Kecheng Tongzhi dui dabaike quanshu "Lin Biao" tiao shiwen de yijian' (Comrade Huang Kecheng's comment on the 'Lin Biao' entry in the encyclopedia [published by the PLA General Political Department]). *Dangshi ziliao zhengji tongxun* (Collected Materials on Party History Bulletin, Beijing), no. 4, 1985.

Huang Yao. 'Luo Ruiqing' (Luo Ruiqing). In *Zhonggong dangshi renwu zhuan* (Biographies of Personalities in CCP History), edited by Hu Hua. Vol. 46, Xi'an: Shaanxi renmin chubanshe, 1991.

Jin Chunming. 'Luelun dang de Jiudahou de zhengfeng' (A brief discussion of rectification after the Party's Ninth Congress). *Dangshi yanjiu*, (Research on Party History), no. 2, 1985.

Lan Sou. 'Weiduizhang jiyi zhongde jiu.yisan qianye' (A guard unit head's recollections of the eve of 13 September). *Zhonghua ernu* (Chinese Children, Beijing), no. 5, 1994.

Li Desheng. 'Cong Lushan huiyi dao "jiu.yisan" shijian de ruogan huiyi' (Certain recollections concerning the period from the Lushan meeting to the

'9.13' incident). *Wenhuibao* (Wenhui Daily, Shanghai), 23 December 1993.

Li Gui. 'Xiao Hua' (Xiao Hua). In *Zhonggong dangshi renwu zhuan* (Biographies of Personalities in CCP History), edited by Hu Hua. Vol. 45, Xi'an: Shaanxi renmin chubanshe, 1990.

Ling Jiajie. '"Wu Zhong you zhong" – "wenge" zhongde Beijing weishuqu silingyuan Wu Zhong' ('Wu Zhong is loyal' – Beijing Garrison Commander Wu Zhong during the 'Cultural Revolution'). *Zhuanji wenxue* (Biographic Recollections Literature, Beijing), no. 6, 1994.

Luo Yingcai. 'Chen Yi zai suowei eryue niliu zhong jiejian guiguo liuxuesheng daibiao' (Chen Yi's reception of a delegation of students returning to the country from overseas during the February adverse current). *Dang de wenxian* (The Party's Documents), no. 4, 1990.

Quan Yanchi. 'Peng Dehuai luonan yu Lin Biao deshi zhenxiang' (The Truth about Peng Dehuai's downfall and Lin Biao's ascendancy). *Yanhuang chunqiu* (The Spring and Autumn of the Chinese People, Beijing), no. 4, 1993.

Su Caiqing. 'Huanhe Zhong-Mei guande zhengque juece – 1971 nian zhongyang gongzuo huiyi qianhou' (The correct policy of relaxing Sino-US relations – before and after the 1971 central work conference). *Zhonggong dangshi tongxun* (CCP History Bulletin), no. 2, 1989.

———. '"Wenhua dageming" chuqi jingji zhanxian sange mianhe de douzheng' (Three rounds in the struggle on the economic front during the initial stage of the 'Cultural Revolution'). *Dangshi wenhui* (Collected Articles on Party History), no. 3, 1993.

———. '"Wenhua dageming" shishi bianwu san ze' (Three rectifications of 'Cultural Revolution' historical facts). *Zhonggong dangshi yanji* (Research on CCP History), no. 5, 1989.

Tan Zhongji. 'Eryue kangzheng jishi – eryue de lishi zhenxiang' (A true record of the February resistance – the historical truth about the Frebruary adverse current). *Dangshi ziliao tongxun* (Party History Materials Bulletin, Beijing), no. 10, 1987.

Wang Dongxing. 'Mao Zhuxi zai fensui Lin Biao fangeming zhengbian yinmoude rizili' (Chairman Mao during the days of smashing the Lin Biao counterrevolutionary coup plot). *Dangdai Zhongguoshi yanjiu* (Research on Contemporary Chinese History, Beijing), no. 1, 1994.

———. 'Yi Jiujie erzhong quanhui' (Recollecting the Second Plenum of the Ninth Central Committee). *Dangdai Zhongguoshi yanjiu* (Research on Contemporary Chinese History, Beijing), no. 3, 1994.

Wang Nianyi. 'Guanyu He Long Yuan'an de yixie ziliao' (Some materials concerning He Long's unjust case). Photocopy of article in unidentified journal.

———. 'Guanyu "Wuchanjieji zhuanzhengxia jixu geming" de lilun de jige wenti' (Some questions concerning the theory of 'continuing the revolution under the dictatorship of the proletariat'). *Dangshi yanjiu* (Research on Party History), no. 1, 1984.

———. 'Ping "pipan zichanjieji fandong luxian"' (An appraisal of 'criticizing the bourgeois revolutionary line'). *Dangshi tongxun* (Party History Bulletin), no. 10, 1987.

———. 'Ping *"Wenhua dageming" shinianshi*' (An appraisal of *History of the 'Cultural Revolution' Decade*). *Dangshi tongxun* (Party History Bulletin), no. 4, 1987.

———. 'Shilun "Wenhua dageming" de zhunbei' (Preliminary discussion on the preparation for the 'Cultural Revolution'). *Dangshi ziliao tongxun* (Party History Materials Bulletin, Beijing), no. 8, 1983.

———. '"Wenhua dageming" diyi jieduan shuping' (An account of the first stage of the 'Cultural Revolution'). *Dangshi yanjiu ziliao* (Research Materials on Party History, Beijing), no. 10, 1984.

———. '"Wenhua dageming" fadong de zhengjie' (The crux of the launching of the 'Cultural Revolution'). *Dangshi yanjiu* (Research on Party History), no. 1, 1985.

———. '"Wenhua dageming" fadong fazhan de mailuo' (The logic of the 'Cultural Revolution's' misguided development). *Dangshi tongxun* (Party History Bulletin), no. 10, 1986.

Xi Xuan. 'Dang de Bajie shiyizhong quanhui shuping' (A commentary on the Eleventh Plenum of the Eighth Central Committee). *Dangshi ziliao tongxun* (Party History Materials Bulletin, Beijing), no. 18, 1981.

Xiao Xiao. 'Changqi bei zhaozao lishi yinying zhongde Lin Doudou: Lin Biao nu'er dadan pilu fuqin chuzou yixie xiangqing' (Lin Doudou in the long shadow of history: Lin Biao's daughter bravely reveals details of her father's flight). *Jingbao yuekan* (The Mirror Monthly, Hong Kong), June 1988.

Xin Ming. 'Guofen qingxing de xianshizhuyi – cong "zhi Jiang Qing de xin" kan Mao Zedong wannian xintai (Exceeding sober-minded realism – viewing the feelings of the later Mao Zedong from the 'letter to Jiang Qing'). *Mao Zedong Sixiang luntan* (Forum on Mao Zedong Thought, Changsha), no. 2, 1994.

Xiong Xianghui. 'Dakai Zong-Mei guanxi de qianzou' (Preamble to the opening of Sino-US relations). *Zhonggong dangshi ziliao* (CCP History Materials), vol. 42, June 1992.

Yu Nan. 'Jingxin dingpo de jiu.yi'er zhi ye' (12 September, a soul searching night). *Dang de wenxian* (The Party's Documents), no. 4, 1994.

———. 'Jiujie erzhong quanhuishang de yichang fengbo' (A disturbance at the Second Plenum of the Ninth Central Committee). *Dang de wenxian* (The Party's Documents), no. 3, 1992.

———. 'Lishi qike waiqu – bo haiwai chubande "Lin Biao zhi si" yishu' (Distorting historical fiction and fact – refuting the overseas-published book 'The death of Lin Biao'). *Dang de wenxian* (The Party's Documents), no. 4, 1989.

——. 'Mao Zedong yijiuqiyi nian nanxun kaoshu' (An investigation of Mao Zedong's 1971 southern tour). *Dang de wenxian* (The Party's Documents), no. 5, 1993.

——. 'Zhou Zongli chuli jiu.yisan Lin Biao pantao shijian de yixie qingkuan' (Some facts about Premier Zhou's handling of Lin Biao's treacherous flight on 13 September). *Dangshi yanjiu* (Research on Party History), no. 3, 1981.

Zeng Tao. 'Zhengyi de kangzheng – suowei "eryue niliu" de qianqian houhou' (Righteous resistance struggle – before and after the so-called 'February adverse current'). *Dangshi tiandi* (The Party History Field, Wuhan), no. 1, 1993.

Zhang Songshan. 'Yige zhongyang zhuan'an zuzhang de chanhui' (The repentance of a central special case group head). *Yanhuang chunqiu* (The Spring and Autumn of the Chinese People, Beijing), no. 9, 1994.

Zheng Qian. 'Zhonggong Jiuda qianhou quanguo de zhanbei gongzuo' (War preparations work in the entire country before and after the CCP's Ninth Congress). *Zhonggong dangshi ziliao* (CCP History Materials), vol. 41, 1992.

Zheng Xiaofeng and Shu Ling. 'Tao Zhu' (Tao Zhu). In *Zhonggong dangshi renwu zhuan* (Biographies of Personalities in CCP History), edited by Hu Hua. Vol. 43, Xi'an: Shannxi renmin chubanshe, 1990.

Chronologies, Documentary Collections, Personnel Directories, etc. (excluding Red Guard Publications)

Dang de jianshe qishinian jishi (1921–1991) (A Record of 70 Years of Party Building, 1921–1991), edited by Lu Cheng *et al.* Beijing: Zhonggong dangshi chubanshe, 1991.

Gongfei wenhua dageming zhongyao wenjian xubian (Supplement to the Communist Bandits' Important Cultural Revolution Documents). Taibei: Guofangbu qingbaoju, 1969.

Guanyu jianguo yilai dang de ruogan lishi wenti de jueyi zhuyiben (xiuding) (Revised Notes on the Resolution on Certain Questions in the History of Our Party since the Founding of the PRC), compiled by Zhonggong zhongyang wenxian yanjiushi. Beijing: Renmin chubanshe, 1985.

Jiefangjun jiangling zhuan (Biographies of PLA Generals). Beijing: Jiefangjun chubanshe, 1985.

Lijie Zhonggong zhongyang weiyuan renmin cidian (Biographic Dictionary of Previous Central Committee Members), edited by Liu Jintian and Shen Xueming. Beijing: Zhonggong dangshi chubanshe, 1992.

Lin Biao shijian yuanshi wenjian huibian (Collection of Original Documents on the Lin Biao Affair), edited by Yuan Yue. Taibei: Zhongguo dalu wenti yanjiusuo, 1973.

Lin Biao Tongzhi guanyu zhengzhi sixiang gongzuo yanlun zhailu (Extracts from Comrade Lin Biao's Speeches on Political and Ideological Work), edited by Jiefangjun Zongzheng (PLA General Political Department). Beijing: Renmin chubanshe, 1966.

Lin Biao zhanji (Special Edition on Lin Biao), edited by Zhongguo wenti yanjiu zhongxin (China Questions Research Centre). Hong Kong: Zilian chubanshe, 1970.

Mao Zedong dazidian (Mao Zedong Dictionary). Guangzhou: Guangxi renmin chubanshe, 1992.

Sixiang zhengzhi gongzuo 70nian (70 Years of Ideological and Political Work), edited by Huang Xiaohui *et al*. Beijing: Guofang Daxue chubanshe, 1991.

'Wenge dashiji' (Chronology of the Cultural Revolution), compiled by Xu Zhengguang. *Gongdang wenti yanjiu* (Research on Communist Party Questions, Taibei), vol. 14, nos 2–6, and vol. 15, nos 1–6, 1988–9.

Xin Zhongguo biannianshi (Chronological History of New China), edited by Liao Gailong. Beijing: Renmin chubanshe, 1989.

Zhejiang wenge jishi: 1965.5–1976.10 (A Chronological Account of the Cultural Revolution in Zhejiang: May 1965–October 1976), edited by Cheng Cao *et al*. Zhejiang: Zhejiang bianjibu, 1989.

Zhonggong dangshi jiaoxue cankao ziliao (CCP History Teaching Reference Materials). Vols 24, 25–6, [Beijing]: Zhongguo Jiefangjun Guofang Daxue dangshi dangjian zhenggong jiaoyanshi, July 1986, October 1988.

Zhonggong dangshi renwu zhuan (Biographies of Personalities in CCP History), edited by Hu Hua. Vols 1–50, Xi'an: Shaanxi renmin chubanshe, 1980–91.

Zhonggong wenhua dageming zhongyao wenjian huibian (Collection of Important CCP Documents on the Cultural Revolution). Taibei: 'Zhonggong yanjiu' zazhishe bianjibu, 1973.

Zhongguo Gongchandang huiyi gaiyao (Outline of CCP Meetings), edited by Jiang Huaxuan *et al*. Shenyang: Shenyang chubanshe, 1991.

Zhongguo Congchandang lishi dashiji (1919.5–1987.12) (History of the Chinese Communist Party: A Chronology of Events, May 1919–December 1987), compiled by Zhonggong zhongyang dangshi yanjiushi. Beijing: Renmin chubanshe, 1989.

Zhongguo Gongchandang zhizheng sishinian (1949–1989) (The CCP's Forty Years in Power, 1949–1989), by Ma Qibin, *et al*., rev. edn. Beijing: Zhonggong dangshi chubanshe, 1991.

Zhongguo Gongchandang zuzhu gongzuo dashiji (Chronology of CCP Organizational Work), edited by Zhao Bo *et al*. Beijing: Zhongguo guoji guangbo chubanshe, 1991.

Zhongguo Gongchandang zuzhishi ziliao huibian (Compilation of Materials on CCP Organizational History), edited by Wang Jianying. Beijing: Hongqi chubanshe, 1983.

Zhongguo Renmin Jiefangiun liushinian dashiji (1927–1987) (PLA 60 Years

Chronology, 1927-1987). Beijing: Junshi kexue chubanshe, 1988.

Zhongguo Renmin Jiefangjun yange he geji lingdao chengyuan minglu (xiudingban) (PLA Evolution and Namelists of Leading Members at Various Levels, rev. edn), edited by Junshi kexueyuan junshi tushuguan (Military Science Academy's Military Library). Beijing: Junshi kexue chubanshe, 1990.

Zhonghuarenmingongheguo dang zheng jun qun lingdao renminglu (Namelists of PRC Party, Government, Military and Mass Organization Leaders). Beijing: Zhonggong dangshi chubanshe, 1990.

Zhonghuarenmingongheguo guomin jingji he shehui fazhan jihua dashi jiyao 1949-1985 (Outline of Events in PRC National Economic and Social Development 1949-1985), edited by 'Dangdai Zhongguo de jihua gongzuo' bangongshi (General Office of 'Contemporary China Planning Work'). Beijing: Hongqi chubanshe, 1987.

Zhonghuarenmingongheguo jingji dashiji (1949-1980 nian) (Chronology of Economic Events in the PRC, 1949-1980), edited by Fang Weizhong, Beijing: Zhongguo shehui kexue chubanshe, 1984.

Zhonghuarenmingongheguo jingji zhuanti dashiji (Chronology of PRC Special Economic Topics), edited by Zhao Desheng. Henan: Henan renmin chubanshe, 1989.

Zhonghuarenmingongheguo shilu (True Record of the PRC), vol. 3, part 1, *Neiluan yu kangzheng – 'wenhua dageming' de shinian (1966-1971)* (Civil Disorder and Resistance – The 'Cultural Revolution' Decade, 1966-1971), edited by Chen Donglin and Du Pu. Changchun: Jilin renmin chubanshe, 1994.

Zhonghuarenmingongheguo zhengzhi tizhi yange dashiji (1949-1978) (Chronology of the Evolution of PRC Political Institutions, 1949-1978), edited by Hong Chenghua *et al.* Beijing: Chunqiu chubanshe, 1987.

Unpublished Mimeos and Photocopies of Printed and Handwritten Speech Transcriptions

Lin Biao's speech to the 7,000 cadres conference, 29 January 1962. Printed text provided by our Chinese sources.

Speeches at the Ninth Congress, April 1969. Printed and handwritten Chinese texts available at the Fairbank Center Library, Harvard University.

Speeches by CCP leaders, October 1968-September 1971, including Mao's several conversations with local leaders and stinging attacks on Lin Biao during his summer 1971 southern trip. Handwritten Chinese texts available at the Sinological Institute, University of Heidelberg.

Red Guard Cultural Revolution Publications

Gaoju Mao Zedong sixiang weida hongqi (Raise High the Great Red Banner of Mao Zedong Thought). Beijing: April 1967.

Gaoju Mao Zedong sixiang weida hongqi kuobu qianjin (Raise High and Advance Far the Great Red Banner of Mao Zedong Thought). Beijing: 1968.

Lin Biao Tongzhi jianghua ji yanlun zhailu huibian (Collection of Extracts from Comrade Lin Biao's Talks and Speeches), edited and published by Niujie renmin gongshe 'cong douyue' zhandoudui (Niu Street People's Commune 'Marching High' Combat Force). n.p.: 1967.

Mao Zedong sixiang wansui (Long Live Mao Zedong Thought). Red Guard collection of Mao's talks and speeches. Beijing: 1967.

————. Red Guard collection of Mao's talks and speeches. Taibei: 1969.

————. Red Guard collection of Mao's talks and speeches covering 1958–9, no publication data. Copy held at the Menzies Library, Australian National University.

Mao Zhuxi de geming luxian shengli wansui – dangnei liangtiao luxian douzheng dashiji 1921–1967 (Long Live the Victory of Chairman Mao's Revolutionary Line – A Chronology of the Two-Line Struggle within the Party 1921–1967), edited and published by Shoudu *Shixue geming* bianjibu (Capital *Historical Studies Revolution* Editorial Department). Beijing: 1968.

Mao Zhuxi de geming luxian shengli wansui – dangnei liangtiao luxian douzheng dashiji (1921.7–1969.4) (Long Live the Victory of Chairman Mao's Revolutionary Line – A Chronology of the Two-Line Struggle within the Party, July 1921–April 1969). Beijing: Red Guard pamphlet, 1969.

Mao Zhuxi de jiebanren – Lin Biao Futongshuai (Chairman Mao's Successor – Deputy Commander Lin Biao). Red Guard pamphlet, n.p.: June 1969.

Mao Zhuxi de wuchanjieji geming luxian shengli wansui (Long Live the Victory of Chairman Mao's Proletarian Revolutionary Line). Red Guard collection, n.p.: n.d.

Tianfan difu kai er kang – wuchanjieji wenhua dageming dashiji (1963.9–1967.10) (Celebrating the World Turned Upside Down – A Chronology of the Great Proletarian Cultural Revolution, September 1963–October 1967), edited by Shoudu dazhong xuexiao Mao Zedong sixiang xuexiban (Mao Zedong Thought Study Class of the Capital's Universities and Middle Schools). Beijing: 1967.

Weida lingxiu Mao Zhuxi zuiqinmi de zhanyou Lin Biao Tongzhi jianghua xuanbian (Selected Edition of Talks by the Great Leader Chairman Mao's Closest Comrade-in-Arms Lin Biao), edited by Hongdaihui Beijing gong-nong-bing tiyuan Mao Zedong sixiang bingtuan xuanchuanbu (Red Representative Congress of the Beijing Workers-Peasants-Soldiers Physical Culture Academy's Mao Zedong Thought Corps Propaganda Department). Beijing: 1967(?).

Wuchanjieji wenhua dageming cankao ziliao (Reference Materials on the Great Proletarian Cultural Revolution), edited and published by Beijing Huagong xueyuan (Beijing Chemical Industry Academy) *et al*. 4 vols, Beijing: 1966.

Wuchanjieji wenhua dageming wansui dazibao huibian (Long Live the Great Proletarian Cultural Revolution Wall Poster Collection), edited and published
by Shoudu hongqi lianhe zongbu xuanchuanbu (Capital Red Banner United
Headquarters Propaganda Department). Beijing: 1967.
Wuchanjieji wenhua dageming yundong zhong shouzhang jianghua (Leaders' Talks
during the Great Proletarian Cultural Revolution Movement), edited and
published by Beijing dizhi xueyuan (Beijing Geology Academy). Beijing:
November 1966.
Xuexi wenxuan (Collected Study Documents). Red Guard collection of Mao's
talks and speeches. 4 vols, Beijing: 1967.
Xuexi ziliao (1962–1967) (Study Materials, 1962–1967). Red Guard collection
of Mao's talks and speeches. Copy hold at the Menzies Library, Australian
National University.
*Zhongyang lingdao ji youguan fuze tongzhi guanyu Wuchanjieji wenhua dageming
de jianghua* (Talks by Central Leaders and Concerned Responsible Comrades
on the Great Proletarian Cultural Revolution). 4 vols, n.p.: December 1966.

PRIMARY CHINESE SOURCES IN ENGLISH

Books and Monographs

*A Great Trial in Chinese History: The Trial of the Lin Biao and Jiang Qing
Counter-Revolutionary Cliques, Nov. 1980–Jan. 1981.* (Oxford: Pergamon
Press, 1981.
'An Insider's Account of the Cultural Revolution: Wang Li's Memoirs', edited
by Michael Schoenhals. *Chinese Law and Government*, no. 6, 1994.
Li Zhishui. *The Private Life of Chairman Mao: The Memoirs of Mao's Personal
Physician.* London: Chatto and Windus, 1994.
'*True Account of Maojiawan*: Reminiscences of Lin Biao's Secretary by Zhang
Yunsheng', edited by Lawrence R. Sullivan. *Chinese Law and Government*,
no. 2, 1993.
Zong Huaiwen (comp.). *Years of Trial, Turmoil and Triumph – China from 1949
to 1988.* Beijing: Foreign Languages Press, 1989.

Articles, Documents, Speeches etc.

'[The] CCP Central Committee's circular on the distribution of the "revised
draft constitution of the People's Republic of China"'. *Issues and Studies*,
February 1972.
Hou Xiufen. 'A flame of ideals in my heart – an interview with General Fu
Chongbi, political commissar of the Beijing PLA units'. *Beijing wanbao* (Beij-
ing Evening News), 12 April 1985, in *Foreign Broadcast Information Service*,
1 May 1985, pp. K9–K10.
'Impromptu remarks by Lin Biao at plenary session of the Ninth National

Congress of the CCP on 14 April 1969'. *The Stockholm Journal of East Asian Studies*, vol. 2, 1990.

Nie Rongzhen. 'Several questions concerning Lin Biao'. *Xinhua ribao* (New China Daily, Nanjing), 18–26 October 1984, in *Foreign Broadcast Information Service*, 5 November 1984, pp. K16–K19, 6 November 1984, pp. K20–K24, 7 November 1984, pp. K20–K26.

'Preamble of the revised draft of the constitution of the People's Republic of China'. *Issues and Studies*, April 1971.

'Revised draft of the "constitution of the People's Republic of China"'. *Issues and Studies*, December 1970.

Shen Tao-sheng. 'The "Gang of Four" and Lin Piao'. *Renmin ribao* (People's Daily), 18 May 1978, in *Foreign Broadcast Information Service*, 24 May 1978, pp. E2–E11.

'Speech by Zhou Enlai at plenary session of the Ninth National Congress of the CCP on 14 April 1969'. *The Stockholm Journal of East Asian Studies*, vol. 2, 1990.

Summary of the Forum on the Work of Literature and Art in the Armed Forces with Which Comrade Lin Piao Entrusted Comrade Chiang Ching, February 1966. Peking: Foreign Languages Press, 1968.

Xi Chen. 'A great struggle to defend Party principles – revealing the true nature of a major political incident, the "February countercurrent"'. *Renmin ribao* (People's Daily), 26 February 1979, in *Foreign Broadcast Information Service*, 28 February 1979, pp. E7–E20.

Chronologies, Documentary Collections, Personnel Directories etc.

Chinese Politics: Documents and Analysis, Volume 1: Cultural Revolution to 1969, edited by James T. Myers, Jürgen Domes and Erik von Groeling. Columbia: University of South Carolina Press, 1986.

Chinese Politics: Documents and Analysis, Volume 2: Ninth Party Congress (1969) to the Death of Mao (1976), edited by James T. Myers, Jürgen Domes and Milton D. Yeh. Columbia: University of South Carolina Press, 1989.

[The] Great Power Struggle in China. Hong Kong: Asia Research Centre, 1969.

History of the Chinese Communist Party: A Chronology of Events (1919–1990), compiled by the Party History Research Centre of the Central Committee of the Chinese Communist Party. Beijing: Foreign Languages Press, 1991.

[The] Lin Piao Affair. Power Politics and Military Coup, edited by Michael Y. M. Kau. White Plains: International Arts and Sciences Press, 1975.

Mao, edited by Jerome Ch'en. Englewood Cliffs: Prentice-Hall, 1969.

Mao Papers: Anthology and Bibliography, edited by Jerome Ch'en. London: Oxford University Press, 1970.

Mao Tse-tung and Lin Piao: Post-Revolutionary Writings, edited by K. Fan. Garden City, NY: Anchor Books, 1972.

Mao Tse-tung Unrehearsed. Talks and Letters, 1956–71, edited by Stuart Schram. Harmondsworth: Penguin Books, 1974.

Miscellany of Mao Tse-tung Thought. Vol. 2, *Joint Publications Research Service*, no. 61269-2, 20 February 1974.

[The] People's Republic of China 1949–79. A Documentary Survey, edited by Harold C. Hinton. Vols 3–5 (1965–79), Wilmington: Scholarly Resources, 1980.

SECONDARY SOURCES

Books

Bachman, David. *Bureaucracy, Economy, and Leadership in China: The Institutional Origins of the Great Leap Forward.* Cambridge University Press, 1991.

Barnouin, Barbara, and Yu Changgen. *Ten Years of Turbulence: The Chinese Cultural Revolution.* London: Kegan Paul International, 1993.

Bonavia, David. *Verdict in Peking: The Trial of the Gang of Four.* London: Burnett Books, 1984.

Byron, John, and Robert Pack. *The Claws of the Dragon: Kang Sheng – The Evil Genius behind Mao – and his Legacy of Terror in People's China.* New York: Simon and Schuster, 1992.

Domes, Jürgen. *China after the Cultural Revolution: Politics between Two Party Congresses.* London: C. Hurst, 1976.

Ebon, Martin. *Lin Piao: The Life and Writings of China's New Ruler.* New York: Stein and Day, 1970.

Garver, John W. *China's Decision for Rapprochement with the United States, 1968–1971.* Boulder, CO: Westview Press, 1982.

[van] Ginneken, Jaap. *The Rise and Fall of Lin Piao.* New York: Penguin Books, 1976.

Harding, Harry, and Melvin Gurtov. *The Purge of Lo Jui-ch'ing: The Politics of Chinese Strategic Planning.* Santa Monica, CA: RAND Report R-548-PR, February 1971.

Lee, Hong Yung. *The Politics of the Chinese Cultural Revolution: A Case Study.* Berkeley: University of California Press, 1978.

Pye, Lucian W. *The Dynamics of Chinese Politics.* Cambridge: Oelgeschlager, Gunn, and Hain, 1981.

Robinson, Thomas W. *A Politico-Military Biography of Lin Piao, Part I, 1907–1949.* Santa Monica, CA: RAND Report R-526-PR, 1971.

Salisbury, Harrison E. *The New Emperors. China in the Era of Mao and Deng.* Boston: Little, Brown, 1992.

Snow, Edgar. *The Long Revolution.* New York: Random House, 1971.

Teiwes, Frederick C. *Leadership, Legitimacy, and Conflict in China: From A Charismatic Mao to the Politics of Succession.* Armonk, NY: M.E. Sharpe, 1984.

——. *Politics and Purges in China: Rectification and the Decline of Party Norms 1950–1965*, 2nd edn. Armonk, NY: M.E. Sharpe, 1993.

——. *Politics at Mao's Court: Gao Gang and Party Factionalism in the Early 1950s*. Armonk, NY: M.E. Sharpe, 1990.

——. *Provincial Leadership in China: The Cultural Revolution and Its Aftermath*. Ithaca, NY: Cornell University East Asian Papers, 1974.

—— and Warren Sun (eds). *The Politics of Agricultural Cooperativization in China: Mao, Deng Zihui, and the 'High Tide' of 1955*. Armonk, NY: M.E. Sharpe, 1993.

—— with the assistance of Warren Sun. *The Formation of the Maoist Leadership: From the Return of Wang Ming to the Seventh Party Congress*. London: Contemporary China Institute Research Notes and Studies, 1994.

Yao Ming-le. *The Conspiracy and Death of Lin Biao*. New York: Alfred A. Knopf, 1983.

Articles

Bridgham, Philip. 'The fall of Lin Piao'. *China Quarterly*, no. 55 (1973).

Hannam, Peter. 'Solved: the mystery of Lin Biao's death'. *Asiaweek*, 2 February 1994.

——. 'Solving a Chinese puzzle: Lin Biao's final days and death, after two decades of intrigue'. *US News and World Report*, 31 January 1994.

Harding, Harry. 'Political trends in China since the Cultural Revolution'. *The Annals*, July 1972.

——. 'The Chinese state in crisis'. In *The Cambridge History of China*. Vol. 15, Cambridge University Press, 1991.

Jammes, Sydney H. 'The Chinese defense burden, 1965–74'. In *China: A Reassessment of the Economy*, by the Joint Economic Commitee, Congress of the United States. Washington: US Government Printing Office, 1975.

Joffe, Ellis. 'The Chinese army after the Cultural Revolution: the effects of intervention'. *China Quarterly*, no. 55, 1973.

Kau, Ying-mao, and Pierre M. Perrolle. 'The politics of Lin Piao's abortive military coup'. *Asian Survey*, June 1974.

MacFarquhar, Roderick. 'The succession to Mao and the end of Maoism'. In *The Cambridge History of China*. Vol. 15, Cambridge University Press, 1991.

Naughton, Barry. 'The third front: defence industrialization in the Chinese interior'. *China Quarterly*, no. 115, 1988.

Parish, William L. Jr. 'Factions in Chinese military politics'. *China Quarterly*, no. 56, 1973.

Pollack, Jonathan D. 'The opening to America'. In *The Cambridge History of China*. Vol. 15, Cambridge University Press, 1991.

Ra'anan, Uri. 'Peking's foreign policy "debate", 1965–66'. In *China in Crisis*, edited by Tang Tsou and Ping-ti Ho. Vol. II, University of Chicago Press, 1968.

Robinson, Thomas W. 'China confronts the Soviet Union: warfare and diplomacy on China's inner Asian frontiers'. In *The Cambridge History of China*. Vol. 15. Cambridge University Press, 1991.

——. 'Chou En-lai and the Cultural Revolution in China'. In *The Cultural Revolution in China*, edited by Thomas W. Robinson. Berkeley: University of California Press, 1971.

——. 'Lin Piao as an elite type'. In *Elites in the People's Republic of China*, edited by Robert A. Scalapino. Seattle: University of Washington Press, 1972.

——. 'The Wuhan incident: local strife and provincial rebellion during the Cultural Revolution'. *China Quarterly*, no. 47, 1971.

Ross, Robert S. 'From Lin Biao to Deng Xiaoping: elite instability and China's U.S. policy'. *China Quarterly*, no. 118, 1989.

Shambaugh, David. 'The soldier and the state in China: the political work system in the People's Liberation Army'. *China Quarterly*, no. 127, 1991.

Sun, Warren. 'The National Defense University's *Teaching Reference Materials'*. *CCP Research Newsletter*, nos 10 and 11, 1992.

Teiwes, Frederick C. 'Interviews on Party History'. *CCP Research Newsletter*, nos 10 and 11, 1992.

——. 'Leaders, institutions, and the origins of the Great Leap Forward'. *Pacific Affairs*, Summer 1993.

——. 'Mao and his lieutenants'. *Australian Journal of Chinese Affairs*, no. 19–20, 1988.

——. 'Peng Dehuai and Mao Zedong'. *Australian Journal of Chinese Affairs*, no. 16, 1986.

—— with Warren Sun. 'The politics of an 'un-Maoist' interlude: the case of opposing rash advance, 1956–57'. In *New Perspectives on State Socialism in China*, edited by Timothy Cheek and Tony Saich. Armonk, NY: M.E. Sharpe, forthcoming.

Uhalley, Stephen Jr., and Jin Qiu. 'The Lin Biao incident: more than twenty years later'. *Pacific Affairs*, Fall 1993.

Whitson, William. 'The field army in Chinese Communist military politics'. *China Quarterly*, no. 37, 1969.

Yahuda, Michael. 'Kremlinology and the Chinese strategic debate, 1965–6'. *China Quarterly*, no. 49, 1972.

Biographical and Personnel Collections

Gendai Chugoku Jimmei Jiten (Modern China Biographic Dictionary). Tokyo, Gaimusho, 1982.

Klein, Donald W., and Anne B. Clark. *Biographic Dictionary of Chinese Communism 1921–1965*. 2 vols, Cambridge, MA: Harvard University Press, 1971.

Lamb, Malcolm. *Directory of Officials and Organizations in China: A Quarter-Century Guide*. Armonk, NY: M.E. Sharpe, 1994.

Who's Who in Communist China. Hong Kong: Union Research Institute, 1966.

INDEX

231

work conference (Beijing), 202;
spring 1965, national industry
and communications work
conference, 206;
September–October 1965, Party
Centre work conference, 208;
January–March 1966, national
conference on industry and
communications, 59; March 1966,
conference on Luo Ruiqing case,
30; August 1966, central work
conference, 65; April 1967,
conference on localities (Beijing),
81; March 1970, central work
conference, 138; December
1970–January 1971, North China
conference, 153, 158; June 1971,
central work conference, 125–6;
see also MAC conferences; PLA
conferences; CCP Politburo
meetings; CCP Politburo
Standing Committee meetings;
State Council conferences;
CCP Congresses: Seventh
(April–June 1945), 170, 186;
Eighth: First Session (September
1956), 20n, 177; Second Session
(May 1958), 179, 180; Ninth
(April 1969), 1, 7, 9, 13, 49,
50, 53, 103–10, 111, 113, 115,
117, 118, 121, 122, 137, 141,
148, 153, 163; and PLA, 127–8;
and Zhou Enlai, 137, 163; Lin
Biao's political report to, 4,
104, 106–9, 114; role of Mao
at, 106–10, 132; Tenth (August
1973), 104n;
CCP Politburo: 11, 13, 25n, 40,
46, 51n, 52, 59, 64, 76, 77n,
107, 112, 113, 114, 115, 126,
128, 135, 137, 138, 139, 140,
141, 142, 143, 153, 162, 170,
172, 174, 175, 176, 177;

meetings of: January 1960
enlarged meeting (Shanghai),
188; May 1966 enlarged
meeting, 15, 56, 58, 60–1, 63;
December 1966 enlarged
meetings, 66, 69; July 1970
meeting, 140; 23 August 1970
meeting, 143; 1969 Politburo,
selection of, 104–6, 108,
109–10, 130;
CCP Politburo Standing Committee:
20, 25n, 68, 108, 110n, 121,
177, 180, 206, 208; meetings
of: June 1958 meeting, 181; 31
July–1 August 1959 meeting,
182–4; December 1965 enlarged
meeting (Shanghai), 25n, 30,
33, 211, 212–13; April 1966
meeting, 61; 22 August 1970
meeting, 141–2; 25 August
1970 expanded meeting, 148
Chinese People's Political
Consultative Committee, 171
Chinese Soviet Republic: 169;
Central Executive Committee,
169
Chongqing, 170
Churchill, Winston, 164
civil war (1945–9), 170
civilian affairs: and CCP, 111,
122, 127, 130; and Lin Biao,
191, 193–4, 205; and Mao,
130–1, 205; and PLA, 59, 131,
133, 191; military dominance
over, 103, 127–30, 133
civilian authority: ix, 7, 8, 16n,
19; *see also* Cultural Revolution
Group; radicals, civilian
civilian radicals, *see* radicals,
civilian
communes, *see* people's communes
Cong Jin, 57n
'conservatives': 43, 80, 81, 82–3,

86, 90, 91, 96, 102, 105; *see
also* mass organizations
counterrevolutionaries, viii, 23, 62,
84, 146, 159
coups, *see* military coups
court politics, ix, 20, 162–3, 168
CRG, *see* Cultural Revolution
Group
'Cultivation of a Communist Party
Member', 18
Cultural Revolution: vii, viii, xi,
1, 2, 3, 4n, 5, 12, 18, 34, 36,
37, 38, 39, 51–2, 53, 56–160,
163–5, 167–8, 169n, 202, 209;
access to official sources on,
2–4; active phase of, 7, 9, 49,
56–102, 115, 154; and
factionalism, 34, 37, 38–42, 90,
92–3, 95–6, 144, 148, 153, 158;
and PLA, 36, 37, 40, 41–2,
44–8, 53, 65–7, 72–4, 76, 87,
88, 128, 152n, 154; and
production, 59, 60, 65, 68, 69,
73, 79, 106, 107, 108, 117; and
students, 58, 60, 63, 67–8;
attacks on military, 24, 42, 70,
72–5, 77, 80, 83; attitudes
towards, 76, 149, 151;
construction phase of, 7,
103–160; extension into
countryside, 56, 60, 65–6, 68–9,
122n; extension into industry,
56, 59–60, 65–6, 68–9, 122n;
extension into military, 56, 60,
65–8, 72–3, 76; leadership of,
66–8; persecution during, 22,
161; role of CRG, 52, 63,
66–7, 68–9, 72, 79, 80, 83, 85,
89, 110; role of Jiang Qing, 52,
57, 67, 69, 86–7, 88, 89; role
of Lin Biao, viii, 1, 2, 7–8, 11,
16, 17, 19, 21, 22–4, 52, 55,
56–69, 72–4, 77, 79, 83–5,

87–9, 90–1, 160, 161–8; role of
Mao, 19–20, 50, 56, 65–9,
73–5, 76, 79, 87, 89, 91, 98,
127–9, 130–2; role of Yang
Chengwu, 89n, 90; role of
Zhou Enlai, 11, 19, 65–9, 72,
76, 87–9, 92, 98, 131–2
Cultural Revolution Group
(CRG): 19, 24, 38, 45, 49, 50,
51, 54, 65, 76, 78, 86, 149;
and Chen Boda, 38, 67, 74,
86–7, 106, 110n, 140; and Jiang
Qing, 52, 90, 91; and Lin Biao,
49–50, 72, 80n, 84, 86–7; and
Tao Zhu, 70–1; and Wuhan
incident, 80, 83–9; and
Yang-Yu-Fu affair, 91–2,
98–102; and Ye Qun, 24, 51;
and Zhang Chunqiao, 51, 149;
and Zhou Enlai, 76, 90;
representation in 1969 Politburo,
104–6; role in Cultural
Revolution, 52, 63, 66–7, 68–9,
72, 79, 80, 83, 85, 89, 110; *see
also* PLACRG
'Cultural Revolution left', 7
culture: 61, 115, 173, 189, 199,
201–2; and Lin Biao, 18; and
Mao, 60, 131, 201–2, 213;
Chinese political, 15, 52, 164,
166–7; literature and art, 53,
57, 58–9, 60, 201; theatre
groups, 42–3, 44n; *see also*
Ministry of Culture; PLA:
literature and art forum
(February 1966)

Dalian, 63, 64, 207
'defend with weapons and attack
with words', 83, 87
de Gaulle, Charles, 164
defence policy: 104, 115, 116,
118–20, 123, 143, 148, 163,

194, 207; and Lin Biao, 103–4,
111–15, 116, 118–20, 124, 125,
167n, 188, 195, 207; and Mao,
118, 124, 207; *see also* industry
policy, defence
Deng Liqun, 16
Deng Xiaoping: x, 18, 20, 27n,
36, 64, 71, 106, 107, 113, 173,
176, 178, 182, 198, 201, 206,
208, 212; and He Long, 34;
and Lin Biao, 18, 59, 175–6;
and Liu Shaoqi, 186; and Luo
Ruiqing, 31; and Mao, 20, 83,
187, 196, 202–3; as Mao's
successor, 20, 83, 187
Deng Zihui: 171, 173, 178; and
Lin Biao, 197
Diaoyutai, 49, 51, 53, 54, 99,
100, 139, 153
dogmatism: 180; and Lin Biao,
178, 181, 189; and Mao, 178,
179, 180; economic, 179;
military, 178, 179
domestic policy: 11, 104, 115–17,
123, 126, 161; and Lin Biao,
126, 161, 172; and Mao, 126,
200; and Zhou Enlai, 126; *see
also* agricultural policy; culture;
defence policy; economic policy;
education policy; industry
policy; military policy
Dong Biwu, 105, 106, 137n, 139
'drag out a small handful in the
military', 12, 81, 84, 85

East China, 84
economic policy: 7, 8, 68, 79,
108, 115–18, 119–23, 126, 143,
148, 194; and international
situation, 118, 120, 121, 123,
163; and Lin Biao, 7, 8, 79,
108, 115–18, 122, 123, 161,
172, 184; and Mao, 69, 120,

121, 122–3, 178, 179, 181, 184;
and Zhou Enlai, 117–18, 120–3,
126, 163; role of military,
120–2, 126
education policy, 57–8, 66, 67, 115
eight-point military directive
(January 1967), 56, 72, 73,
74–5, 79, 81, 161

factionalism: in CCP, 144, 148,
153, 158; in PLA, 34, 37,
38–42, 43, 90, 92–3, 95–6
'February adverse current' (1967):
44, 46n, 53, 56, 72, 75, 79, 81,
82n, 148, 149; second February
adverse current (1968), 92
'February mutiny' (1966), 34
field armies: 38–9, 40, 41, 92–3,
96; *see also* Fourth Field Army;
North China Field Army;
Second Field Army; Third Field
Army
fifth encirclement campaign, 169
5 October directive (1966), 66–8
First Army Corps of the First
Front Army, 39, 94, 95, 96, 169
'first front': 174, 198, 209; *see also*
'second front'
'first ten points': 199; *see also*
Socialist Education Movement
'five principles of giving prominence
to politics': 209, 213; *see also*
politics, role of
Five Year Plan: Third, 118, 207;
Fourth, 120, 121
foreign policy: 7, 11, 89, 104,
115, 116, 117, 123–6, 158, 161;
and Lin Biao, 123–6, 161; and
Mao, 123, 125–6, 158; and
Zhou Enlai, 125–6, 158
'four firsts', 189, 198, 200, 204
four generals: 42, 140, 153, 154,
156, 158, 206; and Jiang Qing,